# WARFARE IN
# ANCIENT
# GREECE

# WARFARE IN ANCIENT GREECE

## ARMS AND ARMOUR
## FROM THE HEROES OF HOMER
## TO ALEXANDER THE GREAT

## TIM EVERSON

SUTTON PUBLISHING

First published in the United Kingdom in 2004 by
Sutton Publishing Limited · Phoenix Mill
Thrupp · Stroud · Gloucestershire · GL5 2BU

British Library Cataloguing in Publication Data
A catalogue record for this book is available from the British Library.

ISBN 0-7509-3318-6

*Endpapers, front:* Mounted hoplite wearing a Corinthian helmet, Taranto, *c.* 550. (*Trustees of
the British Museum, GR 1904.7-3.1*); *back*: a selection of Classical and Hellenistic helmets.
(*Ashmolean Museum, Oxford*).

Typeset in 11.5/15pt Garamond.
Typesetting and origination by
Sutton Publishing Limited.
Printed and bound in England by
J.H. Haynes & Co. Ltd, Sparkford.

For Ellie

Red figure vase by the Achilles Painter, showing a hoplite in a Thracian helmet, linen corslet and greaves, c. 450–440. (*Trustees of the British Museum GR 1843.11-3.1*)

Frieze from the Siphnian Treasury at Delphi, *c.* 525. (*Joint Library of the Hellenic and Roman Societies, Slide G.1467*)

# Contents

The Dendra panoply,
c. 1425. *(Joint Library
of the Hellenic and
Roman Societies,
Slide G.1889)*

# List of Illustrations

# *Preface*

The study of Greek military matters has always come second to Roman in this country, which is hardly surprising since the Romans were actually here for 400 years; but the Greeks have a great deal more to offer us. Work on Greek arms and armour has often been the premiss of German scholars, who have been digging in Greece for well over a hundred years – ever since Schliemann dug up Mycenae. One of the objects of this work is to bring some of this German, Greek and other research to an English-speaking audience. The difference between Roman and Greek warfare is often seen as the Roman legionary versus the Greek hoplite, but Greek warfare is not as simple as that. This book covers a span of nearly 1,500 years, of which only 250–300 at the most are strictly hoplite warfare.

We begin in the late Bronze Age, when heroes battled each other in chariots and their exploits would be remembered and written down by Homer some 700 years later. We cover Homer's own time and try to make sense of the dearth of evidence there is for the Greek Dark Age. After that there was the age of the hoplite, and then the renaissance of arms under Philip II and Alexander the Great of Macedon, when Greek warfare reached its greatest diversity; not only assorted infantry and cavalry, but chariots, elephants and even artillery made their appearance. We then follow the Hellenistic kingdoms until their defeat and/or dominance by Rome.

Recent work, such as that by Connolly, Hanson and Sekunda, has paid much attention to army organisation, strategy and tactics, with some work on the psychology of war and the equipment used. It is with the equipment, the arms and armour, that this book is concerned. The basis of all warfare is arms and armour. What weapons were actually used during which periods, and how effective were they? What was armour made of? Did it work, and why did it change so much? This book endeavours to answer these questions and to give a mental picture of what these soldiers were actually like. Some periods and aspects have been given more coverage than others. There is more controversy about Mycenaean arms and armour (and chariotry) than there is about hoplite warfare and equipment, for example, and so there is more to be written. Similarly, Snodgrass did a lot of work on different types of early spearheads, which does not need repeating in its entirety here. Everyone knows pretty well what a spearhead looks like. Body armour and helmets, on the other hand, show a much greater variety of types, which benefit from full examination and discussion, especially concerning their origins. Body armour is my own particular specialism and I make no excuses if it dominates parts of this book. In general, a sword is a sword, and a spear is a spear. (Not true, of course: please read this book for details!) But helmets, shields and body armour are what change the most, and are what make a soldier recognisable for what he is – heavy infantry, light cavalry and so on – and from what period he comes.

This book is aimed at anyone with an interest in warfare: students, soldiers, wargamers, historians and re-enactors. I hope reading it gives you as much interest as writing it gave me.

Tim Everson
February 2004

# *Acknowledgements*

First and foremost I would like to thank Alastar Jackson, who was my tutor twenty years ago at Manchester University, and who encouraged me to study Greek rather than Roman military equipment. He also kindly read through the first three chapters of this book, and would have read them all if he had not had such a busy excavation schedule at Isthmia, and if I had been a faster writer! Much of his advice has been taken on board and, as the saying goes, any remaining errors are entirely my fault.

I should like to thank my brother, Anthony, for encouraging me to learn Greek at an early age, and Fr St Lawrence (RIP) and Tony Brook for teaching it to me. Also Tony Poole for his inspiring ancient history lessons at Wimbledon College.

I should also like to thank Peter Connolly, whose marvellously illustrated books inspired me from an early age, and who continues to do so much good work in this field. I should like to thank Anthony Snodgrass, who first wrote on this subject in an accessible and comprehensive form and who has given me many sleepless nights wondering about the existence of bronze armour in Dark Age Greece. I would like to thank especially Nick Sekunda for his many books on Greek and Hellenistic warfare. I often seem to disagree with his conclusions, but they really make you think, which is what books are for! Finally, I would like to thank Paul Hill for his advice on spears and javelins and for interesting conversations comparing the many similarities between the Greek Dark Age and the English Dark Age.

Thanks for the pictures go to the British Museum, London; Ashmolean Museum, Oxford; Shefton Museum of Greek Art and Archaeology, Newcastle-upon-Tyne; and to the British and French Schools at Athens. They were all most helpful. I must also thank the combined Library of the Roman and Hellenic Societies and the Classical Institute in Senate House, London, for providing some slides for illustrations and also, of course, for helping with many of the more obscure books and journals consulted during the course of this work. Most other illustrations featured are my own humble artwork.

I would also like to thank my wife Shaan, and my daughters Eleanor and Rachel, for their forbearance during this project, and the musical talents of Jethro Tull and Enya, who have helped to calm my mind when the clash of Greek arms became overwhelming!

## ONE

# The Early Mycenaean Period, 1600–1300 BC

Civilisation in Greece developed rapidly under the influence of Crete in the second millennium BC, when trade was making Knossos, and Crete as a whole, wealthy. There is little evidence for warfare in the Aegean before about 1600, however, and it is sometimes assumed that a general peace existed under the thalassocracy, or sea-empire, of Cretan kings like the legendary Minos. What is perhaps more likely is that Mycenaean Greeks from the mainland wanted more of a share of the lucrative Aegean and eastern trade and that war became more common as a result after about 1650. Halfway through this period, in about 1400 BC, the palaces on Crete were destroyed and only Knossos was rebuilt. Here, the writing changed from local Linear A to Greek Linear B, and it is thought that mainland Greeks, probably from Mycenae, were responsible and that from *c.* 1400 onwards they ruled Crete, or at least central Crete, from Knossos.

For this early Mycenaean period we have much evidence in the way of finds of arms and armour and some useful artistic depictions, although these are not always clear. We also have small sketches called ideograms, which feature in the early Greek writing of the period: Linear B. What we do not have for this chapter and the next is 'proper history' telling us about military equipment and the battles in which it was used. We do have Homer, whose *Iliad* and *Odyssey* were written down in about the eighth century but which seem to refer, at least in part, back to Mycenaean times and which can offer us some help, especially for the late period discussed in Chapter 2. Greece followed Crete in having a society based around palaces, which were the centres of administration. The best known of these, because of excavations carried out, are Mycenae, Pylos and Knossos, but there were also palaces at Thebes and Gla in Boeotia, Athens, Tiryns and elsewhere. Each palace ruled over a hinterland in much the same way as the later city-states, and they were as likely to be at war with one another as with foreign enemies. This is another reason why we have more evidence for warfare at this time than previously.

This evidence shows us that the Greeks of the Mycenaean period fought on foot and in chariots. There is little evidence for horses being ridden and none for cavalry. Some of the Linear B 'chariot' tablets from Knossos show the issuing of armour and horse, but no chariot. This has been interpreted by Worley (1994, p. 7) as evidence for cavalry, but these tablets often show other pieces of equipment missing from the items issued and the chariot explanation is simpler. This theory has supplementary items being issued to a warrior who already has some equipment – for example a horse and cuirass – when he has the chariot, another horse and perhaps another cuirass. This armour is likely to be of a Dendra style (see below), which is completely unsuitable for cavalry use. The best-known evidence for a Mycenaean cavalryman is a thirteenth-century terracotta, but he is not clearly armed as a warrior (Hood 1953). The reason for the lack of soldiers on horseback is that horses of this period were not big enough or strong enough to carry warriors, especially armoured warriors: hence the chariot.

The chariot was devised and used throughout much of the ancient world as fast transport, in peace and war, but was rapidly replaced by ridden horses when these became strong enough to carry a rider. This does not appear to have happened in Greece until the tenth century (see Chapter 2). That chariots were used is clear from the grave stelae at Mycenae, the Linear B tablets at Knossos and various other depictions, although no remains have been found from this period. There is still much argument about how they were used. Greenhalgh (1973, ch. 1), using the evidence of the Dendra cuirass (see below), argues for heavily armed spearmen in chariots charging headlong at one another. Littauer and Crouwel, in their various works, argue that the evidence of Homer, writing several hundred years later, could be valid and that the chariots were used as a 'taxi service', taking warriors to and from battle. They then fought on foot. Littauer and Crouwel (1983) also try to show that charging the enemy with a thrusting spear would have been impractical. The spear is unlikely to have had the reach and, if it did, any contact would send the charioteer backwards out of the chariot. However, this argument was recently disproved by Loades in a Windfall Films documentary on the Hittite chariot (*Machines Time Forgot: Chariot*, 2003). Loades, a re-enactment specialist, had no trouble in using a thrusting spear from the side of the chariot at speed. Anderson (1975) argues for a usage similar to early British chariotry, for which we have good evidence from Caesar. Here the charioteers rode into battle on their chariots, but did not

Fig. 1: Stele from a Shaft Grave at Mycenae, *c. 1550. (From: Karo, 1930, plate V)*

always dismount to fight. They fought from within their chariot as well as alongside it, and charged the enemy in it. Littauer and Crouwel dismiss the charge against infantry and other chariots as myth because it would harm the horses, but that is true of ordinary cavalry throughout history, and they still charged. The answer lies in the nature of the opposition. If a line of infantry holds firm, then chariots or cavalry will shy away from it and the chariot confers no advantage. However, this takes a great deal of discipline. If several hundred chariots are charging at once, it is likely that at least sections of the enemy will break and run. Fighting from the chariot with a spear is then possible, and that is certainly how the Hittites used their chariots, despite Drews's arguments (1993, p. 116) to the contrary. Drews considers that all chariots in the late Bronze Age were used as archery platforms, a stance that is quite irreconcilable with the evidence from Greece.

His idea that one of the Shaft Grave stela from Mycenae shows a charioteer with a bow case rather than a sword, which is the usual interpretation, does not convince (Fig. 1) (Laffineur 1999, pp. 28–9). Drews's other main claim (1993, p. 119) is that Greek armies were chariots and virtually nothing else. This he gets from Linear B, where chariots are listed but there is no sign of infantry.

Fig. 2: Warriors on a fresco from Thera, *c.* 1500.

However, he is ignoring the Thera frescos, which show marching soldiers (Fig. 2), and many warrior graves that show no evidence for their having been chariot warriors. An important point to make here is that the Linear B tablets do not, so far as we are aware, mention shields, the main defence of the infantry, although we know that shields were abundantly used. Either the correct section of a palace archive has not yet been uncovered, or palaces dealt only with the elite chariotry, leaving the infantry to supply themselves with equipment. Even Drews admits (1993, p. 137) that where figures are available for other Bronze Age armies in Egypt and Hatti, infantry outnumber chariots by three or four to one. Estimates for the population of Pylos vary between 50,000 and 120,000 (Drews 1993, p. 148), which would give a combat strength of at least 5,000 warriors, yet chariot numbers are mentioned only in hundreds.

The infantry fought with spear, sword and shield for the most part, whereas the chariot warriors dispensed with the shield and wore heavy body armour instead. Helmets were also reasonably abundant. Javelins were possibly used, and there is evidence for archery and slings. Let us now look at this equipment in more detail, starting with the armour.

## HELMETS

Helmets of beaten copper appeared at Ur in about 3000 BC and were the earliest form of armour developed, as the head is obviously the most vulnerable area. Bronze helmets would have been a natural progression, but many Near Eastern soldiers seem to have made do with protections made of leather or other material for the next thousand years or more, the expense of bronze probably being the cause. The Greeks, however, were not influenced by the Hittites or Egyptians when they developed their own unique helmet design in about 1650: the boars' tusk helmet. Over fifty graves have now been discovered containing small plates carved out of boars' tusks and drilled with holes for attachment to a leather or felt cap. They date from before 1600 to about 1150, and we also have illustrations of such helmets covering the same period, showing that they were the most widely used helmet type. Kilian-Dirlmeier (1997, pp. 35–50) has recently surveyed the fifty-plus known finds of tusks and tusk plates and divided them into two main types.

The earliest type is represented by helmets from Aegina, Eleusis, Argos and Thebes (Fig. 3a, b), which have holes drilled through the tusk plates from front to back and a preponderance of trapezoidal plates to cover the crown of the head. All these pre-date the Shaft Graves of Mycenae, that is before 1600, and their

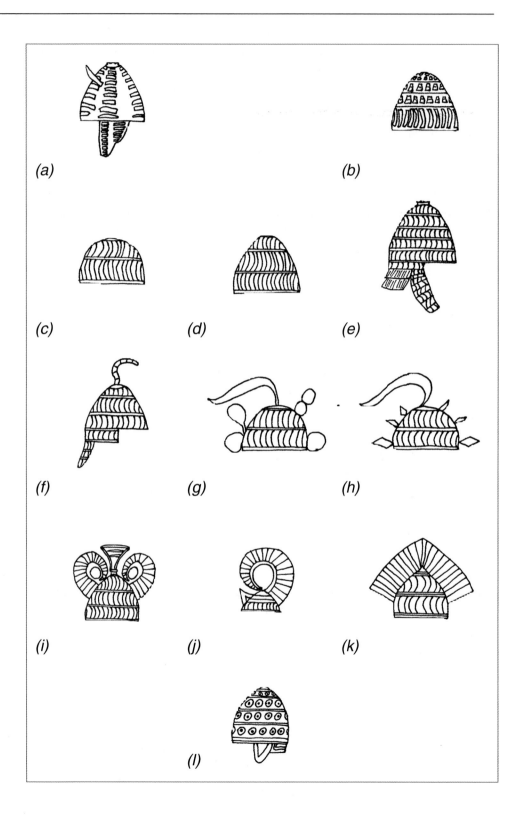

(a)

(b)

(c)

(d)

(e)

(f)

(g)

(h)

(i)

(j)

(k)

(l)

grouping shows the helmet to have been a Greek invention (Kilian-Dirlmeier 1997, p. 47). Later helmets have between two and five rows of curved tusks aligned alternately, as we can see from illustrations and from actual finds (Fig. 4).

These pieces are between 5cm and 8cm in length, depending on the number of rows. An example from Spata, near Athens, had two rows of 7cm and 8cm plates, whereas an example from Armenoi on Crete had three rows of 6.1cm, 5.5cm and 5cm (Fig. 3c, d) (Kilian-Dirlmeier 1997, p. 76; helmets, nos 57, 64). The Spata helmet had forty tusk plates, whereas that from Armenoi had ninety. No evidence of the material onto which the boars' tusks were stitched survives, and the tusks themselves are often poorly preserved. A chamber tomb from Mycenae had only about a third of the tusks surviving (Wace 1932, fig. 38). These are the curved plates with holes drilled through from front to back on which Connolly (1977, p. 13) based his reconstruction of a helmet. Having the holes bored straight through leaves the lacing rather vulnerable and so, in his reconstruction, Connolly covers this with a leather strip, which gives a thin band similar to some of the illustrations. This would have been useful in covering the edges of the tusks as well to stop them catching on a sword edge, for example.

Three of the Shaft Graves at Mycenae had some boars' tusks in them, including a new type in which the holes were skilfully drilled from the side of the tusk plate through to the back. The rows of tusks could then be stitched onto a cap without the stitches being vulnerable (Kilian-Dirlmeier 1997, p. 45). It is this type that continued through to the twelfth century, the latest example known being some fragments in one of the Kallithea warrior graves which will be discussed in Chapter 2 and which date to about 1150. This type of helmet is even mentioned by Homer, writing perhaps three hundred years after it had gone out of use: 'a helm wrought of hide, and with many a tight-stretched thong was it made stiff within, while without the white teeth of a boar of gleaming tusks were set thick on this side and that, well and cunningly, and within was fixed a lining of felt' (*Iliad*, bk. X, ll. 261–5, Loeb translation).

*Opposite page:* Fig. 3: Various boars' tusk helmets and crests. *(a)* Helmet from Aegina, *c.* 1600 (after Kilian-Dirlmeier). *(b)* Helmet from Thebes, *c.* 1600 (after Kilian-Dirlmeier). *(c)* Helmet from Spata, fourteenth century. *(d)* Helmet from Armenoi, fourteenth century. *(e)* Helmet from an ivory model from Mycenae, *c.* 1350. *(f)* Helmet shown on the Pylos frescos, *c.* 1200. *(g,h)* Helmets shown on the Thera frescos, *c.* 1500. *(i)* Crested helmet from the Vapheio gem, fifteenth century. *(j,k)* Crested helmets from a silver cup from Mycenae, *c.* 1550. *(l)* Helmet with bronze discs from an ivory from Knossos, *c.* 1550–1500.

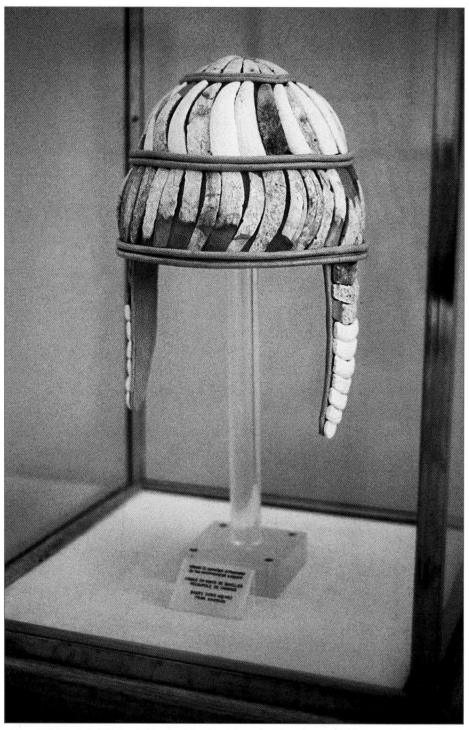

Fig. 4: Boars' tusk helmet from Knossos, *c.* 1400. *(Joint Library of the Hellenic and Roman Societies, Slide G.1160)*

The early helmet from Aegina (Fig. 3*a*) has been reconstructed with cheek pieces, and cheek pieces often seem to feature, usually also made up of small rows of tusks (Fig. 3*e*). The Linear B ideograms for helmets from Knossos dating to *c.* 1400 show a simple cap with cheek pieces. Another common later feature is the neck guard. The carved ivory heads from Mycenae and Cyprus dating to about 1350 seem to have neck guards made of a different material, which Connolly (1977, p. 15) has interpreted as leather strips coming down from the material cap. This seems likely, but the later frescos from Pylos of about 1200 seem to have neck guards also constructed of boars' tusks (Fig. 3*f*). The neck guard does not feature in the Linear B ideograms or other early depictions, although it may be one of the helmet accessories mentioned in Linear B text (see below). We may assume that it was a later addition after 1450, perhaps 1400, and may have been copied from contemporary bronze helmets.

The helmet is frequently depicted in art on frescos, gems and cups. One of the earliest depictions is on the frescos from Thera dating to about 1500 BC, showing that the helmet type was established early in the islands. These helmets have two rows of tusks, horsehair crests and uncertain other decorations, which look rather like pom-poms and perhaps stylised horns (Fig. 3*g*, *h*). The early example from Aegina (Fig. 3*a*) had boars' tusks attached to the sides or front, and horned helmets are known later. A gem from Vapheio (Fig. 3*i*) (Lorimer 1950, pp. 216–17, fig. 20) has an image of a helmet with two horns, which may be rams' horns on the sides, as well as a central, box-like crest, which may be upright horsehair viewed from the front. The horns appear to end in pom-poms reminiscent of the Thera frescos. Another important depiction is on a silver cup from Mycenae, where two more crest styles are seen (Fig. 3*j*, *k*). These appear to be made of stiff horsehair pointing upwards, rather than the floppy horsehair crests of Thera, and are very elaborate in their execution. The similarity of one (Fig. 3*j*) to the Vapheio example (Fig. 3*i*) casts doubt on the side decorations of the latter being rams' horns. They may also be stiff horsehair. Later helmets on the Pylos frescos of about 1200 BC have small crests, which may be made of pieces of tusk or may be rams' horns (Fig. 3*f* ).

The boars' tusk helmet was used throughout Greece and the islands and also Crete, although examples are fewer there, probably because there were no native boar. An ivory carving of the Mycenaean school has also been found on Cyprus (Borchhardt 1972, p. 75) and fragments of one or more helmets have been found in Egypt (Kilian-Dirlmeier 1997, p. 45; helmet, no. 82). Recently an important papyrus picture from El-Amarna in Egypt has been published, which also appears to show boars' tusk helmets. The soldiers wearing them are perhaps

Mycenaean raiders or mercenaries in Egypt, and the date of the papyrus is *c.* 1450 BC (Parkinson and Schofield 1995).

A variation on the boars' tusk helmet is one reinforced with bronze discs instead of tusks. A clear illustration of such a helmet comes from an ivory from Knossos (Fig. 3*l*) (Borchhardt 1972, p. 46, plate 8.3). This shows four rows of horizontal circles on a depiction of a helmet, which must surely represent bronze reinforcements on a material cap. Another interesting depiction of a helmet, or indeed helmets, comes from Katsamba, also in Crete (Alexiou 1954; Borchhardt 1972, plate 8.1). This is a three-handled amphora painted with four pictures of helmets. These helmets have horizontal bands on them, but while some bands have rows of boars' tusks, others have rows of rosettes, which again could represent metal discs. There are also rows with random zigzags, which may perhaps represent the material of the underlying cap. It is important to note that these examples came from Crete and were perhaps a local variant, because boars' tusks were harder to obtain in the island; but there is also one probable example from mainland Greece as well. Shaft Grave IV at Mycenae produced boars' tusks, but also some forty bronze discs, which may have come from a similar combination helmet (Snodgrass 1967, p. 18). Two or more helmets of different types in the same grave could also account for this, of course. A certain combination boars' tusk and bronze helmet comes from the chamber tomb at Dendra, which produced the famous suit of armour discussed later in this chapter. Here the cap of the helmet was made of tusks, now mostly corroded away, but there was also a pair of cheek pieces in bronze (Astrom 1977, p. 49).

Why boars' tusks? To us today it seems a strange material to make helmets from, but metal working was still being developed and, while bronze swords and spears were relatively simple to make, sheet bronze that was light enough to wear without being so thin as to be worthless was a much harder task. Body armour of bronze was developed during this period, but bronze helmets are rare; there is in fact only one definite example (from Knossos), because of the difficulty in hammering out the shape in the somewhat brittle bronze of the period. Also though, the boars' tusk helmet was well established by the time of bronze armour working, and must have been effective enough. Boar hunting seems to have been an important part of Mycenaean warrior culture (Morris 1990), and the decoration of helmets with the tusks of boars was probably done to show off prowess. This then developed into a practical protection. Boars' tusks are made of a much denser material than bone and would certainly have offered a great deal of protection. A blow on the helmet might well have smashed the tusks it hit, but the force would be dissipated in a similar way to the ceramic plates in modern flak jackets. A firm felt base to the cap was certainly essential. The number of tusk plates in a helmet varies from about forty to over 140 (Kilian-Dirlmeier 1997, p. 46), but generally about forty to fifty boars would have been killed to produce each helmet.

There is a suggestion that some warriors would have worn a material cap helmet on its own without additional tusks or discs (Snodgrass 1967, p. 26; Borchhardt 1972, p. 16). Most of the illustrated examples of this 'zoned' helmet, so called because it has horizontal bands or zones, seem to me to be representations of boars' tusk helmets without the tusks drawn in. This is because the object, such as a gem, was too small or because detail was added in a paint that has since worn away (e.g. Borchhardt 1972, plate 7, nos 1, 2, 7). There is only one example on a jar from Crete (Borchhardt 1972, plates 7, 8), which seems to be a clear example of a striped cap with no reinforcements of either bronze or tusks. To what extent such a helmet was used is therefore debatable.

Another obscure type of helmet is that featured on a vase from Hagia Triada in Crete showing boxers (Borchhardt 1972, plate 9.1). It appears to cover the head well and be fitted with cheek pieces but, as Snodgrass says (1967, p. 26), it can hardly be metal in a boxing context. Similar helmets appear on a seal from Zakro, also in Crete, and there is one depicted on a tiny piece of gold foil from Pylos, but that is all. It is generally thought that this helmet type may have been solely for boxing, possibly in a religious context, like Cretan bullfighting (Borchhardt 1972, p. 53). They all date from the period 1550–1500.

The final early Mycenaean helmet to discuss is that made entirely of bronze. This is the helmet from Knossos dating to about 1400 (Fig. 5) (Hood and De Jong 1952). It consists of a bronze, slightly pointed cap with a separately cast knob on the top to hold a horsehair plume, and separate cheek pieces. These have a slightly scalloped front edge, very similar to the bronze cheek pieces from the Dendra helmet. The edges of the bronze on both the cap and the cheek pieces have a line of holes by which they would have been stitched separately to an underlying cap of leather or felt. The bronze smith may have had trouble with the manufacture, as the helmet is wafer thin and would not have offered much protection unless mounted on a substantial leather cap.

Also found with the helmet were about 150 U-shaped pieces of bronze wire (Fig. 6) (Hood and De Jong 1952, plate 52b). These 'staples', and smaller scraps which could be scales, might have been part of a scale armour neck guard, for which there is evidence in the Linear B tablets (see below). A recent find of these 'staples' from a tholos tomb at Nichoria in south-west Greece, shows that they were used to attach small pieces of bronze to one another (McDonald and Wilkie

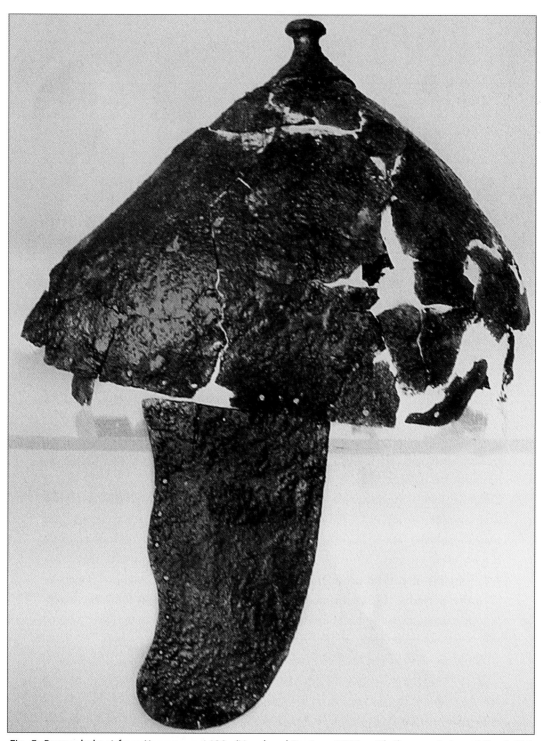

Fig. 5: Bronze helmet from Knossos, *c.* 1400. *(Hood and De Jong 1952, with the permission of the British School at Athens)*

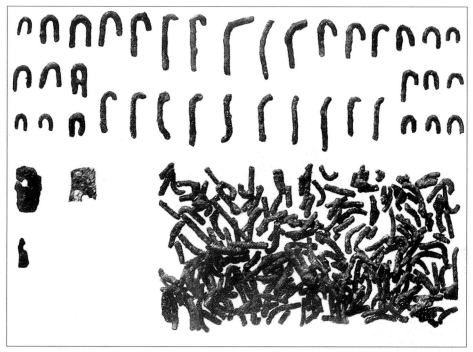

Fig. 6: Bronze 'staples' from the Knossos helmet, *c.* 1400. *(Hood and De Jong 1952, with the permission of the British School at Athens)*

1992, p. 277). The excavators suggest a leather helmet with bronze scales attached but, in that case, the pieces of bronze would probably not be stapled to one another, and the Knossos examples show use of these staples with a bronze helmet. There are a couple of small fragments of bronze from the Knossos tomb which could be bronze scales from this neck guard, but not nearly enough. It may be that the bronze 'staples' connected leather scales, which are known from Near Eastern contexts.

Fragments of two bronze helmets have also been found at Enkomi in Cyprus from this period (*c.* 1425), a time when Greek influence was reaching the island, but are too fragmentary to be of further help (Gjerstad 1935, vol. 1, p. 554, no. 129; Schaeffer 1952, p. 341, no. 2).

The only other piece of armour that has been interpreted as part of a bronze helmet is a 'cheek piece' from Ialysos on Rhodes (Lorimer 1950, p. 211; Borchhardt 1972, p. 74). This probably dates from 1400–1300 BC and is triangular in form, quite different from the scalloped cheek pieces of both the Dendra and Knossos examples (and the later Tiryns helmet). It is also much wider at the 'top' (14cm, as opposed to 10.5cm and 9cm for Dendra and

Knossos), and longer. It is in fact about the same size as, but wider than, the triangular chest protector from the Dendra suit of armour (see below) and I would suggest that it is in fact just such a piece.

As mentioned above, helmets with cheek pieces are shown on the Linear B tablets found at Knossos dating to *c.* 1400. The depiction is too simple to help us decide what sort of helmet is being listed, but the description is informative. It is listed as having four 'helmet accessories' and two cheek pieces. Chadwick (1976, p. 160) suggests that these accessories are four metal plates which make up the cap of the helmet, which is certainly feasible and would have been a stage on the way to constructing the complete helmet bowl out of one piece of bronze. Such helmets were certainly around in eighth-century Greece. But the word 'accessory' really means 'things hung on', some things in addition to the helmet itself, so it is also possible that it refers to the various crests and pom-poms that we see in the artistic representations. My preferred interpretation is 'strip', 'row' or 'things in lines', because the cuirasses in Linear B are also described as having these 'accessories' attached when it clearly refers to the bronze 'belts' which hung in rows from a Dendra-style cuirass (see below). Also, the later Pylos Linear B tablets describe cuirasses with thirty or thirty-four accessories, which are almost certainly rows of scales (see Chapter 2). If these helmets have four rows of scales in addition to the cheek pieces, then it is surely a neck guard that is being referred to. We have seen in the artistic illustrations that this could have been made up of rows of little boars' tusks or leather strips and there is a possibility that bronze scales were used for such a purpose, especially perhaps in Crete. We have the examples mentioned above from Knossos and Nichoria of bronze 'staples', which seem to be linked with bronze scales, perhaps forming just such a neck guard.

## BODY ARMOUR

While evidence for helmets in this period is reasonably common, evidence for body armour is much rarer, resting mostly on the amazing find in 1960 of a complete suit of armour from Dendra, near Argos (Fig. 7). Because this is such a complex piece of work, it must have predecessors, but they are hard to trace. In the Near East, body armour was made up of rows of bronze scales worn by archers and chariot warriors, but there is no evidence for the use of scale body armour by Greeks this early. There is evidence for chariot use, though, in the grave stelai of Mycenae's grave circle A (Fig. 1), showing warriors running down their enemies. It is in these graves, dating to about 1550–1500, that we have

Fig 7: The Dendra panoply, *c.* 1425. *(Joint Library of the Hellenic and Roman Societies, Slide G.1889)*

our only clues to early body armour. One is a small fragment of linen, fourteen layers thick, which may be body armour of a type known in Egypt at this time, although it was not in evidence again in Greece for another thousand years. The other clues are two or three gold pectorals found in the graves (Hagemann 1919, p. 32). These are thin sheets of gold covering the chest and, in one case, decorated with an anatomical design. It is possible that they were merely decoration for the corpse, like the gold face masks which were also found, but they can also be interpreted as representing bronze pectorals, which were worn in battle (Astrom 1977, p. 36). In eighth-century Italy, where bronze pectorals were certainly used, there is an example of a warrior being buried in a gold version of the cuirass of the time (Connolly 1978, p. 12).

So, instead of adopting scale armour from the East, the Greeks invented sheet bronze plate armour. This must have developed from the pectoral into a cuirass of front and back plates to which further refinements were added, and by 1450 there were great suits of armour, which were worn by the chariot warriors of the Mycenaean palaces.

This armour is known as Dendra armour, because the only complete suit we have was found in a chamber tomb there (Astrom 1977, *passim*). This dates to *c.* 1425, and consists of an inner cuirass of back- and breastplates; two large shoulder guards, to which are attached upper arm guards and triangular chest protectors; a high neck guard; and six 'belts' of bronze, three at the front and three at the back, which formed a protective skirt. A boars' tusk helmet with bronze cheek pieces was in the tomb, too, as were a greave and an arm guard, both of which may originally have been in pairs. Two swords were also in the tomb. The bronze of the cuirass is about 1mm thick and holes are punched around the edge at 2–5cm intervals for the attachment of a lining, which would have been folded over the edges of the bronze to stop chafing. Some pieces also have the edges of the bronze rolled over for extra strength. These are the neck guard, the shoulder guards and the chest protectors. The cuirass, consisting of back- and breastplates, is very basic, with no decoration. The backplate has a ridge along the waistline where the bronze is beaten out into a sort of flange, so that the protective belts at the back would hang clear of the buttocks. The holes for attaching the additional plates do not line up exactly, and the whole armour must have been assembled with leather thongs. These could be adjusted to fit a variety of shapes of warrior and made it easy to pass the suit on to someone else. This was essential, otherwise an expensive suit would become useless, or would at least need a lot of work doing to it if it was to fit someone else. It also made the looting of your opponent's armour, such as is recorded in Homer, a practical thing to do. The backplate of the cuirass overlaps the breastplate and slots over upright loops on the shoulders. On the left side are three similar loops through which a bronze rod slid to provide a primitive hinge. The right side has just a single loop and slot, to be secured with a leather thong. This is a very complex system and could not have been managed by the warrior alone; he will have needed a squire to help him.

The two large shoulder guards show a much better attempt at anatomical detailing, fitting the shoulders snugly so as to help deflect a spear thrust, and the bronze edges are rolled over except at the bottom, where the upper arm guard was attached. The top of the right shoulder guard has a bronze ring fitted to it, which has been interpreted as a holder for a sword or a shield strap to prevent it from sliding off the shoulder (Astrom 1977, p. 30). A sword is the more likely answer, since the remains of a shield were not found in the grave and it will be shown later that this warrior neither needed nor used a shield. The two shoulder guards are tied only to the breastplate (not the backplate) by leather thongs, and therefore could probably have been fastened on by the warrior himself, if he was in a particular hurry to arm. Also if the shoulder guards had been fastened to the backplate as well, it would have impossibly restricted upper arm movement.

The two upper arm guards are shaped to fit over the shoulder guards exactly and were again fastened with leather thongs. The left guard is longer than the right, for no good reason, and is possibly a later replacement. These guards seem to be a lot of extra work for what is minimal extra protection, and shows the careful thought that went into making a suit that gave the required balance between protection and mobility.

The shoulder guards meet at the back of the cuirass but not at the front, where the gap is closed by two triangular chest protectors (Fig. 8b). These would have overlapped each other when the warrior's arms were at his side, but would still have covered the central chest area, or protected the armpit if one arm were raised (Taracha 1999, p. 9). These guards have all three edges rolled over bronze wire for extra strength, a feature that would become common in later cuirasses.

The high neck guard is a strip of bronze with the ends soldered together to form a cylinder. The upper edge is bent outwards to allow for head movement, while the bottom edge is carefully shaped to fit snugly onto the cuirass. The shoulder guards are cut away to allow for this.

Lastly, there are six curved 'belts' attached to the bottom of the cuirass, three at the front and three at the back. Each is slightly trapezoid in shape, with the lower edge being longer than the upper, and each overlaps the one above it. They are 16–17cm deep, and vary in length from 64cm for the top of the upper front 'belt' to 78cm for the bottom of the lower front 'belt'. There is some inconsistency in that the middle 'belt' at the back is actually shorter in length than the one above it, and the lowest 'belts' have holes for fitting further plates. This suggests a certain amount of mass production of these 'belts' by the armourer. When an armour came to be assembled, six 'belts' of the right size for the wearer could be chosen and fitted, with each 'belt' having all the holes that might be needed already punched through. Alternatively, or in addition to the above, the extra holes on the lowest 'belts' would come in useful if an upper or middle plate was damaged in battle. This could then be removed and replaced by a lower 'belt' with the knowledge that the required holes would be there. Another problem with these 'belts' is that the upper and middle 'belts' at the front each have three extra pairs of holes punched through on both sides and in the middle, at the centre of each 'belt'. There are corresponding holes in the breastplate, and Connolly (1977, p. 13), quite rightly I think, has interpreted these as a means of obtaining a flexible skirt while retaining full protection. If the 'belts' forming the front of the skirt were tied tightly with leather thongs, as at the back, then the warrior would find it impossible to bend over, or to raise his legs to climb stairs or get into a chariot. These thongs must therefore have been tied loosely, but that would leave gaps between the 'belts'. A solution was to tie leather thongs at the holes in the breastplate and thread them through the holes in the centre of these two upper 'belts'. The thongs were then tied so that the 'belts' were held up in an overlapping position. Mobility was then retained without the loss of protection.

The Archaeology Department at the University of Birmingham has made a reconstruction of the Dendra suit, which Dr Prag kindly let me examine when it was on show in Manchester. It was extremely heavy. The whole weight of the suit sat on the shoulders and it must have been worn with a padded jerkin of some sort. It was also impossible to lift the arm above shoulder height, although with a bent elbow one could wield a spear or even throw javelins over short distances. Sword thrusting was also possible, but not really slashing. We shall see later, however, that swords of the period were indeed used in this way. It would also have been theoretically possible to shoot a bow while wearing this armour, as Taracha (1999, pp. 9–10) has pointed out. However, I believe it would have been difficult – too difficult – to be an archer in combat wearing this armour when arrows would have to be fired repeatedly. There was no evidence for archery in the Dendra grave, and I am convinced that this warrior was a spear- or sword-wielding chariot warrior. Using the Birmingham reconstruction of the armour, it was also possible to work out how the suit was put on. Greaves, if worn, would be put on first. The warrior would then hold the breastplate, with its three 'belts' already attached, in position while a squire fastened on the backplate with its 'belts'. The two shoulder guards, with their triangular chest protectors and upper arm guards already attached, would then be tied on. Finally the neck guard would go on. So, this suit of fifteen pieces would be kept in five sections for reasonably rapid arming.

There are a few other examples of armour from this type of suit. A tomb in Phaistos in Crete produced half a 'belt', which was probably a single piece of armour placed in a tomb to represent the whole (Hood and De Jong 1952, p. 60). A chamber tomb at Mycenae also contained at least two 'belts' in a fragmentary state, and more of the armour may have been present originally (Yalouris 1960, plate 25, 1; Astrom 1977, p. 137). The British Museum has a triangular piece of bronze, from Ialysos on Rhodes, that has always been described as a cheek piece; but it is very similar in size to the Dendra triangular chest protectors, and I would suggest that it is a similar guard since, as mentioned earlier, it does not conform to the shape of other known bronze cheek pieces.

The most interesting finds are of other shoulder guards (Fig. 8). An earlier tomb at Dendra, dating from about 1450, contained a solitary shoulder guard for the right arm, again probably placed in the tomb to represent the whole armour (Fig. 8a). This has a hole for its attachment to the breastplate, but does not have holes to attach triangular chest protectors to it. It is also not cut away to allow for a neck guard, and does not have holes to attach upper arm guards. Indeed, it reaches further down the arm itself to give this protection, which would have made it more restrictive to movement. It is obviously of an earlier and simpler design. In 1965 a pair of shoulder guards with their triangular chest protectors and upper arm guards dating from c. 1375 were discovered in the Cadmeion in Thebes (Fig. 8c) (*Illustrated London News*, 5 December 1965). Details of these have still not been properly published, but they are on display in Thebes Museum. The shoulder guards are of a simple rounded form and again lack a cutaway for a neck guard. The upper arm guards appear to fit snugly to them and have straight ends, rather than the points of the Dendra examples. The triangular guards both curve in the same direction and may not be a pair, but they are certainly longer than the examples from Dendra and Ialysos – probably over 20cm – and could never be mistaken for cheek pieces. It is interesting to speculate as to where the rest of this armour is. Towards the end of this period less elaborate cuirasses were worn, probably consisting of just

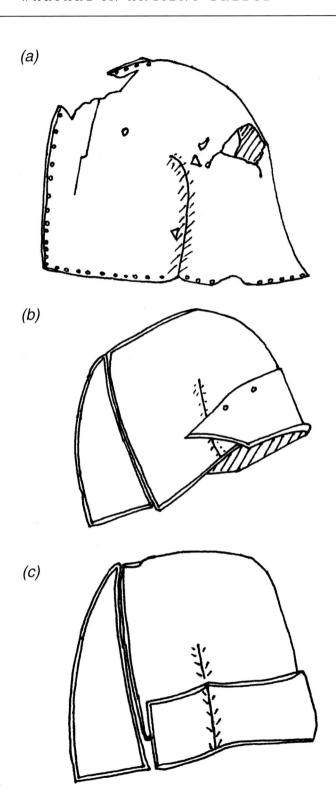

Fig. 8: Shoulder-guard assemblies from Dendra-style panoplies.
(a) Early shoulder guard from Dendra, c. 1450.
(b) Shoulder-guard assembly from the cuirass tomb at Dendra, c. 1425.
(c) Shoulder-guard assembly from Thebes (hypothetical recon-struction), c. 1375.

back- and breastplates (see Chapter 2). Perhaps here we have a pair of shoulder guards, dumped by a warrior in favour of just such a simpler cuirass. In 1992, at Nichoria in south-west Greece, several small pieces of bronze armour were found in a tholos tomb (McDonald and Wilkie 1992, pp. 276–8, 333). These are very fragmentary, but may include parts of a shoulder guard or perhaps a helmet cheek piece. Further small fragments of bronze body armour have been found on the acropolis of Midea near Dendra, but these are too small to identify further (Walberg 1998, p. 158 and plate 143).

Clear artistic representations of this armour are hard to find, and indeed the only undisputed item is a vase, which is clearly shaped like the inner cuirass section of a Dendra suit with shoulder guards but no other additions (Astrom 1977, p. 37). This may show that the armour was sometimes worn without the skirt of 'belts', again pointing the way to the simpler armour of the Late Mycenaean period. The vase dates from about 1450.

The other, most important pieces of evidence are the tablets in Linear B script from Knossos, dating to about 1400. These tablets are written in an early syllabic Greek, and were used as some sort of inventory system. Examples have been found at most Mycenaean palaces. About forty tablets mentioning armour have been found at Knossos, and the accompanying ideogram looks remarkably like the Dendra panoply (Fig. 9). There are horizontal lines representing the

Fig. 9: Linear B ideograms of suits of armour and a chariot from Knossos, c. 1400.

'belts' and curved lines representing the shoulder guards. One example even seems to show triangular chest guards (Fig. 9, third from left). The wording that goes with the ideograms also supports the interpretation as being a Dendra cuirass. Two 'qe-ro' are listed, which are probably the two halves of the inner cuirass; two shoulder pieces; and then an (unknown) quantity of accessories hung on, which must be the 'belts'. The cuirasses are nearly always depicted on Linear B tablets that depict chariots (Fig. 9, bottom) and horses as well, and it is clear that a chariot force was the mainstay of the Knossian army and indeed of other Mycenaean palace forces. It is also clear that these chariot warriors were being armed by the palaces, or at least partly so. The weight of the armour precludes such a warrior from being simply an infantryman, as he would not have been able to walk very far, and apart from the suit itself there is evidence that these charioteers wore still more, additional pieces of armour.

## GREAVES AND ARM GUARDS

The cuirass tomb at Dendra produced a fragmentary greave which may have been one of a pair (Astrom 1977, p. 45), although there is evidence that during the later Mycenaean period single greaves could be worn on the leading left leg only (Fortenberry 1991). Unfortunately the Dendra greave is too damaged to see if it was shaped for either left or right leg. It is 32.5cm long, 8cm wide and paper thin. It has holes around the edge for attachment of a lining, but no evidence for lacing wires such as occurred later. It seems likely that this bronze was attached as a facing to a larger linen or leather greave, which would also have made it a more substantial defence. A similar combination of bronze and material greaves certainly happened later on (see Chapter 2).

Another piece of paper-thin bronze found in the Dendra cuirass tomb has been interpreted as a forearm guard. It is similar in construction to the greave, but much shorter at 20cm. It too has holes along the edge for attachment to a backing, which may have been linen or leather and by which the guard was attached to the forearm, like the greave. This guard also seems not to have been one of a pair, but there were other fragments in the tomb which could not be reconstructed. If the Dendra warrior wore only one forearm guard, it might be thought that this would be on the right, spear-wielding forearm but, if he was not using a shield, the left arm would be just as vulnerable. The piece of armour illustrated in Fig. 10 might support the idea of its being a left arm guard.

This piece of armour came from the same Mycenaean tomb that produced some Dendra-style 'belts' (see above). Yalouris (1960, p. 58) originally

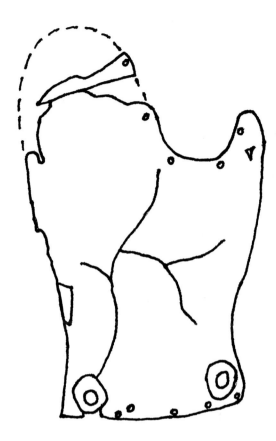

Fig. 10: Armour guard for the left hand from Mycenae, c. 1450.

interpreted the piece as an ankle guard, but examination of the photographs led me to interpret it as a hand guard, an identification also arrived at independently by Wardle and Wardle (1997, p. 64). The piece of bronze is 13.5cm tall and 19cm in circumference at its widest point, with three bronze knobs riveted around the lower edge. These knobs were used to fasten the guard around the wrist, and the bronze then covered the back of the hand, with a separate tongue for the back of the thumb. This shows that the guard was for a left hand and that, to be of any use, it must have been worn with a forearm guard. The cut out semi-circle between hand and thumb allowed for reins or the edge of a chariot to be grasped. It also shows that these heavily armoured chariot warriors did not carry shields, which would have made left arm guards redundant. The large shields used at the time would have been impractical to use in chariots and they are not mentioned on the Linear B chariot tablets. There was no evidence of a shield in the Dendra cuirass tomb and it is generally thought that, during this period, shields and body armour were considered to be alternatives. These supplementary pieces show just how completely covered in bronze armour these chariot warriors were. Apart from the encumbrance factor, especially in the summer heat of the Mediterranean, this armour must have been effective for it to have remained popular for so long; about 100 years or more from *c.* 1450 to *c.* 1350. The only weapons it had to defend against at this time were also made of bronze, with the exception of flint and obsidian arrowheads, and since bronze armour was later used as a defence against iron weapons, we can assume it must have been even more effective against bronze. The curved surfaces of the armour would have helped to deflect glancing blows and, although a direct thrust from a pointed weapon would have punctured the bronze, a strong leather undergarment or lining would have helped to absorb any attack.

## SHIELDS

If the elite chariotry relied on their body armour and helmets for protection, the infantry, who must have formed the vast majority of the soldiery, relied principally on their shields. Shields were generally made of perishable materials and they survive less well in archaeological contexts than helmets and armour do. This is especially true for the early Mycenaean period, from which we have no definite shields or parts of shields. Tomb 15 at Mycenae produced a bronze strip that may have come from a shield, and there are similar strips of gold from the Shaft Graves at Mycenae, although in neither case do they help with reconstructions (Borchhardt 1977, p. 9). To counter this we are fortunate in having several depictions of shields, which show us that there were two main types of large body shield in use at this time: the figure-of-eight shield and the tower shield.

Fig. 11: Warriors on the Lion Hunt Dagger from Mycenae, *c.* 1500. *(After Osgood and Monks 2000, p. 126, and Connolly 1977, p. 14)*

Both are well known from the 'Lion Hunt' Dagger found in the Shaft Graves at Mycenae (Fig. 11). The figure-of-eight shield is composed of two large, joined circles, the lower one usually slightly larger than the upper, with a long vertical line joining both halves like an elongated boss. The sideways views that appear on some gems show that the shield was also heavily convex, giving a great deal of protection from neck to ankle.

The 'Lion Hunt' Dagger and the frescos of shields from Knossos and Tiryns (Fig. 12) are dappled in black and white, and show that the shields were made of, or covered with, cowhide still retaining the hair on the outside. It is likely that this hide was stretched over a wood and wicker framework, with the edge bound in leather or sometimes bronze. The frescos also show circles of stitching by which the hide was attached to the frame behind. On a bead from one of the Mycenaean Shaft Graves, these stitches are replaced by small dots, which might

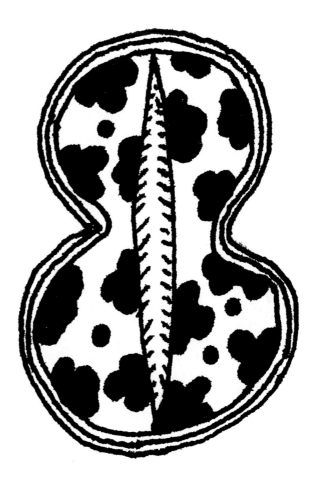

Fig. 12: Figure-of-eight shield from a fresco from Knossos, c. 1400.

represent attachment by bronze rivets (Lorimer 1950, pp. 136, 142, fig. 5). The unusual shape of the shield might have helped in fighting with swords, which could be held in the indentation of the shield to poke at an opponent or, indeed, with a spear held underarm. Unfortunately such a use of the 'waist' of the shield is not depicted. Spears and swords are generally thrust over the top of the shield in the illustrations and, indeed, shields are often omitted from the attacking warrior in scenes shown on gems and seals, either for the sake of clarity or to show extra bravery on the part of the attacker.

Whatever the reason for the shape, it seems that the figure-of-eight shield became something of a religious or ritualistic symbol as well as a practical defence. The frescos in the palaces are one example of this. Others are the use of the design as a decorative feature on a sword and the silver 'siege rhyton', both from the same Shaft Grave (IV) at Mycenae (Lorimer 1950, p. 142, fig. 4). The British Museum holds a gold necklace from tomb 93 at Enkomi in Cyprus on which the beads are shaped like figure-of-eight shields, and also a separate carved gem that shows the convex shape very nicely (Cassola Guida 1973, plates XIV.3, VI.6).

The earliest representation of the shield is a gem dating to *c.* 1600 from Crete, and the latest appears to be a vase fragment from Tiryns dating to *c.* 1250. This shows two bearded warriors with boars' tusk helmets, carrying shields and spears. One has a figure-of-eight shield and the other a tower shield (P. Rehak, in Laffineur 1999, p. 234). The consensus among scholars is that the shield is a Minoan invention in Crete, transported to mainland Greece at the end of the sixteenth century.

The other large body shield is known as the tower shield and also appears on the 'Lion Hunt' Dagger (Fig. 11). It is a rectangular shield and, like the figure-of-eight type, it also reaches from neck to ankle. Some depictions show a straight, flat top, while others show the shield with a curved upper guard to add further protection. The marching warriors on the Thera fresco show us that this shield too was covered in hide with the hair left on (Fig. 2), and gems tell us that it was also convex, like a half-cylinder, to cover the warrior as much as possible (Lorimer 1950, p. 140, fig. 2). However, it does not appear as a religious motif at all and is generally not as common as the figure-of-eight shield, despite the fact that it must have been easier to construct. There are small rectangular shields known from Egypt and Crete at this time and Borchhardt (1972, pp. 25–6) suggests an origin from there. He concedes, however, that all the examples of *body-sized* tower shields are from mainland Greece. (This was before the discovery of the Thera frescos, which places the shield in the islands too.) Both on the Thera frescos and the silver siege rhyton from Shaft Grave IV there appear to be smaller rectangular shields, only half the size of body shields, but my own feeling is that this is artistic error. In the Thera case the shield is on its own, having been lost at sea, and clearly shows a telamon, or shoulder strap, which a small shield would not have had. It is drawn too small, because there is no warrior with it for scaling purposes. The two examples on the silver siege rhyton (Lorimer 1950, p. 142, fig. 4) could be costumes or cuirasses rather than shields, and one cannot be dogmatic about them. The Thera frescos are the earliest depiction of the tower shield, dated to about 1500. The latest depiction of a tower shield is on the same vase fragment from Tiryns that gives us the latest depiction of a figure-of-eight shield, and dates to c. 1250. The two varieties of body shield seem to be quite contemporary and both had disappeared by the end of the thirteenth century.

The final unusual feature to discuss about both these large body shields is the way they were wielded. Where a method is shown, it was by a telamon or baldric over the shoulder, so that when not deployed in front of the warrior the shield could be slung behind over his back, where it would tap the neck and ankles just as it did for Ajax (Homer, *Iliad* VI, 118). Another advantage of having the telamon was that it allowed spears to be wielded two-handedly, and many of the gems/seals and the 'Lion Hunt' Dagger show just this. However, there is no depiction of a central handgrip, which would have been useful in bringing the shield round from the back to the front for combat, and indeed for combat itself. Borchhardt (1972, p. 6) says there must have been a handgrip, and Connolly (1977, p. 15) thinks it likely. Lorimer (1950, p. 135) disagrees, however, and there is an interesting passage in Herodotus which seems to back her up. In Book I, verse 171 of his histories, Herodotus credits the Carians (Greeks on the coast of Asia Minor) with inventing helmet crests, shield blazons and shields with handgrips, all in the time of King Minos, i.e. the Bronze Age, when the Carians were perhaps living on the Aegean islands. Before then, he says, soldiers had to make do with a strap over the shoulder. Is he right, though? Herodotus was writing hundreds of years later and he is clearly wrong about shield blazons, which did not appear until the eighth century at the earliest. Shortly after this, the hoplite shield grip appeared (see Chapter 3), and it seems most likely that Herodotus was getting confused with the introduction of this grip. The next generation of Mycenaean shields clearly have handgrips (see Chapter 2), and it seems most likely that these large shields did too. They would be essential for defensive manoeuvring of the shield, especially one of such size and weight.

## SPEARS

We have discussed the defensive armament of the Mycenaean warrior from 1600 to 1300, and it is now time to turn to the offensive weapons. For hand-to-hand combat the warrior relied mainly on the spear and the sword, which are commonly depicted in art, but there is also some evidence for archery and the use of the sling. All these weapons were used in hunting as well as in warfare, and it is often difficult to decide whether a burial containing certain weapons indicates a hunter or a warrior. It is probably safe to assume that most male adults indulged in both activities using the same or very similar equipment. It also seems to be the case that swords (and daggers), especially, were used as burial items to indicate status, and were not necessarily used by the person with whom they are buried. (See especially the Shaft Graves at Mycenae and the 'Warrior Graves' at Knossos: Karo 1930; Hood and De Jong 1952.)

The sword is often considered to be the primary weapon of Bronze Age Greece because of the number of examples which have been found, and especially of those that are highly decorated. They are depicted as often as the spear in scenes of combat, although not so frequently in hunting scenes (Snodgrass 1967, p. 16). Nevertheless, a man with a spear will always have the advantage over one with a sword, and I am certain that the spear was the primary combat weapon, although the sword seems to have been superior as a status symbol. There are close parallels in Dark Age and Anglo-Saxon England for this (Wilson 1981, pp. 114 ff.).

The examples of spearheads from the Shaft Graves at Mycenae must come from large thrusting spears. They have leaf-shaped blades with strongly marked mid-ribs and can be as much as 50cm in length. None of the Shaft Grave examples is decorated (unlike the swords) and the spear was perhaps more of a practical weapon than a prestige item. The comparative lack of spear finds means that they were too important to dispose of with the dead. The British Museum holds three variant examples of the large thrusting spear from Ialysos in Rhodes, which date towards the end of the fourteenth century, and several large spearheads were found in the 'Warrior Tombs' at Knossos (Hood and De Jong 1952, plate 53b). Evidence from gems, and the 'Lion Hunt' Dagger from Shaft Grave IV, shows these spears being wielded two-handedly, and appears to make them about 3 metres long (Buchholz 1987, p. 39). This ties in well with the surviving heads that we have, although it was also perfectly feasible to wield these spears single-handedly, like the warriors on the Thera frescos. A gold seal ring from Shaft Grave IV shows a spear with three or four tassels along its length, and there are similar gems from Crete showing this decoration. A spear from Vapheio in Crete also had a long length of bronze tubing running from the head down the shaft for some distance, which would have served as a reinforcement as well as a decoration. The spear would have been used by infantry, as shown on the Thera frescos (Fig. 2), and by chariot warriors, although it is clear that spears could not have been used two-handedly from the chariot itself. The warrior would have had to dismount first, as discussed above, if he wished to wield his spear in this way. Since our best evidence for using a spear with two hands is the 'Lion Hunt' Dagger, and that is clearly a hunting situation, it is possible that combat spears were always used with one hand. This seems the most likely, since warriors would be holding on to their shield or the edge of a chariot with their left hand. Some smaller spearheads are known from this period, but there are no clear representations of javelins used in battle, and they may be purely hunting spears. After 1300 spears wielded with two hands no longer appear, and the single-handed spear, whether thrust or thrown, became the norm for both hunting and combat. This will be discussed in Chapter 2.

## SWORDS

The Mycenaean sword seems to have been another Minoan development. Plenty of daggers are known from the early Cretan Bronze Age, but these are handy tools as much as weapons and certainly seem to be status symbols too (Fig. 13*a*) (Papadopoulos 1998, *passim*). From these, however, were developed the earliest bronze swords, known as Type A (Fig. 13*b*). The earliest examples are a pair from Mallia in Crete dating from perhaps 1700, which are some 90cm long. Some examples in the Mycenaean Shaft Graves are even longer. The type is distinguished by a short tang (where the handle fits the blade) like the earlier daggers, which was very prone to breakage. This has happened in many of the discovered examples. There is a high mid-rib running down the length of the

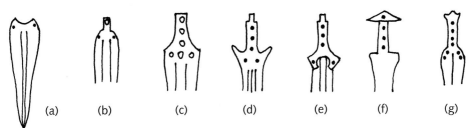

(a)        (b)        (c)        (d)        (e)        (f)        (g)

Fig. 13: A selection of Mycenaean swords, seventeenth to twelfth centuries.

blade, and the narrowness of the blade has led to their being termed rapiers (Snodgrass 1967, p. 15). Peatfield has pointed out (in Laffineur 1999, p. 68) that the swords do have a distinct edge, however, and could be used for long-distance slashing as well as for thrusting. I find this unlikely, owing to the damage that would have been caused to the edge of the sword and because of the weakness of the tang. The weapon seems far more likely to have been used to thrust at people from behind a body shield, like a short spear. The sharpening of the edges would help to inflict damage using this manoeuvre and does not mean that the sword had to be used as a slashing weapon. The weakness of the weapon has led some to see this sword as a ritual rather than an actual weapon, but it seems to me that it is the sword's function that gives it its ritual status. That there was a ritual significance to the sword is clear from some examples found in a cave at Arkalochori in Crete, which were decorated but had no rivet holes for the attachment of the hilt and had obviously been offered as a non-functioning sword (Kilian-Dirlmeier 1993, plates 4–5, nos 22–5). Other examples of the ritual function of swords, or their significance as status symbols, are the Shaft Graves at Mycenae, where grave IV had five bodies with forty-six swords, and grave V had three bodies and ninety swords (Sandars 1961, p. 24). Many of these swords have ivory handles and gold-capped rivets, as well as blades which are sometimes decorated down the central rib with spirals and, in one case, with depictions of figure-of-eight shields.

The Type A sword was soon improved upon by the Mycenaeans with the development of Type B (Fig. 13c). This tends to be a shorter sword at some 60cm on average, with distinct square or slightly pointed shoulders where the blade joins the tang (Sandars 1961, p. 17). The tang is longer and broader, and the riveting is more secure. The blade also tends to be slightly wider, without such a pronounced central rib. These changes brought the centre of balance further towards the handle than in Type A and made the sword much more easily wielded. More varied cut-and-thrust strokes could be employed, and the sword could be used for longer before tiring (Peatfield, in Laffineur 1999, p. 69). Most of the examples of this type of sword are from the Mycenaean Shaft Graves, and it seems likely that this was a Greek improvement on the originally Cretan Type A. The Type A sword lasted from perhaps before 1700 until c. 1450. Type B came into use just before 1600 and lasted until about 1375.

Alan Peatfield (in Laffineur 1999, pp. 69–70) has shown through experimental sword fighting that bronze swords chip easily, and that to prevent such damage a warrior would not try to parry the opponent's sword too roughly.

Rather, if blades were in contact, he would slide his sword down the opponent's blade to attack the sword arm. This led to the development of swords with protective hilts, known as Horned swords (Fig. 13*d*) and Cross-hilted swords (Fig. 13*e*) (Kilian-Dirlmeier 1993, *passim*, developing from Lorimer 1950; Sandars 1961, 1963).

The Horned swords can be divided into a further five varieties. Type 1a has small projecting horns of rolled-over bronze to act as a hand guard and was around from *c*. 1450 to 1350. Type 1b has flat horns for easier manufacture and hilt attachment and lasted from *c*. 1400 to 1300. Towards the end of the period studied here, in the second quarter of the fourteenth century, types 2a and 3 emerged. Type 2a has the horns curving downwards in an attempt to catch an opponent's blade, and continued in use until about 1200. Type 3 has very long horns of rolled-over bronze set almost at right angles to the blade, and continued in use until *c*. 1300, maybe a little later. Some of the last Horned swords have a cross-guard of bronze at the top of the hilt (a T-flange) for further strength and for improving the balance (as in Fig. 13*f* ). All these swords are long, mainly thrusting weapons at 60–70cm on average. (Horned sword Type 2b has the same hilt as 2a, but is a short-bladed version which did not appear until *c*. 1230 and so is considered in Chapter 2.)

From a similar period is the Cross-hilted sword (Fig. 13*e*), which makes do with simple bumps where the blade joins the tang to deflect an opponent's blade. This comes in two varieties: Type 1 with a simple tang, and Type 2 which has a T-flange at the top of the hilt (as in Fig. 13*f* ). These swords also average about 60cm in length and lasted from *c*. 1430 to *c*. 1300. Both Horned and Cross-hilted swords are found throughout Greece, Crete and the islands; the Horned sword is evenly and widely distributed, while the Cross-hilted sword is found mainly in Crete, Mycenae and Rhodes. The swords are heavy and difficult to use, and are further evidence for a warrior elite at this time. Only those aristocrats who had no labouring work to do would have had the time to put into sword practice. This seems to be confirmed by swords always being found in graves that are wealthy in other ways, for example they contain gold and jewellery. After 1300 shorter, more effective and more easily used swords came into use and these will be discussed in Chapter 2.

## MISSILE WEAPONS

Let us now turn to missile weapons: the javelin, the bow and the sling. Evidence for javelins or throwing spears for this period is slight. There are some examples of small spearheads, which may have been for such weapons, but it is not possible to tell whether they were merely hunting spears. There are no definite depictions of javelins in the art of the period. There are some Linear B sealings from Knossos, originally thought to mention arrows, which may be javelins (Chadwick 1976, p. 172), and some 'arrowheads' from Enkomi in the British Museum that are rather large and may also be javelins. These date from *c.* 1300, however, and may be considered to belong to the later Mycenaean period covered in Chapter 2, when evidence for throwing spears or javelins is greater.

There are no surviving Greek bows from this or indeed any other period, and we have to rely on the evidence from arrowheads and a few illustrations. In *c.* 1600 arrowheads were generally of flint or obsidian, like the six found in a Shaft Grave at Aegina (Kilian-Dirlmeier 1997, p. 28). The nearest source for obsidian was the Cyclades, which suggests an expense more consistent with arrows for warfare than for hunting. The barbed heads of the arrows also suggest warfare; they do more damage and are harder to withdraw. In hunting, it is preferable to do less damage and to be able to retrieve used arrows easily. By the fifteenth century, arrowheads were also being made of bronze, which is better suited to mass production (Reboredo Morillo 1996, *passim*). The palace at Knossos produced 110 bronze arrowheads dating from *c.* 1400 and that at Pylos, 500, although these are of a later date. Most of our other finds are from graves. Shaft Grave IV at Mycenae had twenty-six flint and twelve obsidian arrowheads. Tomb Delta in Grave Circle B at Mycenae had seventeen flint heads, and tomb Lambda, twenty-four flint and twenty obsidian. Shaft Grave IV also produced the silver siege rhyton (Cassola Guida 1973, plate III.1), which shows three archers in battle using simple bows. Bows and arrows are also featured in Linear B from Knossos, though perhaps in a hunting rather than a warfare context (Chadwick 1976, p. 172). Evans (the original excavator) thought that these bows might be composite bows, which were reinforced with sinew and horn to produce more power, but that is now considered to be a later development and it is believed that Mycenaean Greeks used the simple or self bow of plain wood (Reboredo Morillo 1996, p. 12). The evidence of the silver siege rhyton shows that Mycenaean Greeks did use the bow as a weapon of war. Although many of the finds of arrowheads may be associated with hunting, those from warrior graves and the large numbers from the palaces are just as likely to be for use in warfare.

Slings were in use throughout Greece by the early Bronze Age, but only in a hunting or flock-defending capacity until the middle of the second millennium BC. The missiles used were shaped stones, natural pebbles or baked clay. The Thera frescos may show drowning slingers (Vutiropoulos 1991, p. 283), but the first (and only) clear example of slingers in combat is the same silver siege rhyton from Shaft Grave IV at Mycenae, which depicts three archers. Three slingers are also shown on this, working with the archers. By 1300 slingshots made of lead were also being manufactured and have been found in Knossos and Cyprus. Lead shots carry greater weight for a smaller size, and travel farther and faster. The sling was to remain a weapon, albeit a fairly ephemeral one, throughout the period covered by this book (Pritchett 1991).

In this period then, we have seen that the Greeks adopted and adapted some items of military equipment from Minoan Crete and perhaps beyond, while also improving and inventing items themselves. The elite force of each palace seems to have been a chariot force numbered in the hundreds, armed with helmets, thrusting spears and swords, with body armour also being introduced after *c.* 1500. In support of this force was the infantry, armed with body shields, spears and swords. They probably fought as a skirmishing group with the chariot warriors, or maybe even as a primitive sort of phalanx. Most of these warriors also seem to have possessed helmets. Archers and slingers were clearly used in siege contexts, and it seems likely that they would have featured on the battlefield as well. Such light troops were very effective at breaking up cavalry charges in the Hellenistic period, and it seems probable that they fulfilled a similar function at this time. With this equipment Greeks, probably from Mycenae, conquered Knossos in *c.* 1400 and began to spread across the islands of the Aegean to Asia Minor and Cyprus. These movements led to increased fortifications at the palaces (Connolly 1977, pp. 20–1), and there seems to have been a general increase in levels of warfare, which led to several military innovations. These will be discussed in Chapter 2.

# TWO

# The Late Mycenaean Period, the Dark Age and Homer, 1300–900 BC

The period covered by this chapter, although only 100 years longer than that covered by Chapter 1, was a period of turmoil and change. The Greek palaces grew in economic wealth, and many of them built or improved impressive fortifications, showing that battle was very much a common occurrence. Greek influence was extended to south-west Asia Minor and to the island of Cyprus. Then, shortly after 1200, the great catastrophe happened. The palaces were destroyed and only some were rebuilt. At the same time the Hittite civilisation was overrun, and Egypt had to battle with invading 'Sea Peoples', some of whom may have been Mycenaean Greeks. This calamity was originally thought to be some great natural disaster like an earthquake, but it is unlikely that one such event could have caused such an impact. The main reason seems to have been population movement, probably caused by overpopulation after a long period of relative peace and prosperity. A good parallel is the Viking period in north-west Europe.

Overpopulation at home caused the Vikings to leave in search of plunder to support a way of life, followed by settlement in England, Normandy and elsewhere. Was Mycenaean Greece overcrowded? The increase in prosperity might suggest that, but there is also evidence from linguistics that Greeks from further north, the Dorians, came south and caused the collapse of the Mycenaean palaces and the emigration of some Mycenaeans, forming part of the 'Sea Peoples'. Whole books have been written on this subject (Drews 1993, *passim*; see also Sandars 1964 and Snodgrass 2000, p. 311 ff.) and there is not the space to go through all the arguments here. Suffice it to say that the evidence for Greece points to warfare causing the collapse of the civilisation, and that it was warfare among Greeks. The palace system did not disappear overnight. Pylos was destroyed in *c.* 1200 and never rebuilt, but Mycenae and Thebes were rebuilt and struggled on for perhaps another 100 years or more. Athens, a smaller settlement, seems to have remained unaffected. Many other smaller settlements were simply abandoned, and there is evidence for Mycenaean population movements to Achaea in the Peloponnese and to Cyprus, where there was a final flourishing of Mycenaean civilisation until about 1050.

After this, Greece entered a Dark Age, by which we mean that there is little evidence for what was going on, although it is certain that overseas trade and contacts diminished dramatically, as did the population. To help enlighten us, we have the *Iliad* and the *Odyssey* of Homer, epic works written down in the eighth century, but preserved in an oral tradition for generations before. These refer to the Trojan War, traditionally fought in the 1180s, and preserve some memory of those calamitous times and their aftermath. The wanderings of Odysseus in the *Odyssey* perhaps preserve some memory of the population movements and strife in the homeland, and the *Iliad* perhaps tells us of Mycenaean expansion eastwards. It also tells us much about how Greek soldiers were thought to have fought at the end of the Mycenaean period, written by Greeks just a few hundred years later. Mixed up with this is the combat of Homer's own day, and sorting out true Mycenaean memories is difficult. This evidence, as well as the archaeology, will be examined in this chapter.

Fig. 14: Warriors from a fresco at Pylos, *c.* 1200. *(After Connolly 1977, p. 10)*

The form of combat with chariots and infantry appears to have remained virtually the same in this period, except for the demise of the chariot following the final collapse of the palace civilisation in the eleventh century (Crouwel, in Laffineur 1999, p. 456). The last certain use of the chariot is an example excavated at Lefkandi in Euboea, dating to *c.* 1000 (Popham, Touloupa and Sackett 1982), and by then it may have been a status symbol rather than a weapon of war. At around the same time there is the first certain evidence for cavalry, in the form of a picture on a vase of a mounted warrior with a spear (Greenhalgh 1973, pp. 46–7).

Evidence from vases and frescos seems to show an increase in the use of infantry over chariots, which may have been caused primarily by an increase in the size of armies in general. Chariotry was expensive, and larger armies would be made up of more infantry, especially after the catastrophe when the palace system gradually broke down. Let us now look at the equipment and its use in detail.

## HELMETS

As far as helmets go, the boars' tusk helmet still seemed to be the main form of head protection. As discussed in Chapter 1, it features on the Pylos frescos of *c.* 1200 (Figs 3*f*, 14), and three plates from a helmet were found in Chamber Tomb B at Kallithea in Achaea, dating from *c.* 1150 (Yalouris 1960, p. 44 and plate 31; Papadopoulos in Laffineur 1999, p. 269). It is perhaps safe to assume that, with the end of the palaces and their elite warriors/hunters, the boars' tusk helmet ceased being manufactured. It does of course survive in literary form in the *Iliad*, as mentioned above, but as a rare helmet whose method of construction has to be explained to an unfamiliar audience. The Pylos Linear B tablets of 1200 continue to mention helmets with four 'strips' or 'things hung on' (as well as cheek pieces), which we interpreted in the earlier period as scale armour guards for the back of the neck on bronze helmets.

Other evidence for bronze helmets continues to be slight. The Mycenaean Warrior Vase (Fig. 15) of *c.* 1150 shows lines of warriors marching off to battle. The helmets are black with white dots, which has been interpreted as bronze studs on a leather helmet (Snodgrass 1967, p. 31) or an embossed bronze helmet (Connolly 1977, p. 22), which latter was certainly in use further north in the Balkans and Central Europe at this time. Indeed, the helmets are remarkably similar to the Pass Lueg crested helmet from Austria (Borchhardt 1972, plates 39.1, 39.2). Some other warriors on the vase have a low crest on the helmet, which has been described as a hedgehog crest, probably made of stiff horsehair.

Fig. 15: The Mycenaean Warrior Vase, c. 1150. *(Joint Library of the Hellenic and Roman Societies, Slide G.1868)*

The main surviving line of warriors have high crests with white dots, which seems to favour the idea of an embossed bronze helmet. These also appear to have a flowing horsehair crest behind, and horns on the front.

We have seen that earlier boars' tusk helmets could have horns, and there is no reason for these not to have been fitted to bronze helmets. Indeed, Homer mentions such helmets in the *Iliad* (XXII, 314). Mention has been made of Central European helmets of embossed bronze which appeared possibly as early as the twelfth century, and it is likely that they received the idea of bronze plate armour from the Greeks. The fact that helmets were more common in Central Europe, in this and later periods, is because of the abundance of the raw materials there and the greater likelihood of being buried with such items, or of such items being offered in votive deposits (Snodgrass 1971, *passim*). Greece, by contrast, has little copper, and most would have had to be imported from Anatolia and Cyprus – hence the Mycenaeans' interest in the island.

The embossing of bronze does seem to be a form of decoration clearly derived from that of reinforcing leather with bronze studs, and so it would seem that leather helmets reinforced with bronze were certainly in use at this time, as well as completely bronze helmets. The evidence of the Mycenaean Warrior Vase shows that foot soldiers during this period were being armoured to a greater extent with body armour and greaves (see below), and there was perhaps more of a demand for bronze than could be met by the supply. The only find of a Late Mycenaean bronze helmet has occurred just recently at Portes-Kephalovryson in Achaea, where many Mycenaeans went after the initial catastrophe of *c.* 1200. Here in Chamber Tomb 2 a helmet of a 'tiara'-like construction was found. It consists of strips of embossed bronze in layers or rows built up to form a helmet, and must have been over a leather cap. It is in fact more of a bronze-reinforced leather helmet than an actual bronze one. It has not yet been reconstructed or fully published (Papadopoulos, in Laffineur 1999, p. 271). Similar embossed bronze strips occurred in Chamber Tomb A at Kallithea and were interpreted as part of a cuirass (Yalouris 1960, p. 43 and plate 29). They too could be part of a 'tiara' helmet, especially as there was no sign of a helmet in this otherwise very rich grave. Further bronze studs, but no studded strips, have also been found in a tomb at Lakkithra on the island of Kephallenia (Marinatos 1932, plate 16). To confuse the situation, Chamber Tomb 3 at Krini, also in Achaea, had bronze studs and strips which were clearly the decoration for a scabbard (Papadopoulos, in Laffineur 1999, p. 271), so the Kallithea and Lakkithra finds could now be interpreted as scabbards! We will need to wait for the 'tiara' helmet from Portes-Kephalovryson to be fully published before we can properly reassess these other finds.

The Mycenaean civilisation based on the palaces seems to have petered out by 1100, and from just after then, perhaps from 1050, we have a helmet find from Tiryns (Fig. 16) (*Bulletin de Correspondance Hellénique*, 82, 1958, p. 707, fig. 26; *Mitteilungen des Deutschen Archäologischen Instituts*, 78, 1963, pp. 17–24). Although often described as a bronze helmet, this too is really a bronze-reinforced leather helmet. It consists of four plates. There are two triangular side plates which have a decorative border of triangular holes punched right through the plate, presumably the means by which it was attached to its leather or fabric cap; and two long, curved, rectangular plates running along the central ridge from the forehead to the back of the neck. These would leave a join running down the middle, where we might imagine a short horsehair crest was fitted like the 'hedgehog' crests on the Mycenaean Warrior Vase. The border of each side plate is also decorated with rows of small, embossed bronze studs, and the centre of each side has a large, embossed bronze stud surrounded by circles of

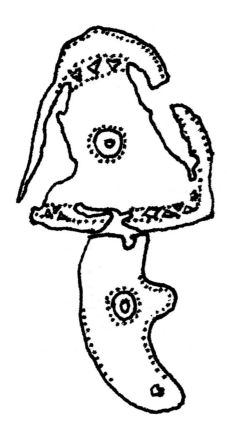

Fig. 16: Bronze helmet from Tiryns, *c.* 1050.

smaller studs. Such decoration is very similar to that found on greaves of the period (see below). The cheek pieces are bronze plates of a scalloped shape, very similar to the earlier helmets of Dendra and Knossos, and were not attached to the helmet plates but separately attached to the lining, just like the Knossos helmet. They have a row of holes all around the edge for attachment to the lining and a central embossed stud and circles matching the helmet plates.

For the next 200 years there is no evidence for helmets in Greece, almost certainly due to a great shortage of bronze following the loss of contacts with the outside world. Bronze or bronze-reinforced helmets may have continued in use, but were simply never buried or lost for archaeologists to find, because the bronze was too precious. However, the evidence we do have, for the period 1025 to 950 roughly, shows that many artefacts which were previously made in bronze, like pins and fibulae, were now made in iron, which was just coming into use. When Greek contacts overseas began again towards the end of the tenth century, these pins and fibulae were again made in bronze (Snodgrass 1971, p. 42). If there was not enough bronze in Greece for such small items, it seems even less likely that there was sufficient to make helmets, and warriors must have resorted to caps made of leather or other perishable materials.

The evidence of Homer adds a little to our knowledge of helmets, apart from the evidence already quoted for the boars' tusk helmet. Most importantly, the other helmets used in the *Iliad* are invariably made of bronze or reinforced with bronze (Lorimer 1950, p. 238). An occasional epithet is 'with bronze cheek pieces', reminding us of the Dendra boars' tusk helmet, where only the cheek pieces were of bronze. 'Bronze helmets' reminds us of the late fifteenth-century Knossos helmet, whereas 'bronze-reinforced helmets' is closer to the Tiryns helmet, and perhaps those shown on the Mycenaean Warrior Vase. There is no detailed description to show us the construction of the helmet, but there is some information on decoration. Horsehair crests are frequently mentioned and must have been of an upright, stiff form rather than just hanging naturally loose, because they are said to nod downwards (*Iliad* III, 336–7). Achilles' helmet also has additional golden crests at its sides (*Iliad* XIX, 382–3). Some helmets are described as four-horned, *tetraphalos*, and others with four plates, *tetraphaleros*; Lorimer (1950, p. 241) probably rightly asserts that there may be some confusion between these two words. The Tiryns helmet is constructed of four main plates, so Homer may be remembering a reality there, but there is also evidence for horned helmets from early seals of boars' tusk helmets, through to the Mycenaean Warrior Vase. Those helmets appear to have just two horns, and Homer also uses the term *amphiphalos* for this sort of helmet. A problem with this interpretation of *phalos*, meaning horn, is that it is sometimes described as 'shining', which is more suggestive of metal (*Iliad* XVI, 216). Another passage suggests that the horn is supporting a horsehair crest (*Iliad* XIII, 614), which also suggests a metal projection. Perhaps the word could mean either; or perhaps we have a mistake here, with *phaleros* meaning a bronze plate, like the central plates on the Tiryns helmet which would have supported a crest. A final word, which Homer uses in connection with the four-horned helmets, is *aulopis*. This word is unknown but is related to *aulos*, meaning a socket, and presumably means that the four horns or crest supports on these helmets were tube-like, which is easily understandable if crests were to be fitted into them. While some of these descriptions can be related to late eighth-century helmets of Homer's own day, the horns, and certainly the description of a boars' tusk helmet, seem to be connected only to Mycenaean helmets. With the shortage of bronze in the Dark Age, Mycenaean helmets – or at least their memory – may have been passed down the generations; or old pieces of armour may have been discovered in Mycenaean tombs, as is discussed below.

## BODY ARMOUR

When we turn to body armour we again have to rely on artistic depictions, supplemented by finds from Central Europe and the evidence from Homer. A short cuirass seems now to have been the order of the day, replacing the much heavier Dendra-style armour, and was being worn by infantry as well as chariot warriors. It was suggested in Chapter 1 that the warrior who wore the Dendra-style armour found at Thebes may have discarded the subsidiary plates to be left with a short bronze cuirass. Unfortunately there is no Greek bronze cuirass of that date to support this theory, although some vase paintings of around 1200 suggest metal cuirasses rather than the leather corslets they are usually described as. Three examples at least seem to be shown by Vermeule and Karageorghis in their book on vase paintings (1982, figs XI.31, XI.57, XI.64.1). One has the nipples marked out especially and there is a high neck guard, which suggests that this piece of equipment lasted longer than the other Dendra attachments (Greenhalgh 1980, *passim*).

Fig. 17: Linear B corslet ideograms from Pylos, *c.* 1200.

A bronze neck guard implies a bronze cuirass, and the continued use of the neck guard is also shown by the Pylos Linear B tablets (Fig. 17). Another picture of a warrior on a vase fragment (Vermeule and Karageorghis 1982, fig. XI.57), lacks a neck guard, but his cuirass is clearly marked with curved lines representing the pectoral muscles, as well as having the nipples marked. These fragments all date from *c.* 1200.

Two gold breastplates of this period have also been found at Enkomi in Cyprus with anatomical details; they remind us of the Shaft Grave finds and the possibilities of bronze versions for use in combat (*Fasti Archaeologici* 4, 1949, no. 1817). As far as I am aware, these finds have not been published further, so I cannot ascertain whether they were full breastplates or just small pectorals.

There are no surviving Greek bronze breastplates from the Late Mycenaean period, but there are two fragmentary examples from Slovakia that are worth looking at, as they are of the same period and were probably derived from Mycenaean examples (Snodgrass 1971, p. 37). The Urnfield peoples of Central Europe certainly had contact and trade with the Mycenaean Greeks and may have been introduced to plate armour in the course of that trade. Lack of evidence prevents us from deciding whether the Central Europeans adapted their simple cuirass from the inner thorax of the Dendra panoply, or whether the Greeks first adopted this short cuirass which was then in turn passed to Europe; this latter reason seems more likely.

The Čaka cuirass from East Slovakia was the first to prove that Urnfield cuirasses really did stretch back to the late Bronze Age, as it was firmly dated to the end of Bronze D or the beginning of Hallstatt A, that is c. 1200 (Snodgrass 1967, p. 42). It consists of only four or five fragments, and the overall shape is indeterminable. It is possible that it was short, ending at the waist, and perhaps with a separate belt below that, rather than a proper bell shape with a flange over the hips as developed later. It has a decorated border of embossed studs and zigzag lines, and over each breast it has a star-shaped design, cut out of a separate piece of bronze and riveted on. It was thought that this was a unique piece of armour, possibly an import from Greece, but further finds now argue convincingly for local manufacture; there was after all a plentiful supply of copper. Most importantly, two large fragments of another cuirass were found at Ducové in Slovakia in a context datable to 1150. Again the overall shape eludes us but, like Čaka, it has a decorated border, this time a double line of small bosses, and star-shaped designs on the breasts. These were executed with a fine punch and, below the design, one of the fragments shows that a repoussé curve was hammered into the metal to delineate the pectoral muscle, as has been described above on one of the Mycenaean vase fragments. In the centre of the chest was a circular design executed, like the border, by embossed studs on a raised line. A point worth noting here is that the remains of both these early cuirasses are from the breastplate only. It is possible that backplates were a luxurious extra and that sometimes a breastplate was worn on its own, simply tied on with leather straps.

Before we return to the Greek evidence, we should examine the significance of the decoration on these cuirasses. The most important things to note are the studs around the edges, which show they were translations into bronze of leather breastplates, which would have had their edges turned over and riveted with bronze to stop them fraying. The separate bronze breast stars from the Čaka cuirass also have bronze studs at each of the points, showing that such stars were originally riveted to leather corslets. This leather corslet with bronze reinforcement reminds us of the evidence we have discussed for Late Mycenaean helmets, and it would seem that bronze-reinforced leather was also in use for body armour. The surviving evidence is rather stronger for this than for bronze cuirasses.

As with helmets, the Mycenaean Warrior Vase is our best evidence (Fig. 15). The soldiers, marching with spears over their shoulders, apparently have leather corslets with long sleeves since there is no line at the shoulder (Snodgrass 1967, p. 36). The warriors on the opposite side, however, do have a pair of white lines at the shoulder showing, perhaps, that the corslet they wear has no sleeves and maybe a bronze edging. They also have a series of white lines and dots on the chest that look like bronze attachments and studs. Connolly (1977, p. 22) has argued for these being bronze cuirasses, which remains a possibility but, as we have noted, the decoration – if in bronze – implies derivation from bronze-reinforced corslets, and I think that is what we have here. Astrom, in his work on the Dendra armour (1977, plate XXXII), examined several other pottery fragments featuring warriors, which he thought might show bronze cuirasses. Most are painted black like those on the Warrior Vase, although one is white, and one illustrated by Greenhalgh (1980, p. 202, fig. 1) is decorated with geometric designs. This latter possibly represents embossed or painted bronze, but the other examples are more likely to be leather. They mostly appear to have integral long sleeves. An argument in favour of bronze is that most depictions (including the Warrior Vase) have an outward-turning flange at the waist, very similar to the much later bell cuirasses in bronze. This flange may just be artistic style, however, or it could be that the bell curve did develop at this early period. There is no evidence at this time for *cuir-bouilli*, that is, leather stiffened and moulded through boiling; but a bell shape could be made from leather by the use of bronze edging or simply through the cut of the leather. This would have given the warrior more freedom of movement.

The most convincing evidence for bronze-reinforced corslets used to be the finds of strips and studs from Kallithea (Fig. 18), published by Yalouris (1960, p. 47) but, as mentioned above, it seems that these now came from a scabbard or a 'tiara' helmet. Some of the pieces of embossed bronze are curved rather than flat so a helmet is perhaps more likely, as this grave had two swords and a pair of greaves but no sign of a helmet. The only other possibility comes from Cyprus, where Catling assembled a large shield from fragments from a tomb at Kaloriziki dating to the eleventh century (Catling 1964, p. 144 and plates 17, 18; Snodgrass 1967, p. 44 and plate 14). As reconstructed this shield has one

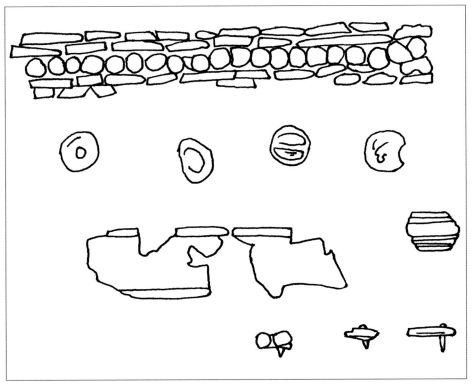

Fig. 18: Fragments of scabbard casing (?) from Kallithea in Achaea, *c.* 1180.

large central boss and two small side bosses, but I know of no other shield that has three bosses, and Borchhardt (in Buchholz and Wiesner 1977, p. 34) has suggested that the smaller two bosses are quite possibly breast ornaments from a leather cuirass. The bronze 'shield edging' may also have belonged to a cuirass, although it is perhaps too wide for this. Most important are the fragments of bronze, decorated with embossed circle patterns, which Catling (1964, p. 144 and plate 17) also places on the reconstructed shield, although he admits that they could have come from anywhere. These remind one of the cuirasses from Slovakia, but also of contemporary Greek greaves which will be discussed later. They too, then, may be from body armour, although greaves are perhaps more likely. Perhaps the important thing to note is that the find is from Cyprus, which did not suffer the bronze shortages that mainland Greece had at this time. The name of the island means 'Copper', and finds of bronze armour are more common there as a result of the occurrence of the metal.

It has been suggested that these bronze or bronze-reinforced leather corslets may have been short, ending at the waist, instead of the flanged bell shape that appears later, although this flanging appears to be shown in some of the contemporary vase depictions. The reason for believing in a short corslet comes from Homer (see below), who occasionally seems to suggest an armoured belt worn below a cuirass of bronze, and also from finds of bronze figurines going through into the Dark Age, which show warriors wearing only a bronze belt and a helmet for protection (Snodgrass 1967, p. 42). A possible example of such a belt was found in a twelfth-century chamber tomb at Mycenae. This example consists of the two surviving ends of a waist belt, 29cm and 16cm long with a width of just over 5cm – much narrower than the earlier Dendra 'belts'. There are holes along the edge for the attachment of a lining, but no sign of a clasp. We must suppose that this was also attached to the leather backing, but not to the bronze itself. If a leather corslet was worn with this belt, it could have reached down to the hips and the belt could have been worn over it. Of course, the belt could have been worn on its own or perhaps with a short bronze cuirass. A similar usage of plate armour appeared among the Samnites and other Italians in the fourth century (Connolly 1978, pp. 22–7).

Fig. 19: Vase fragment showing chariot warriors with kilts and round shields, c. 1200.

Travelling further down the torso, there is good evidence in this period for the wearing of heavy kilts, made of leather or thick material, perhaps reinforced with bronze studs, for the protection of the pelvis and upper thighs. The warriors on the Mycenaean Warrior Vase (Fig. 15) wear them, and some have the same white dot decoration as on their helmets and corslets, which we have interpreted as bronze reinforcement. Other kilts are shown as plain black (Fig. 19), or with a black-and-white check pattern suggesting a woven or quilted material. These kilts often have a fringe on the lower edge (Vermeule and Karageorghis 1982, figs XI.1A, XI.18, XI.42, XI.43, XI.44, XI.59). The warriors on the Pylos frescos appear to be wearing similar black-and-white kilts but with a diagonal pattern (Fig. 14). They wear no other body armour, which suggests that a kilt might have been a preferable piece of armour to a corslet. This would have made sense if a small shield was carried, and there are similar examples of kilts being worn in the later hoplite period (see Chapter 4). The body shield seems to have gone out of favour after *c.* 1300, and smaller shields meant the legs especially became vulnerable. These kilts would have protected the thighs, and we see a greater use of greaves in this period to protect the lower legs (see below).

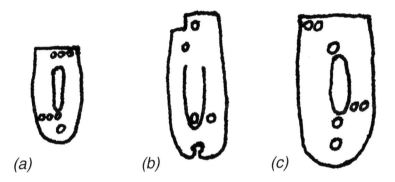

*(a)*        *(b)*        *(c)*

Fig. 20: Bronze armour scales from *(a)* Alaas in Cyprus; *(b)* Mycenae; *(c)* Lefkandi in Euboea.

A final type of corslet to be considered, which would not have required a separate kilt but would have been worn with a belt, is the scale corslet. This was armour made from small plates of bronze called scales, sewn in rows onto a backing material, presumably leather, and was invented in Egypt or the Near East as early as the seventeenth century. There are two possible large scales from Phaistos in Crete dating to *c.* 1200, which are trapezoidal in shape and not of Eastern origin. They measure 5 × 4cm and were perhaps a local idea, possibly made by a man who had heard of scale armour but not seen it, and had attempted his own design (Hood and De Jong 1952, p. 261; Snodgrass 1965c, p. 99). Mycenaeans at this period, especially as they colonised south-west Asia Minor and Cyprus, would have seen and perhaps fought warriors wearing scale armour, and would have noticed its advantages.

Each bronze scale is usually 2–3cm wide, 5–6cm long and about 1mm thick, with a reinforcing central spine (Fig. 20). Since each scale covers the top half of the scale below, the warrior was protected by two layers of bronze as well as by the coat of leather onto which they were sewn. The design also meant that the corslet was almost as flexible as one made simply of leather, and it did not need too skilled a craftsman to make it, although many hundreds of scales would have been needed for each suit. As might be expected, our main evidence for Mycenaean Greeks using scale armour comes from Cyprus. Here there was a ready supply of bronze, and the influence from the Near East was closest. Two bronze scales have been found at Enkomi dating from *c.* 1150 (Popham, Sackett and Themelis 1980, p. 251), four more in an eleventh-century tomb on the Karpos Peninsula, and three more from *c.* 1100 at Alaas in the south of the island (Fig. 20*a*) (Karageorghis 1975, pp. 6 ff.). These late dates are all contemporary with, or after, the great catastrophe that destroyed the mainland palaces. Cyprus and Achaea seem to have had an influx of Mycenaean Greeks at this time. After this period, Cyprus was very much on the periphery of the Greek World, often succumbing to invaders and influences from the East such as Assyria and Persia. As a result it did not always follow armour developments elsewhere in Greece and, unlike Greece, it was to continue to use scale armour for many centuries (see Chapter 3).

For the rest of Greece we have just two examples of scales. A solitary scale of twelfth-century date was found at Mycenae (Fig. 20*b*) (Connolly 1977, p. 23), and there is also an example from Lefkandi on Euboea dating to *c.* 900 (Fig. 20*c*) (Popham, Sackett and Themelis 1980, plate 239.1). Both these scales are small at 5 × 2cm, which means they came from high-quality suits. Smaller scales meant more of them were needed, and so the suit became more expensive. The example from Lefkandi comes from a period when Near Eastern and Cypriot scales were being made from iron, and the excavators suggest this might have been an antique piece kept as a souvenir. Even so, it seems that some Greeks at least had access to scale corslets throughout this Late Mycenaean and early Dark Age period.

For artistic representations of scale corslets we must turn to Egyptian paintings and Assyrian reliefs. These generally show a short-sleeved garment, which reaches down to the ankles and is worn with a belt at the waist to take some of the weight off the shoulders. When first introduced, this armour was used as an alternative to a body shield by those soldiers who needed both hands free, like archers and chariot warriors. This is why the armour covers so much of the body, although it must have hampered movement somewhat. It is unlikely, however, that such a long garment was worn in Greece and Cyprus, since we know that the Mycenaeans of the period also wore greaves (see below). The only clear representation of scale armour we have in the Greek sphere is that worn by an archer in a chariot, on a carved ivory box from Enkomi in Cyprus. This shows Hittite influences, however, and does not seem to be of local manufacture. The scale corslet worn here reaches to midway down the warrior's thighs; this is more likely to be the type worn by Greeks.

Further evidence for the use of scale armour in Greece is provided by Homer. Cinyras of Cyprus gives Agamemnon a unique armour described in detail by Homer (*Iliad* XI, 15). It is described as being made up of forty-two strips or bands (*oimoi*). Ten strips were of dark cyanus, that is blue enamel or glass paste, presumably on a base of bronze. Twelve strips were of gold and twenty strips were of tin; both these also must have been plating on bronze. Since this corslet was a gift, the method of manufacture and the materials used were perhaps uncertain. The word *oimoi* has been interpreted by most scholars as 'rows', and this corslet as being a scale corslet. (See Connolly 1986, p. 7 for an alternative interpretation.) Support for this theory is the fact that the corslet was a gift from Cyprus, where we know scale armour was in use. It seems that some wealthy Greeks may have used them. It is interesting that Homer takes the trouble to write about the armour in detail, suggesting that it was a piece of equipment rarely seen or used in his day. However, he does the same with the boars' tusk helmet, and we have seen that that was a very common piece of equipment in Mycenaean times. Perhaps in the Late Mycenaean period scale corslets were common, but they are a rarity in the Dark Age and into the eighth century. There is certainly no evidence for their use on the mainland after the Lefkandi scale of *c.* 1000. Returning to the description of Agamemnon's corslet, if we assume a scale length of 5cm with a good overlap, this gives a width of 2cm per row, and a total length of *c.* 84cm. As surmised earlier, this means that Agamemnon's corslet reached down to just above the knees and would have been worn with a waist belt and greaves. The different colours of the rows of armour scales are paralleled in Egyptian paintings of scale corslets worn by Ramses III and Tutankhamun (Yadin 1963, pp. 240–1). These could simply be painted scales, but the tomb of Tutankhamun did produce a scale corslet incorporating gilding and blue glass enamelling (Carter and Mace, 1923–33, plate XXXVIII). Agamemnon's corslet is further described as having had three serpents of iridescent cyanus on either side of the corslet, writhing towards the neck. This armour was a splendid piece of equipment, then, and it is fitting that it should have been a gift to the great Greek king from one of his allies.

For this period (*c.* 1200) we also have Linear B tablets from Pylos, twelve of which show corslet ideograms (Fig. 17). These differ from the earlier Knossos ones in several important ways. Firstly, they are now named using the classical Greek word *thorax* implying a simpler piece of equipment than the list of parts accompanying the Knossos ideogram, which was describing a Dendra panoply. Secondly, they are not listed with chariots, although these (or at least their wheels) are listed elsewhere. This implies that the cuirasses could be and were used by infantry as well as charioteers, and were therefore less cumbersome and more widely available. Apart from the word *thorax*, the Pylos corslets are described as having 'things hung on': twenty large and ten small or, in four cases, twenty-two large and twelve small (Chadwick 1976, p. 162). Snodgrass (1965c, p. 99) has interpreted these as quilting or layers for a material armour, but the number seem too large. He backs this idea up by interpreting the horizontal lines on the ideograms as quilting. However, we have seen that the earlier Linear B ideograms from Knossos had these lines because they were representing a Dendra cuirass. It must be remembered that these Linear B ideograms are not accurate illustrations, but a shorthand form. It is clear that by the time of the Pylos ideograms, Dendra cuirasses were no longer used, but the ideogram remains similar because to change it would have been confusing for the scribes.

Chadwick (1976, pp. 162–3) interprets the 'things hung on' as scales, but since that gives him only thirty or thirty-four scales, instead of the hundreds needed, he proceeds to design a theoretical armour with a very small number of large scales. It is much more likely that these 'things hung on' equate with the *oimoi* in Homer, and that the numbers refer to rows of scales. Homer describes Agamemnon's armour by giving the numbers of rows, and it seems reasonable to assume that that is how these Linear B scribes are describing armour in the Pylos tablets. Here we have only thirty or thirty-four rows compared to the forty-two of Agamemnon's suit, but his was a suit fit for a king and would have had a greater number of smaller scales. If we interpret the Pylos large 'things hung on' and small 'things hung on' as 6cm scales and 5cm scales, we get rows mostly of 3cm width each after overlapping, with 2cm rows only where the small scales are used, presumably at the neck. This gives suit lengths of 80–90cm, pretty much the same as calculated for Agamemnon's armour, and giving a knee-length cuirass that would have been supported with a waist belt. If this interpretation is correct, then the palace at Pylos was issuing scale corslets as body armour to its charioteers and foot soldiers in the thirteenth century. The scale from Mycenae and the description in Homer suggest that scale corslets may have been more popular in twelfth-century Greece than has been previously thought rather than just in Cyprus.

The Pylos ideograms differ slightly from the earlier Knossos ones in that they show no shoulder guards, but short sleeves (or the wearer's arms: it is unclear which), and neck guards and helmets. If the neck guard appears on these tablets, but not on the Knossos ones, it suggests that the guard was a later addition to the panoply, as was suggested in Chapter 1. It is also further evidence for the Pylos corslets being metal, since a bronze neck guard would be unlikely with material armour. There is an illustration from Egypt showing a high, bronze neck guard being worn with a scale armour corslet, which is just the armour I am suggesting these Pylos tablets show (Connolly 1986, p. 30, fig. 1).

Apart from his description of Agamemnon's scale corslet, all other mentions of armour by Homer are of bronze plate armour, and before the discovery of Mycenaean bronze armour it was thought that these mentions of bronze were later additions or interpolations. With the discoveries of Dendra, Knossos, Tiryns and Achaea, and the realisation that commonly occurring epithets such as *Achaion chalkochitonon* (bronze-corsleted Achaeans) could not possibly be interpolations, as they are the basic structure upon which the epic is built, this idea can happily now be dismissed (Sheratt 1990, p. 814). We still have the problems of uncertain translations, words that later change their meanings and words for which the translation can be guessed only from the context.

The use of the word *guala* (hollow) in describing this armour shows that the armour consisted of back- and breastplates forming a cuirass, and was not a bronze scale cuirass. Other passages prove that the *thorax* covered the shoulders (*Iliad* V, 98–9) and reached to the waist (*ibid.* IV, 132) but no further. Supplementary pieces of armour were also worn, as is explained below, and we must decide whether they are describing a Dendra-style suit or are just additions to a short cuirass of bronze or bronze-reinforced leather, as has been suggested. The latter seems more likely, and Snodgrass (1965a, pp. 171–2) even equates *guala* with the later bell cuirass of Homer's own day. The wide bell curve of such cuirasses does not always fit well with these armour additions, however, as Snodgrass admits (1967, pp. 55–6), and I would see the Homeric cuirass as ending at the waist.

One of the most enlightening passages in the *Iliad* is in Book IV, 132, when Menelaos is wounded by an arrow. This arrow strikes the golden clasp of his *zoster*, which is made of bronze. It passes through this, and his cuirass, and then pierces the *mitra*, which he wore as a last defence against missiles. Describing the incident later (*Iliad* IV, 186), Menelaos says that the arrow was stopped by his *zoster*, his *zoma* and his *mitra*, which was either made by the bronzesmiths or had bronze put on it. Either translation is possible. The first passage gives us clearly enough the order in which the armour was worn. The word *zoster* means a belt in later times and that seems a reasonable translation here. It is described as well-wrought and shining, which tells us that it is metal, or perhaps metal plates on a leather belt (Liddell and Scott 1968, p. 760). It is worn over the cuirass, and the *mitra* was worn under the cuirass. In later times *mitra* can mean a boxer's girdle, which is perhaps closest to its meaning here. Buchholz and Wiesner (1977, p. 127) associate it with the belts worn by Dark Age warrior statuettes and say it was overlapped sometimes by a metal cuirass. They say that the *zoster*, on the other hand, was a bronze belt worn over a tunic of linen and the *zoma* was a synonym for either word (*ibid.* p. 142). The objections to these conclusions can be found in the two above passages concerning Menelaos that we have been discussing. It is clear that Menelaos was wearing all three pieces of armour at the same time, and with a bronze cuirass.

The word *zoma* is also used by Homer as something worn by boxers, and it is clear that it must be a loincloth. The *zoster* was a belt worn over the cuirass, whether it was bronze or linen. It is possible that it was a baldric rather than a waist belt, but I think this is unlikely. The *mitra* remains a problem. It was a visible part of the armour and perhaps attached to it, as seems likely from the epithet *amitrachitones* (literally 'mitra-corsletted' or mitra-tuniced') (*Iliad* XVI, 419), and its use as a last defence against missiles suggests to me something more substantial than a waist belt. There is no archaeological evidence until the seventh century for the semicircular abdominal guards found mostly in Crete and misnamed *mitras*, and I think the word is most likely describing an armoured kilt such as is worn on the Mycenaean Warrior Vase (Fig. 15). This would allow for the three layers of armour in the region of the waist for Menelaos's arrow to penetrate, and fits well with the phrase 'with the bronze they put on it', since these kilts are generally agreed to have been leather with bronze studs.

King (1970, p. 294) has taken a different line, in which she compares Homer's descriptions to the Dendra-style armour. She argues that *zoster* is in fact the armoured skirt from the Dendra suit, which is why it is never mentioned separately in the arming scenes, since it was attached to the cuirass. King also interprets *guala* as the shoulder guards as well as the inner cuirass. These arguments can be rejected on the following grounds. *Guala* is too general a word to represent a specific item of equipment, and for something not to be mentioned in the arming scenes is not a strong argument. King makes no mention of the *mitra*, and I imagine that it would have been superfluous to wear an armoured kilt under the Dendra-style skirt of bronze. The most telling argument perhaps is that Amphius wore a *zoster* with a linen corslet (*Iliad* II, 830 and V, 615), which is perfectly acceptable for a bronze waist belt, but not for an armoured skirt of Dendra style. Also the *zoster* is often described as having a golden clasp, which Dendra 'belts' did not have. Finally, Dendra-style armour had gone out of use by 1300 and Homer rarely mentions items that were in use only in that earliest period; the large body shield of Ajax is one of the few exceptions. Most Homeric references can be securely dated to the Late Mycenaean or Dark Age periods.

When talking about corslets made of a material backing reinforced with bronze, I have referred to bronze-reinforced *leather*, because such illustrations as we have seem to suggest this. When we come to greaves, however, we will see that there is evidence for the use of linen, and there is also evidence for the use of linen body armour at this time, although it is less practical to attach bronze reinforcements to linen. There was a fragment of multilayered linen in the Shaft Graves at Mycenae, which has been interpreted as armour, but our first real proof for its use comes from Homer. The lesser Aias and Amphius are both described as *linothorex* (linen-corsletted), but Homer neglects to go into details and they could have been made in a variety of ways: either woven from thick cord, built up of many thin layers, or padded. I will discuss these various designs later when the linen corslet gained in popularity in the Archaic period, and we have more evidence for its design. For the present, it is interesting to note the two characters who did wear this armour. The lesser Aias could be insolent and unpleasant, and Amphius is a nondescript, second-class character. All the great heroes wore bronze, and this shows the secondary position of linen armour in the Late Mycenaean period – or perhaps just Homer's opinion of it.

On a couple of occasions Homer also mentions gold armour (*Iliad* VI, 234 ff. and X, 439), and implies that it was of the same design as the bronze armour but more costly. It was worth one hundred oxen, as opposed to the nine oxen that a normal panoply was worth. Both sets of armour were worn by non-Greeks: Glaucus the Trojan and Rhesus, King of Thrace. Homer despises such armour, saying it was fit only for the gods. It no doubt occurred to him that gold armour was useless as a defence, and it is plain that he is not describing gilded armour. The passages remind me of the gold pectorals from the Shaft Graves of Mycenae and from Enkomi, and it seems possible that Dark Age tomb robbers had found such items, and believed that some warriors of old had in fact worn gold breastplates in battle. It is possible, of course, that gilded bronze armour was worn by the exceedingly rich, but it would have been expensive and also impractical in battle, where the gilding would soon have been damaged.

As we have seen, the evidence for body armour in this period is slight, especially considering the lack of it in the otherwise rich Achaean tombs. After 1100 there seems to be little evidence for bronze armour apart from Homer and, with the collapse of the palace system and the lack of bronze coming into the country, we must assume leather or linen corslets, if any, down to the reintroduction of bronze armour in *c.* 800.

## GREAVES

The evidence for greaves and leggings is clearer than that for body armour, but still problematical in parts. Schauer's study (1982, *passim*) still gives the best overall picture, although there have been important recent finds which were not known about when he wrote. The plain bronze greave type that was found in the Dendra cuirass tomb seems to have disappeared, but illustrations of 'leggings' abound (Vermeule and Karageorghis 1982, figs XI.3, XI.7, XI.18, XI.28, XI.42, XI.43, XI.49, XI.53, XI.59, XI.63). Those on the palace frescos at Pylos are long, covering the knee, and clearly tied on (Fig. 14) (Bossert 1937, p. 31, fig. 42). They are painted white, which has suggested to some that they were made of metal, but considering the shape of surviving metal greaves this seems unlikely. I would suggest that they are made of linen but, since most of the pottery depictions show black leggings, it would seem that leather was commoner, perhaps particularly after the great catastrophe of *c.* 1200 which would have disrupted trade. Leather leggings are in fact mentioned in the *Odyssey* (XXIV, 228), but they are worn by a farmer to protect him from thorns, and it is speculative to stretch this to a military use.

We do have some examples of short metal greaves of an elliptical form from this period, and the Pylos frescos show such an elliptical form on one leg of each of the Pylos warriors who wears 'linen' leggings. Because of the style of the fresco painting, it is difficult to ascertain whether the elliptical shape is on the left or right leg. Fortenberry (1991, *passim*) opts for the right, but Schauer (1982, p. 149) is surely right to suggest the leading left leg, which would have been more exposed in combat. The early Roman republican army often wore single greaves on the left leg, which was cheaper than a matching pair (Arrian *Ars tactica*, as quoted by Connolly 1998, p. 133). I suggested that because the Dendra greave was so thin, it was probably stitched to a material legging. The Pylos frescos seem to support the idea of a metal greave or greaves being worn over a much larger material legging, rather than directly on the leg like later Archaic and Classical greaves.

Many such elliptical greaves have been found in the Urnfield culture of Central Europe, and the Greek examples are thought by some to have originated from there (Yalouris 1960, p. 49). However, there are two reasons why this does not seem to me to be the case. Firstly, the greave appears in Greece over 300 years before it does in Europe with the Dendra example, and the later Mycenaean ones I am about to discuss still probably pre-date the earliest Hallstatt greaves, although dating the latter is tricky. The second reason is design.

Let us consider the Late Mycenaean examples. The earliest known greaves of this period, dating to *c.* 1200, are from the tombs at Enkomi in Cyprus, but

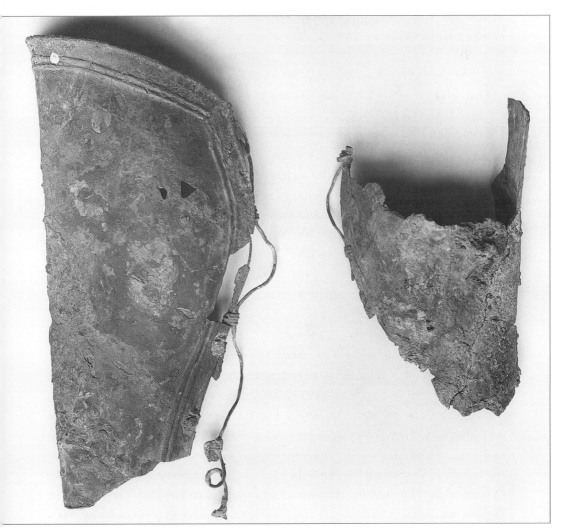

Fig. 21: Greaves from Tomb 15 at Enkomi in Cyprus, twelfth century. *(Trustees of the British Museum, GR 1897.4-1.1531 & 1532)*

were not found with the scales mentioned above. A greave from Tomb 18 is badly corroded and fragmented, and only the lower half is preserved (Catling 1955, p. 23). It is 2mm thick, with the bronze rolled over at the edges for extra strength. The border is 6mm thick and decorated with diagonal lines. Riveted to the edge is a piece of bronze wire lacing, through which leather thongs would have been threaded to tie the greave at the back of the leg. There is no visible decoration on this piece, but other fragments show heavy embossed lines similar to the decoration on the Kallithea greaves (Fig. 22), and the original decoration may have been of this nature.

Tomb 15 at the same site produced a non-matching pair of greaves of similar design (Fig. 21). The best preserved is almost the complete right side of a greave which was probably for the left leg, as there is a bulge for the calf muscle (Fig. 21, right) (Catling 1955, p. 30). This greave is also 2mm thick and is decorated with two repoussé lines running around the greave, 1cm from the edge. Although not visible in the photograph, there was also a repoussé line running vertically from top to bottom down the middle of the greave, the first few centimetres of which still survive. There is also some decoration on the face of the greave, which is hard to detect owing to the corrosion. On the upper half of the greave is an embossed stud surrounded by a circle of fine punched holes. The use of embossing is reminiscent of the helmets and corslets in use at this time, and the fact that such decoration follows on from the direct use of bronze studs on leather leggings. Indeed, the embossed circle is very similar to the later Tiryns helmet mentioned above (Fig. 16). The edges of the greave are rolled over, but the bronze lacing wire is not riveted directly to the greave. It is riveted to a long strip of bronze, which is in turn then riveted to the greave. This suggests to me that the original lacing had become damaged, and that a bronze lacing section had been taken from another greave (old or damaged), and riveted onto this one. The extra work of riveting the lacing onto a strip of bronze and then riveting that strip onto the greave would have made no sense unless it was a repair. All other known laces like this are riveted directly to the greave.

The second greave from this tomb (Fig. 21, left) is only a fragment and, at first glance, the two look like a pair. However, this second greave has double repoussé lines much closer to the edge (6mm) and, like the Tomb 18 example, the bronze lacing wire is attached directly to the greave. Catling (1955, p. 30) suggested that they are the remains of two pairs of greaves, but given that the Dendra warrior perhaps had only one greave, that Tomb 18 at Enkomi had only one greave, and that the Pylos frescos show the use of one greave, then perhaps we have two single greaves here rather than a pair. There may have been two warriors buried in this tomb, each with his own greave, or perhaps a wealthy warrior who possessed two greaves in the same way as he might have had two spears or swords. If we accept that one greave had been repaired after being damaged, it is also possible that this was a pair of greaves worn by a single warrior, which just no longer matched. That they would be reused and repaired also gives us some indication of the value of these items.

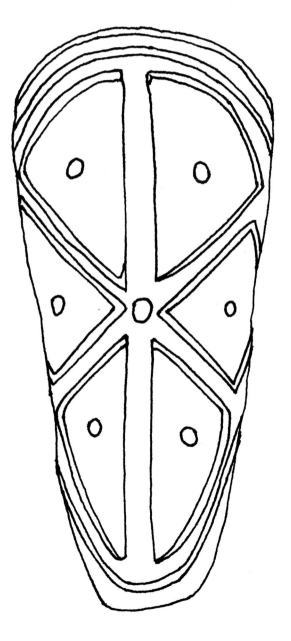

Fig. 22: Greave from Kallithea in Achaea, *c.* 1180.

The other Greek greaves we have are all matching pairs, two from Achaea and a pair from Athens. Tomb B at Kallithea in Achaea, which produced the bronze strips now thought to be from a 'tiara' helmet or scabbard, also produced a pair of greaves dating from perhaps 1180 (Fig. 22). These are of a more oval design than the Enkomi greaves (although they have been heavily restored), and are more heavily embossed with repoussé borders and embossed studs. They also have lacing wires almost identical to the Cypriot examples and riveted directly onto the greaves. Yalouris (1960, p. 46) has cleverly interpreted the design as being derived from bronze-reinforced leather greaves. He suggests the space in between the repoussé lines going around the edge and down the centre of the greave as being representations of bronze strips on a leather backing, and suggests the diagonal lines as being representations of fastening straps held in place by a central stud.

A further pair of greaves was found at Portes-Kephalovryson in Achaea, in the tomb which produced the 'tiara' helmet (Papadopoulos, in Laffineur 1999, p. 271 and plate LIX*a*). Their discovery is yet to be properly published, but from the excavation photograph they appear to be of a similar shape to the Enkomi greaves, and also to have the elaborate lacing wires. According to Papadopoulos they are undecorated, but after cleaning we may discover some slight decoration like the Enkomi ones. They are certainly very different from the Kallithea pair.

The final pair of Late Mycenaean greaves came from a tomb on the slopes of the Athenian acropolis (Fig. 23). They were originally thought to be from the Geometric period, that is tenth or ninth century (Snodgrass 1971, p. 47 after Platon 1965, *Archaeologikon Deltikon* 20, B.1, p. 32), but have now been fairly conclusively proved to be from *c.* 1200 like the Cypriot and Achaean examples (Mountjoy 1984, *passim*). The greaves are very fragmentary, and there are no surviving lacing wires. The bronze was not rolled over at the edges, and there are a couple of edge holes on one piece. These may have been for loops to hold lacing wires, but the greaves may have had more simple fastenings, like some of the Central European specimens. Apart from that they resemble the Kallithea greaves in that they are oval in shape, and the Enkomi greaves in that they have fine, punch-marked decoration. In this case it consists of a border and central vertical line and six circles on each greave.

Very similar decoration was found on some bronze fragments from Kaloriziki on Cyprus, and it is quite likely that they came from another greave or greaves, although Catling (1964, p. 144 and plate 17*e*) restored them as part of a shield. Holes are visible at the edge for attaching to a backing, or for bronze lacing

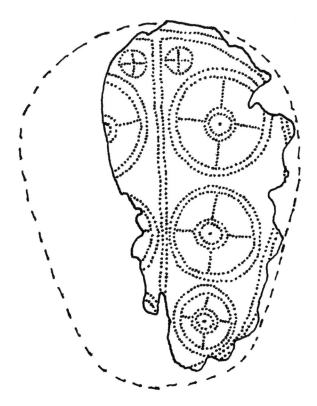

Fig. 23: Greave from Athens,
twelfth century.

wires, although these were not found and may not have existed. The pieces are
very fragmentary and the tomb had been much disturbed.

The European greaves of this period and later have decoration similar to the
Kallithea and Athens greaves, which has led some scholars to believe that the
Greeks got the idea of greaves from Central Europe. Schauer (1982, pp. 152–3)
points out that the main difference between Greek and European greaves is the
fastening. All the European greaves, except for one late Italian copy of the Greek
design, have only single rings or loops of wire at the edges of greaves, which do
not fold around the leg to such an extent. They are much more basic plates of
bronze protecting the front of the leg. Although dating is difficult, they
probably did not appear until 1100 at the earliest, in the Hallstatt A period.

It is much more likely that the Central Europeans copied the Greek greaves,
including their decorations, but simplified the shape and the fastenings.
Yalouris (1960, p. 47) suggested that greaves, like many military developments,
came from the Near East via Cyprus, but this can be refuted. There are no
artistic representations, and the only literary reference is Goliath the Philistine

in the Bible (I Samuel 17: 4), who wears a pair of greaves with his scale armour. This episode is set in the eleventh century and may well have been written later, so it does not count for much. Also, the Philistines are quite possibly descended from the Peleset, one of the Sea Peoples, who brought war to the Near East and may have had a Greek or Central European origin (Astrom 1977, p. 48; Sandars 1964, *passim*).

Homer mentions the 'well-greaved' Achaeans some forty times in the *Iliad*, which rules out later interpolation as suggested by Lorimer (1950, pp. 253 ff.) who was writing before the discovery of Bronze Age greaves on mainland Greece. Homer also mentions greaves three times in a standard phrase (e.g. *Iliad* III, 330–1) which tells us that they were put on first, followed by the cuirass. This was because once the cuirass or corslet was on, the warrior would be unable to bend easily to fasten his greaves. These greaves are presumably bronze, although Hephaestus made a special tin pair for Achilles (*Iliad* XVIII, 613) and these had close-fitting silver guards or clasps (*episphuriois*) at the ankles. There is no evidence for ankle guards until the seventh century (see Chapter 3) and ones made of silver are unlikely. A silver peg was apparently found near the Dendra greave and could have been part of a fastening (Schauer 1982, p. 148), or perhaps the word refers to the elaborate lacing wires that we have seen on the excavated examples, although these are not connected only at the ankle.

All the evidence we have for Late Mycenaean metal greaves fits into the period from *c.* 1220 to *c.* 1150 (*c.* 1050 if the Kaloriziki fragments are greaves), and the decline of the palace system must have been responsible for their disappearance. Bronze greaves continued in use in Central Europe, and this must have been because of the availability of bronze locally. As with body armour, bronze greaves seemed to disappear from Greece completely, to emerge in a quite different form in *c.* 800. For the rest of the period covered by this chapter, perhaps from 1100 down to 900, we must assume that leather leggings were the only armour available.

## SHIELDS

If there seems to have been a reduction in body armour in the Late Mycenaean period, there was certainly a reduction in shield size. The great body shields ceased to exist in art by *c.* 1300 and were replaced with smaller, mostly round shields. Rather strangely, the frescos at Pylos (Fig. 14) do not show shields at all for the warriors armed with helmets and greaves, but shields are more common on pottery fragments. Small round shields of perhaps 50–60cm are being carried by chariot warriors on three separate vases illustrated by Vermeule and Karageorghis (1982, plates XI.1A, XI.1B and XI.28). These were presumably carried by a central handgrip (Fig. 19).

The Mycenaean Warrior Vase (Fig. 15) and Stele, which definitely show infantry, include rather larger shields. The better-preserved side of the Warrior Vase shows 60–70cm round shields with a segment cut out from the bottom. The artist does not show how the shield was carried and, when it was held up in combat, this cut-out may have been on the warrior's right-hand side to make a gap for an underarm spear thrust. Otherwise its purpose is uncertain. The warriors on the other side of the vase and on the stele have even larger oval shields, measuring perhaps as much as a metre across. One of these shows a handle which is not being gripped, implying the existence of a shoulder strap (Lorimer 1950, p. 146; Snodgrass 1967, p. 32). So it seems there were smaller shields carried by chariot warriors, and larger shields with shoulder straps carried by infantry. Lorimer (1950, pp. 148–9, fig. 9) illustrates a vase fragment showing two men on foot holding small shields, but it is most likely that they have just disembarked from their chariot, which is also shown.

Archaeological evidence for shields comes in the form of bronze shield bosses which were used on at least some of these shields, although they are not clearly shown in the art. Mouliana in Crete has produced a twelfth-century example (Snodgrass 1967, p. 32), and eleventh-century examples have been found in Grave XXVIII at Tiryns, which produced the helmet, and Tomb 24 at the Kerameikos in Athens (Snodgrass 2000, p. 319). These are generally domed with a flat edge or border, sometimes decoratively embossed, and would have covered a central handgrip on a round shield. Kaloriziki in Cyprus also produced an example of a shield boss of the eleventh century with a dome and large spike (Snodgrass 1967, p. 45). Found with this shield were two further discs which were interpreted as additional bosses on the shield, and bronze edging, giving a shield shape with an alleged cut-out similar to that on the Mycenaean Warrior Vase (Catling 1964, plate 18; Snodgrass 1967, plate 14). The shape is more exaggerated than the vase and the shield reconstruction looks too wide to be practical. The 'edging' does not exist at the top of the shield where it would have been most needed, and the two smaller bosses are more likely to have come from somewhere else: perhaps a corslet or maybe a pair of cymbals, which are also occasionally found as grave goods. Only one sharp bend in the bronze edging is visible in Catling's plate and I would place this at the bottom of the shield, making a kite shape. This would then look very similar to the larger oval shields on the Mycenaean Warrior Vase. The pieces would obviously benefit from re-examination. Unlike the evidence for helmets, armour and greaves, there is evidence for the existence of shield bosses throughout the Dark Age, to *c.* 900 and beyond, showing that the round shield continued in use (Snodgrass 1967, p. 44). Shields with bronze bosses were, nevertheless, prestige items. The very rich warrior graves of Achaea, which have produced two out of the three known pairs of Late Mycenaean greaves, have produced only one bronze shield boss (Papadopoulos, in Laffineur 1999, p. 271). Since chariots ceased to exist after about 1000, it seems likely that the small shield used by chariot warriors went out of use, leaving only the larger round or elliptical shield used by infantry. This would eventually develop into the hoplite shield.

## SPEARS

The spear became a lighter weapon after 1200. Gone were the 3-metre examples used with the body shield, and now there were only one-handed spears, as clearly depicted on the Mycenaean Warrior Vase (Fig. 15). The spear seems to have been about 2 metres long, with a 20–30cm leaf-shaped blade of bronze. Many of the warrior tombs of Achaea contained a single spear (as well as a sword) of bronze with this type of blade (Papadopoulos, in Laffineur 1999, pp. 267 ff.). Tomb B from Kallithea was also provided with a butt spike of bronze to protect the other end of the spear, and possibly for use as a secondary weapon should the spearhead break off (Papadopoulos, in Laffineur 1999, p. 269 and plate LVII*b*). This is the earliest example of the spear-butt in mainland Greece, but there are also some contemporary examples in Cyprus (Snodgrass 1967, p. 29). A grave from the Kerameikos in Athens produced a similar bronze blade dating from *c.* 1050, but this was paired with a much smaller blade (9cm), suggesting a throwing spear or javelin (Snodgrass 2000, p. 223). A flame-shaped spearhead type, which was an import from the Balkan area, has also been found in parts of north-west Greece, Kephallenia and Crete. Clearly a combat spear, the type does not seem to have caught on (Snodgrass 2000, pp. 306–7, fig. 103).

The soldiers on the Mycenaean Warrior Vase hold one spear, and are using it overarm as a thrusting spear; but another vase fragment (Vermeule and Karageorghis 1982, Plate XI.28) clearly shows a chariot warrior carrying two spears, suggesting that one at least might be thrown. However, his companion has no spear as he is driving the chariot, so perhaps the first warrior is just holding his companion's spear until they both dismount and fight. Other fragments seem to show chariot warriors with only one spear, which seems to be more practical with a small, hand-held shield (Vermeule and Karageorghis 1982, plates XI.1B, XI.16, XI.57). Later on (see Chapter 3) two or more spears, including one for throwing, seem to have been the norm, so this system could have occurred at the end of the Mycenaean period. In the eleventh century, iron started to be used for daggers and swords but not yet for spears, possibly because of the difficulty in fashioning a spear socket; but in the tenth century iron spears began to appear as well (Snodgrass 2000, p. 224). By *c.* 900, bronze spearheads had died out except in some of the more remote regions, but butt spikes, where used, continued to be made of bronze.

From *c.* 1050 until *c.* 900, it often seems to be the case that a warrior was buried with either a sword or a spear, but it is difficult to know whether this was some measure of status or whether the weapons were indeed used as alternatives. Looking at the soldiers on the Pylos frescos fighting the 'barbarians' by the river (Fig. 14), we can see that one has just a sword, and one just a spear. After *c.* 900 spears were more common in multiples (and were buried with swords) and must have been used as throwing weapons as portrayed in the *Iliad* (Snodgrass 1967, pp. 37–9). Homer often describes warriors carrying pairs of spears and throwing them in battle. Even when warriors have only one spear, it is just as likely to be thrown (Lorimer 1950, pp. 258–9). The spearheads in Homer are always made of bronze, and Hector's is mentioned with a gold band around the joint between head and shaft (Homer, *Iliad* VI, 319). The only other evidence for spear decoration at this time is the Mycenaean Warrior Vase, which appears to show flags or large tassels attached to the spears.

## SWORDS

The sword also became a shorter and lighter weapon during the thirteenth century. The long Cross-hilted sword went out of use by about 1250. Swords of Horned Type 2a developed into weapons with shorter blades, usually of 35–40cm, known as Horned Type 2b. Another short sword also appeared in about 1250, known as Type F after the classification by Sandars (1961, 1963, *passim*; Kilian-Dirlmeier 1993, pp. 76 ff.). These swords also averaged 35–40cm in length for the most part and had similar hilts with cross bars at the top, but no sign of horns, which were perhaps no longer considered essential (Fig. 13*f* ). A similar, but even shorter weapon, called Type E by Sandars, was really only a dagger and is not generally considered to be a weapon of war, but a tool (Kilian-Dirlmeier 1993, plates 66–7). It is probably a Type F short sword that is being wielded by a warrior on the Pylos frescos (Fig. 14), and perhaps also on a

Late Mycenaean vase fragment (Vermeule and Karageorghis 1982, plate XI.49). These short weapons were much more practical for cut-and-thrust fighting and for general carrying about in these troubled times (Snodgrass 1967, p. 28) but, although they lasted into the twelfth century, they were ousted by a new sword from the north (Fig. 13*g*).

This new sword is known as the 'Griffzungenschwert' or, more usually, the Naue II Type. It seems to have been invented in Central Europe, where the earliest and best examples have been found (Snodgrass 1967, p. 29), and came into Greece before the great catastrophe: that is, before *c.* 1230. It had a flanged hilt, with a distinctive curved outline where rivets fasten the grip to the sword, making it a very strong cut-and-thrust weapon. The known examples are usually 60 to 80cm long, but daggers with the same handle type are also known. The earliest examples must have been imports and, since they pre-date the great catastrophe, cannot have been brought in by invaders as was once thought. The Greeks were soon making the Naue II Type sword themselves, and the design was so effective that it became virtually the only sword used in Greece for the next four or five hundred years. It was also widely adopted in Italy, Cyprus, Egypt and the Near East. The only change that happened to the sword was its translation into iron from the middle of the eleventh century. Tomb 28 at Tiryns produced a Naue II Type dagger in iron and there is a 48cm sword from the Kerameikos in Athens, which both date from *c.* 1050 (Snodgrass 2000, pp. 220–3). From this time down to 900, nearly every Greek sword is a Naue II Type in iron. There are a few examples in bronze from outlying parts, but these are just as likely to have been heirlooms as contemporary weapons (Snodgrass 2000, p. 241). Iron is stronger than bronze, and can be given a sharper edge. It is also slightly lighter, and some of the iron Naue II Types are longer than any known bronze example, approaching 90cm in length. This is the combined cutting and slashing weapon that features in the *Iliad*, capable of cutting off an arm or a head (Lorimer 1950, p. 270). Only an iron sword could do that, although swords in the *Iliad* are always described as being of bronze, in a throwback to an earlier time.

Homer often describes the swords as silver-studded, which reminds us of earlier Mycenaean swords from the Shaft Graves with their golden rivets. Swords with silver rivets are also known, but are rarer and none is known after 1200 (Lorimer 1950, pp. 273–4). Homer also describes swords as well hilted (*kopeis*) and, on one occasion, bound with black thongs (*melandeton*) (Homer, *Iliad* XVI, 332; XX, 475; XV, 713). Evidence we have for hilts at this time shows they were mainly made of ivory or wood, but thongs would generally not have survived. They would certainly have helped to give a good grip. A recently discovered, rare survival is a wooden scabbard from Krini in Achaea, dating from *c.* 1150 (Papadopoulos, in Laffineur 1999, p. 271 and plate LVIII*c*). This was covered in leather and further decorated with cut-out strips and studs of bronze. Similar studs and strips have been found at Kallithea and Lakkithra (as mentioned above) which may also be from scabbards, and this shows the care with which these swords were treated, and the value they must have had. Swords, like spears, could also be decorated with tassels, as is shown on a vase fragment of *c.* 1200 (Vermeule and Karageorghis 1982, plate. XI.59).

## MISSILE WEAPONS

Archery continued to be practised in the Late Mycenaean period; the palace at Pylos produced 500 arrowheads, showing they were produced for the military. Other finds and depictions are rare. None of the warrior graves from Achaea has produced any arrowheads. A vase in the British Museum from Enkomi dating to the twelfth century shows archers presumably marching to war, but maybe they are going on a hunt (Fig. 24). Vermeule and Karageorghis, in their corpus of Mycenaean pictorial vase painting (1982, plate XI.58), illustrate only one archer, which also tells us little. After the great catastrophe of *c.* 1200, evidence becomes even slighter. There are a few large bronze arrowheads from Greece, including a tenth-century example from the Kerameikos in Athens (Snodgrass 2000, p. 233), but most examples come from Crete, which seems to have begun now to develop its later reputation as a land of archers (Snodgrass 1967, p. 40). Tiryns has also produced two obsidian examples (Snodgrass 2000, p. 274).

By the tenth century arrowheads in Crete are made of iron, and the simple bow is replaced by the composite bow. This has pieces of horn attached to the inner edge of the bow, and sinew attached to the outer edge. When the bow is drawn the sinew is stretched and the horn is compressed, both of which give the bow greater power. Homer (*Iliad* IV, 105 ff.) mentions such a bow but seems to have an incomplete understanding of it, thinking it was made entirely of horn. It is possible that the composite bow did not reach mainland Greece until the eighth century, when there is a great increase in its depiction in art (see Chapter 3). In the *Iliad*, Homer often depicts arrows being shot in the thick of the fight (XV, 313–14; XIII, 711–20), but they were not used in hand-to-hand combat by any of the great heroes. Indeed they frequently had negative connotations (Reboredo Morillo 1996, pp. 16–19) such as in the depiction of Teucros, who hides behind Aias's shield and comes out to shoot

Fig. 24: Vase from Tomb 45 at Enkomi in Cyprus, thirteenth century. *(Trustees of the British Museum, GR 1897.4-1.928)*

(*Iliad* VIII, 265–72). With the archery it is really unclear to what extent Homer is remembering the Late Mycenaean period or is mixing in contemporary material of the eighth century, when there was a brief flourishing of archery after the apparent lapse in the Dark Age. There is no further evidence for the military use of the sling in this period (Pritchett 1991).

To conclude: the Late Mycenaean period was one of expansion and prosperity, probably leading to an increase in armed forces put into the field by the palaces. Perhaps as a result of this, soldiers were less well equipped with body armour, and infantry outnumbered chariots by a larger margin. The chariot also seemed to become lighter and faster (Bloedow, in Laffineur 1999, p. 456). The chariot warriors wore greaves and carried small shields, while the infantry also wore greaves but carried larger, oval shields. These 'greaves' were mostly non-metallic leggings. Most actual fighting was done on foot with the thrusting spear used in combat, supported by the short cut-and-thrust sword, or the longer Naue II Type which was coming into use. Archers and slingers also played their role. After the great catastrophe of *c.* 1200, the palace system gradually collapsed, and that seems to have led to a reduction in chariotry and archery (and slingers?). The infantry continued to fight in the same way, with the richest still being able to afford metal greaves and other armour, and perhaps a personal chariot. Gradually the chariot died out and was perhaps replaced with horse riding. Our evidence for this comes from Homer where, in some passages, he clearly confuses chariots with horses, apparently showing that mounted warriors were in use in Homer's time, i.e. by *c.* 800 (Delebecque, quoted in Greenhalgh 1973, pp. 67–8). We will see evidence for this in Chapter 3. Actual combat was still on foot, even if the warrior arrived by chariot or horse. Also after *c.* 1200, the thrusting spear was replaced by two or more throwing spears. The Naue II Type sword also became the sword of choice and was manufactured in iron. These long cut-and-thrust swords, small shields and the throwing spears suggest a skirmishing type of warfare. Metallic body armour, including helmets and greaves, seemed to die out entirely, due to the economic collapse and the cessation of overseas trade to obtain copper and tin for bronze making. Greece slipped slowly into the darkest part of the Dark Age after *c.* 1050.

THREE

# The Emergence of Hoplite Warfare, 900–525 BC

The darkness of the Greek Dark Age – and indeed the meagreness of all our sources up until that point – are suddenly replaced by an overload of information, beginning as a trickle in the early eighth century and turning into a flood by the following century. The Dark Age produced the occasional warrior grave with sword, spear and perhaps shield. There was almost no figurative art. After 800 we start to get votive statues of bronze warriors. The Late Geometric period (after *c.* 750) produced battle scenes on vases, showing the equipment used, and this tradition in art continued throughout the rest of the period covered by this book, albeit sometimes fitfully. Finally, and most importantly of all, archaeology has produced much more evidence of military equipment, especially in the weapons and pieces of armour found in Greece's sanctuaries, most notably Olympia. There are even some literary fragments to help us, although no major surviving historical works until the end of the period. This chapter examines the emergence from darkness and follows the development of the equipment that changed the face of Greek combat from the skirmishing of individuals and small groups into the hoplite phalanx of the city-state.

The phalanx is a body of men in close order, standing shoulder to shoulder, and closing on the enemy with the thrusting spear. They are called hoplites by ancient Greek authors, after *hopla*, meaning 'arms' or after the name of the large round shield they used, which was sometimes called the *hoplon*. This is more usually – and confusingly – called the *aspis*. Missile weapons became much less common, while the soldiers became more heavily armoured. It was a gradual process and, as Snodgrass (1965a, *passim*) has shown, all the pieces of equipment for hoplite warfare made their appearance before hoplite warfare itself was known to be in existence, in around 675 to 650 BC.

Our earliest evidence for what warfare was like, rather than just what the equipment was, comes in the depictions on Late Geometric vases of Athens

Fig. 25: Vase by the Anavysos Master, a follower of the Dipylon Master, c. 735–720.
(Trustees of the British Museum, GR 1927.4-11.1)

Fig. 26: Corinthian *aryballos* showing a hoplite in padded linen armour (?) with a hoplite shield, and other warriors with Dipylon shields, *c.* 680.

dating from *c.* 760 and later (Fig. 25). Here there is no evidence for the hoplite phalanx, but all the signs of skirmishing warfare, which was assumed to be the norm throughout the Dark Age. Warriors are depicted in small groups or individual combats, carrying a variety of shield types and weapons. The composite bow is seen as often as the spear, and swords are also frequently depicted (Ahlberg 1971, p. 44). On the Corinthian *aryballos* (vase) in Fig. 26 we can see a hoplite in armour with a hoplite shield and spear, but he also carries another spear for throwing and is certainly not fighting in a phalanx with other hoplites. He is supported by an archer, and by one other whose weapon is unclear. His opponents also carry more than one spear, have helmets and perhaps body armour, but carry Dipylon shields (see below), and appear to be throwing spears rather than fighting in a phalanx.

As we shall see from the evidence outlined below, although all the equipment worn by later seventh-century hoplites was available from *c.* 700 or a little before, the hoplite phalanx did not appear in art until the Chigi Vase of *c.* 650 (Fig. 27). Here the men are shown fighting together in ranks with the thrusting spear, in a body known as the phalanx, which in later times was usually eight men deep. The heavy shield and the bronze armour, which some warriors had adopted for personal protection in the later eighth century, made it harder to run in any sort of skirmishing warfare, and it gradually became the rule to stand by your fellow warriors to avoid becoming isolated. This procedure then gradually developed into the phalanx, which became the mainstay of Greek warfare for the next 250 years, although there were subtle changes. Even on the Chigi Vase there is evidence of second spears (for throwing) still being carried.

Literary fragments also tell us about hoplite warfare. Tyrtaeus, a Spartan writing in the later seventh century, says: 'Everyone should close up to his man with his great spear or sword and wound and kill his enemy. Standing leg to leg, resting shield against shield, crest beside crest, and helmet to helmet having

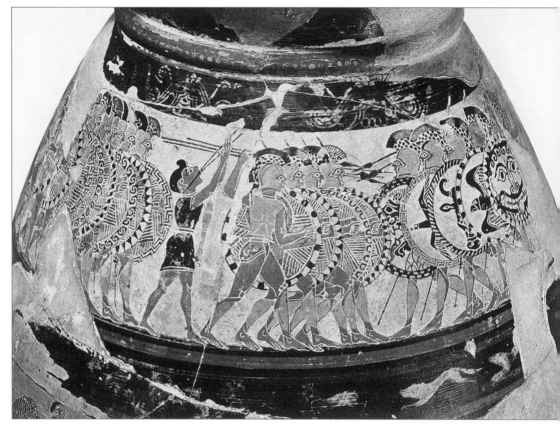

Fig. 27: The Chigi Vase, showing the hoplite phalanx in action, *c.* 650. *(Joint Library of the Hellenic and Roman Societies, Slide G.2776)*

drawn near, let him fight his man with his sword or great spear. And you, O light-armed fighters, crouching behind the shields on either side, hurl your great boulders' (Tyrtaeus, frag. 11, in Sage 1996, pp. 28–9). The mention of light-armed troops is interesting. We have seen how common archery seems to have been, at least at Athens in the later eighth century, from the depictions on Geometric vases. The slow-moving phalanx would have been particularly vulnerable to missiles, but there is a great lack of evidence for archery and slingers in the seventh and sixth centuries. It seems that there was a continuing doubt about the suitability of killing an opponent from a distance, which we noted in Homer's *Iliad*. It was not regarded as brave or heroic and, to help stamp it out, some city-states even made formal agreements not to use such weapons (Hanson 1999, p. 38). The idea that only close, hand-to-hand combat was 'civilised' probably led to the eventual abandonment of the second spear, which could be thrown, in the later seventh century. Hoplite warfare then settled down into an almost ritual battle between city-states, with unchanging equipment and tactics until the later sixth century.

## HELMETS

There is no evidence for Greeks using bronze helmets following the Tiryns example of *c.* 1050 (see Chapter 2) until the middle of the eighth century. At that point, bronze was imported into Greece again with the widening of trade, and bronze artefacts began to reappear in some numbers. Indeed, it seems that the earliest Greek 'colonies' at Pithecusae in Italy and Al Mina in Syria were trading posts founded particularly to import metals into Greece (Boardman 1980b, pp. 43–5). A series of bronze votive statuettes, mostly from Olympia, which show otherwise naked warriors wearing bronze waist belts and helmets of a simple cap form, is our earliest evidence (Snodgrass 1967, p. 42). After *c.* 750 we also have the art of the Dipylon Master on vases from Athens, and his contemporaries (Fig. 25), showing warriors in combat or funeral processions (Ahlberg 1971, *passim*). Some of these have helmet crests, but the style of the art makes it difficult to interpret the helmets (Snodgrass 1965a, pp. 5–6). Securely dated to *c.* 725, however, is our earliest actual example of a post-Dark Age helmet, found in a tomb at Argos with a bronze cuirass and possibly greaves (Courbin 1957, *passim*). The helmet is known as a Kegelhelm, or Kegel helmet, from the German for cone, and it is clear that this is the sort of helmet portrayed on some of the earliest bronze statuettes.

The helmet is constructed in five pieces plus a large curving crest (Fig. 28). There is a cap for the top of the head to which are attached a forehead guard, back of the head/neck guard, and two cheek pieces. All these have repoussé lines at the edges for extra strength. Other examples of Kegel helmets have been found at Olympia; these have a simple pointed cap, an attached crescent-shaped crest, or a curving forward crest made as one with the skull of the helmet (Dezso 1998, p. 31 and figs 16–23). These crest forms are clearly Assyrian and feature on friezes from Assyrian palaces (Snodgrass 1967, p. 43; Dezso 1998, pp. 31–3). The helmets are definitely of Greek manufacture, however, probably made after seeing Assyrian helmets in Cyprus or Asia Minor as trade routes opened up. An Assyrian helmet is also known from a grave at Argos (Dezso 1998, fig. 9). No Assyrian helmets are made in five pieces, and by this period they were starting to manufacture their helmets in iron anyway (Dezso 1998, p. 9). If we examine the other Kegelhelms we see that some examples, like the one in Budapest Museum of Fine Arts (Dezso 1998, figs 16–17), have a repoussé ridge halfway

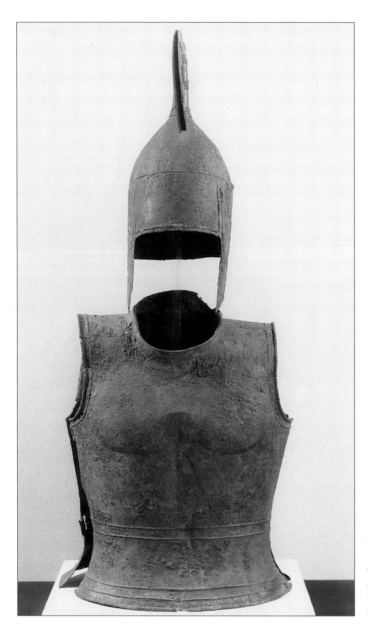

Fig. 28: The Argos helmet and cuirass, *c.* 725. *(Photograph by P. Collet, no. 46869, French School at Athens)*

down the neck guard for extra strength, and a lower cap and broader cheek pieces. The plates on this helmet also overlap by more than the Argos helmet to give greater strength to the welded joints. This is obviously a late example, dating to perhaps *c.* 675, giving the Kegelhelm a lifespan of only about fifty years. The Argos helmet, dating from *c.* 725, is of much poorer quality and its high crest sits on a tube made of cast bronze, making it top heavy and precarious (Snodgrass 1965, pp. 14–15).

Fig. 29: Crested helmet on a plate from
Tiryns, *c.* 700.

Returning to the crests on these helmets, Dezso (1998, pp. 35–6) lists a few
helmets from Olympia with crescent crests, but from which the crest part is
actually missing, so the final form must remain uncertain. Three examples with
a forward-curving crest have been found in Italy but there must have also been
Greek examples, as they are portrayed on some of the bronze statuettes and on a
terracotta model shield from Tiryns dating from *c.* 700 (Fig. 29). Dezso (1998,
figs 26–7) shows that this crest, too, is derived from Assyria. The Kegel helmet
had such a short life because its multi-piece construction made it very weak
compared with other helmets that were being developed in Greece. The helmets
were prone to break apart at the joins, as can be seen from the many 'parts' of
helmets that have been retrieved from Olympia. The crests, especially when
cast, also made the helmets difficult to wear; they must have had chin straps to
keep them on. Crests were an important part of psychological warfare. They
made you look and feel taller and more threatening to an opponent and, later
on, there is also some evidence for their being used as badges of rank.

The first improvement on the Kegel helmet was the so-called Illyrian helmet,
which was clearly derived from the Kegelhelm (Fig. 49*c*). It had a very similar

outline, but was made initially in just two halves. These were joined from front to back and reinforced by two parallel repoussé lines, between which a crest would have sat. It is this design of helmet which probably led to the common fore-and-aft crest we find on most later Greek helmets, and to the phasing out of the more precarious 'Assyrian' crests, although raised crests did persist for some time. The Illyrian helmet was open-faced, like the Kegel, with cheek pieces that became more elongated over time, and a neck guard that got lower and more protective. The lengthened cheek pieces helped to protect the throat area, which was particularly vulnerable to spear thrusts above the breastplate; and a lower neck guard would protect against slashing swords. This helmet would probably not have needed a chin strap, as it had a lower centre of gravity. From the evidence we have today, it would seem that it was developed towards the end of the eighth century in the Peloponnese. It must have followed on from the Kegelhelm and cannot be placed much before 700 (Jackson 1999, p. 161). Later helmets were beaten out of a single piece of bronze for even greater strength and, by the end of the sixth century, some examples have cut-outs for the ears and even hinged cheek pieces to make a more comfortable design (*Olympia Bericht* VIII, pp. 66–71). Towards the end of the sixth century, the phalanx was becoming more lightly armed and more mobile. It seems that more commands were being used in the phalanx and, for that, the hoplites had to have their ears uncovered to be able to hear. The Illyrian seems to have been a popular helmet in the seventh and sixth centuries, especially in the Peloponnese. It may even have been a Spartan development. By the time of the Persian Wars it was in only occasional use in southern Greece, but remained very popular in northern Greece, Macedonia and Illyria: hence the name by which it is known today (Snodgrass 1965, p. 20).

Meanwhile, Crete and the islands developed their own 'Insular' helmet, which consisted of a simple cap brought down at the back and sides leaving an open face, and surmounted by a very tall crest. This was not cast like the Argos crest but made of two thin sheets of bronze, so it was much lighter. This crest was often adopted by Corinthian helmet wearers (see below). These helmets were also made in two halves, like most Illyrian ones, and are best represented by some miniature votive helmets found at Praisos in Greece (Fig. 30). There is also a fragmentary, full-sized example now in Hamburg Museum, and published by Hoffman and Raubitschek (1972, pp. 5–6 and plate 13). This too appears to have had some Assyrian influence. Like the Argos helmet, it must have been somewhat top-heavy to wear, and this sort of crest seems to have disappeared soon after 650, perhaps because of the adoption of the hoplite phalanx.

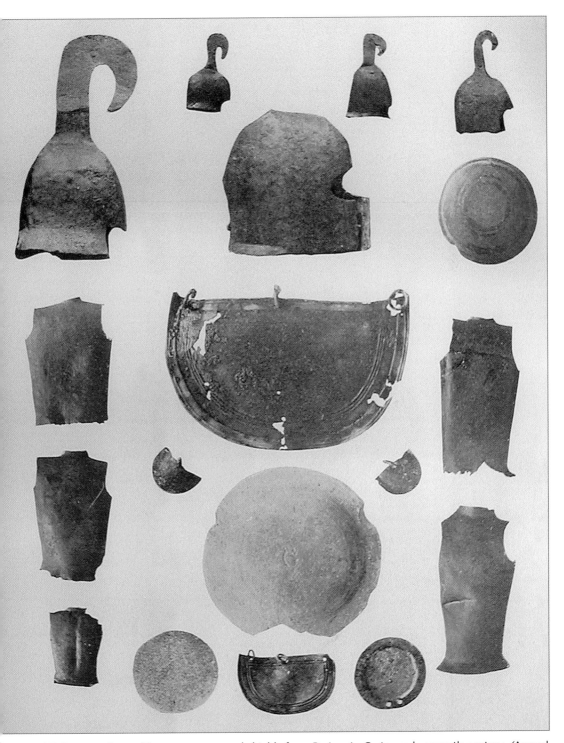

Fig. 30: Miniature votives of bronze armour and shields from Praisos in Crete, early seventh century. (Annual of the British School at Athens *VIII, 1901–2, plate X)*

Fig. 31: Frieze from the Siphnian Treasury at Delphi, *c. 525*. *(Joint Library of the Hellenic and Roman Societies, Slide G.1467)*

Also popular in the islands and on the coast of Asia Minor was the 'Ionian' helmet, which features in many helmet-shaped vases of the seventh century and later. It had an offset neck guard and separate hinged cheek pieces with scalloped edges (Snodgrass 1967, p. 65 and plate 25). Some examples of the cheek pieces have been found at Olympia, and examples are shown on the Siphnian treasury frieze at Delphi (Fig. 31) (*Olympia Bericht* VII, fig. 38). Similar cheek pieces were worn with Assyrian-style conical helmets on the island of Cyprus (Pflug 1989, p. 10 and figs 6–7; Dezso 1998, figs 6, 7, 14, 15), and it is tempting to think of them as a Mycenaean survival, although there is no evidence for the scalloped cheek piece between the Tiryns helmet of *c.* 1050 and Cypriot helmets of *c.* 700. Cyprus was heavily influenced by Assyria in the ninth and eighth centuries, and by 709 was incorporated into the Assyrian Empire (Boardman 1980b, pp. 38, 44), although the population remained largely Greek.

Fig. 32: Early Corinthian helmet, *c. 700–675*. *(Trustees of the British Museum, GR 1920.3-31.1)*

By far the most popular helmet in Greece was the one known today as the Corinthian (Figs 32, 33, 46, 49*d*). There was a helmet known to the ancient Greeks as Corinthian (Herodotus IV, 180), and since the helmet about to be described appeared first and most frequently on Corinthian vases, most scholars agree that it is one and the same with Herodotus's Corinthian helmet (Snodgrass 1967, p. 51). This is the most commonly found helmet in Greece, and lasted from the late eighth century well into the fifth century. Apart from Greece and Magna Graecia (Italy and Sicily), examples have been found on the Black Sea coast, in North Illyria and in southern Spain. Its popularity stems from its almost complete protection for the head and its (usually) one-piece construction, which made it very strong. The Corinthian helmet is a much more competent piece of work than the Kegelhelm or Illyrian types. It covers the entire head, leaving just a T-shaped slot for the eyes, nose and mouth. A problem with this, of course, is that it must have made seeing, and especially hearing, difficult. The introduction of this helmet may have persuaded soldiers to keep close together so they knew what was going on, which in turn helped lead to the close combat of the phalanx. The helmet first appears on early bronze statues (Snodgrass 1967, plate 15) and votive miniature helmets from Praisos (Fig. 30), and it is clear that the earliest examples of the type date to *c.* 700 or shortly before. The earliest full-sized examples known make few concessions to anatomy or to comfort (Connolly 1998, p. 61 and figs 2, 10). They are taller than they are broad, with perhaps a slight neck guard (Fig. 32). Some are made in two halves, like Illyrian helmets, and have the same crest holders (Pflug 1989, p. 14; Sekunda 2000, p. 11).

By *c.* 680 the helmets had become lower, with more of a neck guard, and indentations to help the helmet sit on the shoulders better (Figs 33, 46) (Snodgrass 1965, p. 23). This may have come about with the more frequent use of bronze body armour. The helmets also had nose guards by this time. The earliest Corinthian helmets had a row of holes around the edge for attaching a lining and the padding that would need to be worn with the helmet, but later Corinthian examples simply had the bronze edges rolled over, or thickened, for extra strength. The other designs of helmet mentioned seldom had these edge

*Opposite page:* Fig. 33: Corinthian helmet from Dodona, *c.* 650–570. *(Trustees of the British Museum, GR 1904.10-10.2)*

Fig. 34: Menelaos and Hector fight over the body of Euphorbos. Plate from Rhodes, *c.* 600. *(Trustees of the British Museum, GR 1860.4-4.1)*

holes, and it is likely that padding and linings were glued in. There appears to be no pictorial evidence from this time for a separate 'arming cap' to have been worn under the helmet.

Crests on the Corinthian helmets were front to back like the Illyrian ones, although they could also be mounted on a raised stilt like the warrior with the hoplite shield on the proto-Corinthian *aryballos* in Fig. 26. Lower stilts still

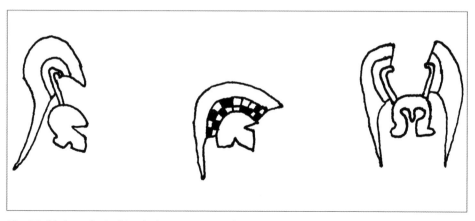

Fig. 35: Various Corinthian helmet crests, sixth century.

featured in art as late as 600 (Fig. 34). Examples of these stilts have been found at Olympia (*Olympia Bericht* VIII, plate 31.1), and may have remained popular until the Persian Wars.

There are even some vase pictures of the mid- to late sixth century showing two stilted crests on either side of the same helmet, or other even more elaborate creations, some of which may be fanciful (Fig. 35) (Boardman 1980a, figs 47, 86; 1998, fig. 470). A transverse crest is also occasionally seen, such as that on the well-known bronze statue of a Spartan warrior wrapped in his cloak (Sekunda 1999, pp. 10–11). A bronze of a warrior on horseback in the British Museum (Fig. 36) also originally had a transverse crest. It has been suggested that this may have been a form of rank recognition, like the Roman centurion's crest, but no one knows for sure. It was perhaps just a personal choice. In the course of the late seventh and sixth centuries, the Corinthian helmet developed elaborately decorated borders (Fig. 33), and by *c.* 530 the whole crown was raised up with a repoussé ridge for greater strength and to allow for more padding (Fig. 46). The cheek pieces followed the Illyrian style of becoming longer and more pointed.

The rounded form of the Corinthian helmet, especially by the later sixth century, was a great asset in the deflection of missiles and spear thrusts, and the padding underneath would have helped to absorb heavier blows. A crest raised on a stilt could be top-heavy and was also perhaps liable to be seized by an opponent in combat, which is why the lower fore-and-aft crests gradually became more popular. A crest was certainly considered essential at this time, and all helmets had crests until the fifth century.

Fig. 36: Mounted hoplite wearing a Corinthian helmet (originally with a transverse crest), Taranto, c. 550. *(Trustees of the British Museum, GR 1904.7-3.1)*

The Cretans seem to have adopted the Corinthian helmet at an early stage, when it was still made in two halves and had no nose guard. They then went on to develop their own form throughout the next two centuries. This helmet has no indent at the shoulders, no nose guard, and usually an extra bronze forehead guard attached to the brow. The cheek pieces are usually scalloped to leave a proper gap for the mouth (Hoffman and Raubitschek 1972, plates 1–12), but occasionally have the straight front edge of the standard Corinthian helmet. The factor that particularly distinguishes the Cretan helmets from other Greek helmets is their heavy decoration.

Hoffman and Raubitschek (1972, Helmet 3, plate 11) have published details of four helmets from Afrati, one of which is plain except for an embossed and incised decorated lower border, and incised rosettes on the cheek pieces. Another has embossed human ears on the sides of the helmet, while the remaining two have very elaborate pictures of men and horses embossed around the helmet, with further detailed decoration inscribed (Hoffman and Raubitschek 1972, Helmet 4, Helmet 1 and Helmet 2, plates 1–10, 12). They also publish a helmet from Axos and some further fragments. The Axos helmet has embossed winged pegasi on either side and incised border decoration. Its forehead guard is also intact and is decorated with embossed and incised rosettes and dragon heads (Hoffman and Raubitschek 1972, plates 14–15). These helmets must have looked stunning when first made, and it is possible that the decoration was enhanced by painting. These Cretan helmets all date from just before 650 until the end of the seventh century, and the fashion probably continued through the sixth century because we have other pieces of decorated Cretan armour with later dates.

Evidence for helmet painting and decorating in mainland Greece at this time comes mainly from vase paintings. Early examples of the Corinthian helmet in art (which accounts for 90 per cent of all helmet illustrations in the seventh and sixth centuries) are generally painted in the natural bronze colour, as on the Chigi Vase of *c.* 650 (Fig. 27). Where there are helmets in a different colour, it is not really safe to assume that they are necessarily painted, because of the limited number of colours available – especially when dealing with black figure vases. However, from about 650 we start to come across vases where the helmets on different warriors are painted in different colours on the same vase (Fig. 34); here I think it is safe to assume that helmet painting, or perhaps even tinning or gilding, is taking place (Boardman 1980a, figs 47, 52, 67; 1998, fig. 290). By *c.* 530 two colours start to appear on the same helmet (Boardman 1980a, fig. 134). Two Illyrian helmets with gold-leaf borders around the face openings have been discovered in Macedonia, dating from *c.* 525. However, the fact that another helmet has been found with a gold face-mask seems to suggest that this was applied as a funereal addition, and was not present on the helmet during its practical lifetime (Vokotopoulou 1995, pp. 116–17, 122–3). From *c.* 530 a general lightening of armour began, and new helmets such as the Chalcidian and 'Attic' were introduced, along with more elaborate decorative techniques. These will be examined in Chapter 4.

## THE BRONZE BELL CUIRASS

Although the Greeks seem to have developed their bronze helmets through copying Assyrian examples, they did not – with some exceptions (see below) – adopt Assyrian body armour made of bronze or iron scales. The first certain evidence for body armour after the Dark Age is bronze plate armour in the form of the Argos cuirass, which was found with a crested Kegelhelm and is dated to *c.* 720 (Fig. 28).

Since the Greeks certainly used bronze plate armour in the Late Mycenaean period, it might be thought that they used bronze armour right through, especially given the proximity of Argos to Dendra. However, in Chapter 2 I showed that there was an almost complete lack of bronze in Dark Age Greece, to the extent that items such as fibulae were made in iron instead; but they began to be made in bronze again when it became available in the ninth century. In Merhart's mammoth 1969 work, *Hallstatt und Italien*, the author argues that the Greek cuirass must have been descended from the cuirasses of the Urnfield culture, such as Čaka and Ducové mentioned in Chapter 2. We certainly know that there was contact between these cultures in the Late Mycenaean period, when the Greeks adopted the Naue II sword from there. But the Urnfield-Type culture does not have such a securely dated pottery sequence as Greece, and even those finds that are in context can be only approximately dated. It seems that, with the exception of Čaka and Ducové in the early twelfth century, no European cuirass can be placed before 800 BC, making their reappearance very similar to the Greek model.

European corslets come from two separate groups called West Alpine and South East Alpine by Merhart. These two groups are quite separate in design, and both have Greek and non-Greek features. The South East Alpine Group from Austria and former Yugoslavia is represented by the cuirasses from Vorlagen, St Veit, Saint-Germain-du-Plain and a now-lost example originally in the Mecklenburg Collection (Merhart 1969, p. 162, plate III). These corslets have a clear bell shape, like the Argos cuirass, and are similarly decorated, except for the Saint-Germain-du-Plain one, which is closer to the Ducové example (Snodgrass 1971, p. 39). Unlike the Argos cuirass, though, these corslets were fastened by simple bronze rings for leather straps, or by long tubes through which wire was threaded. They almost certainly date from the sixth or fifth centuries BC and so derive their advanced shape from the Greek cuirasses, while using simpler fastenings.

The cuirasses of the West Alpine Group are from Switzerland and Italy, although the find locations of the two 'Italian' cuirasses are very uncertain. These have been used by Merhart and Snodgrass to suggest that the Greek bell cuirass was derived from them, despite the dissimilarities. The Greeks founded Pithecusae as a trading post/colony in the early eighth century BC (Boardman 1980b, p. 165) and Snodgrass regards this as the conduit through which knowledge of bronze cuirasses travelled. When we look at the Argos cuirass in detail, however (see below), we see that it is an advanced piece of work. Since it dates from *c.* 725, then the Greeks must have had simpler cuirasses earlier in the century, perhaps even before Pithecusae was founded. The West Alpine cuirasses are short and without the bell flange curving out at the bottom; they are also decorated in a completely different fashion from the others mentioned, being covered with heavy embossing and bronze studs. Their only similarity to the Argos and later Greek cuirasses is that they are generally fastened with hinges and loops. Merhart dated these cuirasses by typology to *c.* 800 at the earliest, but Snodgrass thinks they are too crude and dates them later, bringing them even closer to the Argos model. He still thinks that Argos and other Greek cuirasses must have been derived from them, despite the technical superiority of the former (Snodgrass 1965, p. 82; 1971, p. 35). It seems much more likely to me that the exchange was the other way around. If that is so, then when and how did they rediscover the art? Let us examine the Argos cuirass in detail (Fig. 28).

Like the European cuirasses, the Argos cuirass is of beaten bronze, with the edges at the bottom, neck and armholes rolled over wire. The bronze is about 2mm thick, rather thicker than later examples, and the edging wire is of iron, whereas it is usually of bronze later on. Also, for extra strength, there is a repoussé line parallel to each armhole and two lines parallel to the lower edge. A further two embossed repoussé lines run around the middle of the corslet in imitation of a belt. They would have added much-needed reinforcement in this expanse of undecorated bronze. On the breastplate the repoussé lines stop 1.6mm short of the edge at the shoulders, and it is clear that the backplate overlapped the breastplate here (Courbin 1957, p. 342). A hole in the middle of each shoulder piece on the backplate slotted over a corresponding pin on the breastplate. This is a simple fastening, but the fastenings at the sides display a high level of technical achievement, the like of which has not appeared so far in any of the Central European finds. The relief lines on the backplate at the sides stop some 4cm short of the front edge, and so here it is clear that the breastplate overlapped the backplate. The right side of the breastplate has two hinge tubes which are pushed through slots in the backplate and a hinge pin is then inserted on the inside, thus protecting it from damage in battle. The left side of the breastplate has a small bronze loop on the inside of the corslet near to the lower edge, which matches a corresponding loop on the outside of the backplate. These loops would have been fastened together by a piece of bronze wire or a leather thong, and the resultant join would have been covered by the breastplate. To make the join firmer, the piece of rolled-over bronze on the bottom edge of the backplate on this side is wider and lacks the iron-wire core for the last few centimetres, so that the bottom edge of the breastplate could slide into the channel thus made. This same slot technique is used on the lower edge of the left armhole as well (Courbin 1957, p. 344).

Courbin suspects that the wearer would have needed a fellow warrior or squire to help him put on this cuirass, and I think that is quite right. The right side of the cuirass would have had to be fastened before it was put on, because of the internal pins. Another man would then have had to put it on the warrior's torso and fasten the shoulders, while also slotting the breastplate into the grooves at the armpit and lower edge, and then tying the two bronze loops together before the two halves of the cuirass were fully closed. Such a complicated system might even have required two or three assistants to accomplish it. The corslet was lined with linen, presumably padded, which was probably glued to the inside of the armour rather than stitched through tiny holes as Courbin thought (1957, p. 350).

I have said that such a system was not in use among contemporary European corslets, where their simple loop and wire attachments would have been very susceptible to battle damage, and so the Archaic Greeks must have learned it from elsewhere. No one else used bronze plate armour, so it must have been an indigenous invention. Going back to the Dendra panoply of 700 years earlier, we remember that it possessed a primitive hinge and very similar shoulder fastenings, and some of the pieces of armour had rolled-over edges (though not over wire). As has been mentioned, it is very unlikely that armour use continued through the Dark Age, and even less likely that knowledge of armour making survived. The simplest explanation is that the idea for bronze plate armour and its method of manufacture came from Mycenaean tombs themselves, an idea first suggested to me by Dr A.H. Jackson, formerly of Manchester University. There is much evidence that later Greeks made shrines for 'Hero Worship' at several Mycenaean tombs, and they would have known about the bronze panoplies worn by ancient warriors from these tombs, as well as from the memories preserved by Homer (Whitley 1988, *passim*). Apart from this evidence there is also the story of the 'Bones of Theseus', which were recovered from a presumably Mycenaean tomb by Cimon on Skyros in 476–5 (Plutarch, *Life of Cimon*, 10; *Life of Theseus*, 36). So, the reintroduction of bronze plate armour in the eighth century was almost certainly a Greek phenomenon. The fastening systems were Greek and the decoration was almost entirely of a new style, which the Central Europeans were themselves to borrow.

This decoration, apart from the repoussé strengthening lines already mentioned, consisted of the marking out of basic anatomy on the cuirass. Repoussé lines mark out the shoulder blades and breast muscles and also the lines of the ribcage, known as the omega curve. An indented line marks the linea alba (the line from the sternum downwards) and another the spinal furrow on the backplate. The only non-anatomical decoration other than the repoussé lines is a line of 3.5mm-diameter circles around the lower edge of the cuirass, incised with a compass (Courbin 1957, p. 342). In his thesis 'Bronze Armour and the Earliest Greek Kouroi', Hartmann shows that these anatomical features are indigenous to Greece and appear on seventh-century *kouroi* (statues) as a result of the Greek armour-making tradition; they do not come from Egypt, whence came the idea of stone statuary. He describes several *kouroi* which are carved in detail only on the head, torso and lower leg, precisely the areas where the Greek hoplite wore his armour. This decoration appears uniformly on Greek *kouroi*, and must have already developed into a standard convention before the first stone statuary appeared in Greece in the 660s BC. This was noticed by Hagemann in studying the *kouroi* of Cleobis and Biton (Hagemann 1919, p. 18, fig. 15), and is well illustrated by an example in Bury and Meiggs (1980, p. 125, fig. 4.3). This gives further confirmation that the Argos cuirass is Greek, not a European import, and that since it had already reached the basic anatomical conventions, it must have been pre-dated by cuirasses of a more primitive design. This idea is supported by the technical qualities of the bronze work, which show that it is not an early piece of work by its maker (Snodgrass 1965, pp. 75–6).

The evidence for cuirasses earlier than Argos (*c.* 725) is slight. It used to be thought that the cuirass did not appear in Greece until well into the seventh century, and it was only after the Argos find that Late Geometric pottery was examined for traces of the bell cuirass. The silhouette technique and exaggerated forms used on such pottery make it difficult to reach definite conclusions, but there are some illustrations which show a flange either side of a warrior's waist, and it is possible that the artist was trying to depict a bell cuirass (Snodgrass 1965, p. 73, and p. 234 n. 5; but see his plate 4, especially figs *b* and *d* ). Perhaps the most convincing example is on a large Late Geometric vase in the British Museum (Fig. 25). Here there are warriors in chariots, whose torsos seem to be wearing some sort of body armour marked with separate breasts. These could well be bell cuirasses. The bell cuirass in its simplest form must certainly have been in use by 750, if not before, and it would have travelled with the first Greek colonists rather than being discovered by them. There is also the case of General Timomachus, who had a bronze cuirass called a *hoplon* – apparently from the later eighth century – which was later carried in procession by the Thebans (Cartledge 1977, p. 25).

If we have decided upon where the bronze cuirass came from, we have yet to decide why. As Hanson (1989, pp. 56–7) has pointed out, these cuirasses, along with the helmets and later the hoplite shield, were very heavy, and bronze armour in the Aegean heat seems very impractical. The Mycenaean warrior had occasionally worn bronze, but only chariot warriors wore large amounts of body armour and they would not have had much walking to do. The large numbers of infantrymen in the Late Mycenaean period do not seem to have adopted bronze body armour (apart from greaves), and that may have been because of the heat and weight. If our theory about eighth-century Greeks adopting bronze plate armour because Mycenaeans wore it is correct (they had heard about it in Homer), then that would explain why an armour was adopted that was otherwise perhaps unsuitable. Once adopted, bronze armour did have many advantages for the Greek warrior and later hoplite. As we have seen with the helmets, bronze – especially in the curving forms of the bell cuirass – is very effective at deflecting attacks, and the padding behind would have absorbed many blows. The warrior would have felt like one of Homer's heroes in his shining panoply, which would have given him great confidence on the battlefield. Also it seems likely that hoplites, burdened by their shields as well as by this bronze armour, may have been able to fight only for an hour or so (Hanson 1989, pp. 55–6). This would have led to fewer casualties as both sides quickly became exhausted, and explains why much effort was put into winning the battle in the initial charge. Hoplite battles at this time were about winning and losing, collecting the dead and putting up trophies. They were not meant to lead to the annihilation of the other side, and bronze armour may have played its part in this ritualisation of hoplite warfare.

The bell cuirass remained virtually unchanged for two centuries, but it does become commoner in both finds and illustrations in the middle of the seventh century, at the point when hoplite warfare emerges (Jarva 1995, pp. 24, 27). It seems that bronze for cuirasses became easier to obtain and so more people were able to fight, although cuirass finds do not come close to the number of helmet finds. This may show that many warriors did not wear this body armour, but artistic depictions such as the Chigi Vase tend to suggest that bronze cuirasses were fairly universally worn after c. 650. The evidence from the sanctuaries shows only that helmets (and perhaps shields) were more likely to be dedicated than cuirasses. They probably had more visual appeal. Only the Argos find is securely datable, because our other finds come from sanctuaries like Olympia and Delphi, and the Afrati group from Crete. Armour captured from the enemy was dedicated at these sanctuaries, and inscriptions on the armour relating to such battles can, very occasionally, be used in dating (Jackson, in Hanson 1991, pp. 228 ff.). The dating problems stem from the fact that when a sanctuary building became packed, offerings were cleared out and thrown into pits, wells, rivers, etc., removing any stratigraphical dating material. At Olympia several pieces of armour have been found built into the bank supporting the stadium, or thrown into a nearby river (Snodgrass 1965a, pp. 73–4; 1967, p. 49).

Courbin tried to devise a typology based on the cuirass becoming shorter in height over time, with a less pronounced bell curve, and the anatomical detail on the shoulder blades becoming more elaborate. Jarva has shown these dating methods to be illusory (Jarva 1995, p. 25). Although highly decorated shoulder blades tend to be found later, there are some demonstrably late cuirasses that have shoulders of a simple form like the Argos model. One cuirass which can be dated is the 'Crowe' Cuirass from Olympia, and there is a companion piece almost certainly by the same armourer; these can be dated by their decoration to c. 630–610 (Hoffman and Raubitschek 1972, p. 52). These pieces are both backplates, heavily decorated with incised pictures of animals and figures like the Cretan cuirasses (see below), but the technique is simple and more closely related to Corinthian work (ibid., p. 50). The 'Crowe' Cuirass has added interest because of several square holes, which were originally thought to have been caused by arrows. Hoffman and Raubitschek (1972) have now shown that these holes were made with a chisel, and it seems that the cuirass was nailed up on a post, probably in a sanctuary as a battlefield trophy. The decoration shows that it belonged to an officer or a wealthy hoplite, and was presumably chosen as a trophy because of its splendid decoration.

Jarva (1995, p. 24) has shown that the height of cuirasses is not really determinate of age, but more of the size of the man wearing it . A variant of the bell with a jutting flange rather than a gentle bell curve does seem to have become more usual towards the end of the life of the bell cuirass (*c.* 525), but some examples with such a flange could equally be from the seventh century (Jarva 1995, p. 22, no. 3; Connolly 1998, p. 55, no. 6). The cuirass illustrated by Connolly (from the Olympia Museum) has a highly defined omega curve which is a late feature (Mallwitz and Herrman 1980, p. 93; Jarva 1995, p. 26), and semi-spirals on the breast that also appear to be a late design. Certainly a late feature is a hinged joint at the shoulder that appears on one breastplate from Olympia (Jarva 1995, p. 20, no. 8), but it is otherwise attested only for the muscle cuirass (see below) (Snodgrass 1965a, p. 75).

In Crete, evidence for bell cuirasses begins with a large group of miniature votives from Praisos (Fig. 30). As mentioned earlier, this group includes miniature Insular, as well as Corinthian, helmets and must date from *c.* 700 (Bosanquet 1901–2, *passim*). Miniature armour would have been cheaper to dedicate than the real thing, and examples tend to be from the earlier seventh century; but there is also a preponderance of finds from Crete, where it may have been a popular custom (Jarva 1995, pp. 15–16). I know of just two miniature votives from the mainland: at Sparta and Bassae in Arcadia (Snodgrass 1965a, p. 74; Cartledge 1977, p. 14).

From Praisos, we have two complete miniatures marked with repoussé breasts and omega curves, and with the breastplate attached to the backplate at the shoulders. There are also ten other single cuirass halves of a long tubular form, as well as miniature helmets, abdominal guards and shields. No full-sized examples of this long, undecorated tubular cuirass have been found, although there is another miniature from Gortyn, also on Crete (Snodgrass 1965a, p. 74). This latter cuirass does have anatomical markings, however. The Cretans seem to have adopted the cuirass, like the helmet, at an early stage and then went ahead with their own tubular design, which reached down to the thighs for extra protection while sacrificing some freedom of movement. It may have had anatomical markings, which are absent from these miniatures (perhaps they were only painted on), and this seems likely given the amount of decoration that Cretan cuirasses had later. On a scale size, some of these tubular plates are excessively long. If this is not a distortion caused by re-creation in miniature, or a stylistic convention, then I would suggest these plain pieces must be backplates. They would reach down past the buttocks, but could be worn with a breastplate of normal length and an abdominal guard (see below). Miniature abdominal guards were found at Praisos but, since they were not attached to the cuirasses, it is difficult to connect them definitely with the tubular cuirasses. Abdominal guards are a peculiarly Cretan item, and the early use of tubular backplates might explain their origin. Only one 'full-sized' breastplate was found at Praisos and is about 22cm wide (it is badly crushed). Snodgrass (1965a, p. 74) suggests it might be a large votive, in which case it is the only one known. It could equally well be a proper piece of armour for a small man or even a boy. Armour for children is well known from the Middle Ages, and this could be an ancient Greek example of the practice.

Later seventh-century Cretan cuirasses come mostly from Afrati in Greece and their details have been published by Hoffman and Raubitschek (1972). Apart from the helmets already mentioned, there are nine cuirasses and sixteen abdominal guards. The absence of greaves is particularly noteworthy. Perhaps they took a while to become popular in Crete, or perhaps Cretans never really took to them. Corslet no. 1 in Hoffman and Raubitschek 1972 (plates 19–23) is the most elaborate. It has repoussé figures of lions on the breasts and a pair of griffins marching up the omega line. On either side of the griffins, a warrior wearing an Insular helmet kneels on a curved tendril; and the breasts are marked out with sea dragons. A pair of uncertain animals is below the omega curve. All this repoussé decoration is supplemented with incised lines, and the style dates it to about 660 (Hoffman and Raubitschek 1972, p. 43). The other corslets are plainer, but three have the curved repoussé lines around the breast bulges ending in lotus flowers, with another lotus flower below the neck. Corslet 8 (Hoffman and Raubitschek 1972, plates 28–9) is unusual, in that instead of a repoussé omega line the entire upper thorax is raised in high relief above the stomach region; this shows a very skilled technique. It probably dates from shortly after 600, like some of the abdominal guards (Hoffman and Raubitschek 1972, pp. 44–5). The bronze on these cuirasses is thinner than the Argos cuirass at 0.6–1mm, giving a weight of about 5kg rather than the 7–8kg that the Argos cuirass would have weighed. The edges are also rolled over bronze wire, rather than iron. Where tube slots survive on these cuirasses they show that the breastplate overlapped the backplate, but that hinge pins were now inserted on the outside of the cuirass, making the cuirass easier to put on. The warrior could certainly have taken it off by himself if he needed to, such as to aid flight.

The bell cuirass was the main form of body armour – when body armour was worn – from *c.* 750 to about 525 or 500, and it seems to have gained in popularity throughout that period, judging by the examples illustrated in art and indeed the dedications at sanctuaries. Examples of the cuirass in seventh-century art invariably show it in its natural bronze colour and with the simple anatomical decoration that we have described (Figs 27, 34). In the sixth century there is some evidence for painting the cuirass, just as we have seen with the helmets. Many cuirasses show spiral curves on the breasts that are much longer than actual examples. Jarva (1995, p. 25) thinks we are dealing with artistic exaggeration here, but it seems quite possible that the repoussé lines were continued with painted lines to give the long spirals that we see. An example on a vase dating to *c.* 540 (Boardman 1980a, p. 80, no. 98) shows double lines of spirals on the breasts, one painted in red, as well as red lines below the omega curve. The white lines could be repoussé work in bronze, while the red lines were painted to enhance the effect. Another example has white dots painted along the spiral (Arias 1962, fig. 59). There are also examples on vases of bell cuirasses painted in two different colours, often with the omega line as a boundary (Boardman 1980a, p. 50, no. 57). The vase featuring the cuirass with white dots also shows another hoplite in a gold-coloured cuirass. These cuirasses are often worn by Homeric heroes on vases and remind us of Homer's mentions of gold armour. It is possible that some wealthy hoplites gilded their helmets and armour.

Some late illustrations of 'bell' cuirasses show a cuirass stopping at the waist, with the hips protected instead by pteruges, a row of leather or linen flaps probably adapted from the shoulder-piece corslet that was then becoming popular (Jarva 1995, p. 29 Type II). It seems likely that these flaps were attached directly to the cuirass or its lining, rather than being part of a separate arming jack. These late bells date from around 520. An example on a tomb painting at Elmali shows a large circular pattern of scales or feathers on the chest which could be embossed or painted decoration, and also clearly shows the join at the left shoulder where the armour covers the shoulder at the left side. This would have restricted movement a lot, but the shield arm did not need to be so flexible (Boardman 1979, p. 13, no. 1.2).

Jarva also lists another cuirass (Type V) (1995, pp. 46–7), which appears to have features of both bell cuirasses and shoulder-piece corslets, generally showing the breast spirals of the former and the horizontal, decorated bands and pteruges of the latter. A well-known 'bilingual' vase (i.e. featuring both black and red figure work) of Ajax and Achilles at play shows one of these, but the horizontal line could be embossed or painted decoration on a normal bell. Even the Argos cuirass had parallel horizontal lines like a belt. Jarva (1995, fig. 17) features two further examples, also from the last quarter of the sixth century.

This figure clearly shows a linen corslet, because it is painted white and the 'breast spiral' is both small and actually on the back of the hoplite; it could be the sort of woven or embroidered decoration that appears on these (see below). His other example looks more like a mixed bronze and linen cuirass. A black figure vase now in Rome (Jarva 1995, fig. 16) shows a hoplite wearing a cuirass which has breast spirals and an omega curve; but there are two or three bands below that which look much more like a composite corslet, and possible pteruges below those. Altogether, Jarva lists sixteen examples on vases of this kind of mixed corslet, which he sees as a transitional piece of armour. As I have shown, some of these can be assigned to either a bell or a shoulder-piece cuirass, whereas many others are of such poor artistic quality that it is likely that the artist is in error (Jarva 1995, p. 47). There is no archaeological evidence for a cuirass made only partly of metal at this time, which is particularly significant given the amount of armour discovered at sanctuaries dating from this period. The bell cuirass continued to be shown in art until *c.* 480 (Boardman 1980a, p. 164, no. 283), but these last examples are very crude and are probably cheap copies of earlier vases. It would be safe to assume that the bell cuirass was last made in about 500 and did not see action in the Persian Wars. The shoulder-piece corslet became the popular form of body armour, and bronze armour workers went on from the late sixth century to develop the muscle cuirass, which will be examined in Chapter 4.

## BELLY GUARDS

Another piece of body armour in use at this time was the abdominal or belly guard, a usually semi-circular piece of bronze hung from a waist belt. It is sometimes called the *mitra*, after a Homeric piece of armour, but the two items are probably not equivalent. Around about fifty of these guards are known, outnumbering the forty or so known cuirasses, but it is significant that two-thirds are from find spots certainly or probably in Crete. The remaining examples are mainly from Olympia, and it is possible that they were all dedicated by Cretans, or taken from Cretans, but the number is such that we can say that the belly guard was probably also used to a small extent by other Greeks (Jarva 1995, pp. 51 ff.). The guards we have date from about 675 for an example from Axos to *c.* 525 for some examples featuring engraved winged horses (Jarva 1995, pp. 54–6). There are also some miniature belly guards known from Praisos and Gortyn on Crete (Fig. 30), and some of these may date from as early as *c.* 700 (Bosanquet 1901–2, *passim*).

Unlike cuirasses, belly guards were not made to fit the body and are not lined or padded. For extra protection they are made much thicker than other pieces of armour – generally 5mm to 7.5mm thick – and they do not normally have edges rolled over bronze wire, although this is present in some examples. The belly guards are suspended from a belt by three bronze rings and are generally 25cm wide along the top edge and 15cm deep in the middle. Jarva has noticed a change in shape from the earliest examples, which were shallow crescents. These became longer and squarer before developing into a more aesthetically pleasing true semi-circle (Jarva 1995, pp. 54–5). As with Cretan helmets and cuirasses, many of these belly guards are highly decorated with both repoussé work and engraving. The commonest decorations are facing-horse or winged-horse protomes, but there is also an example with a double-bodied panther, and one from Rethymnon decorated with four youths (Hoffman and Raubitschek, pp. 24–5). The belly guards generally have two or more lines of heavy repoussé decorating the borders.

A second type of belly guard is represented by just two examples from Olympia and one complete example from a tomb in Bulgaria, ancient Thrace (Venedikov 1976, p. 51, no. 193; Webber 2001, p. 34). This type is more of a trapezoidal shape, much longer and with a long horizontal hinge at the midpoint to allow bending. One Olympia example dates to *c.* 520 and the Thracian example is late fifth century (Jarva 1995, p. 57), so they really fall into the scope of Chapter 4. With only two examples at Olympia, one could see this late belly guard as being used only on the fringes of the Greek world. The dates correspond with the general use of the stiff linen and composite cuirass in Greece, and the two are not compatible. I think it is much more likely that the two examples from Olympia have come from Thrace or from Italy, where the bell cuirass and its descendants continued to be used.

Returning to the Cretan pieces, the finds from Afrati are inscribed for the most part as dedications, often with the dedicator's name. This enables us to see that in four cases we have pieces from the same panoply: two cases of helmet and belly guard, and two of cuirass and belly guard (Hoffman and Raubitschek 1972, p. 16). Even allowing for missing pieces, this evidence and the number of belly guards compared to cuirasses suggest that some hoplites chose a belly guard rather than a cuirass as an extra piece of armour. This may well have been on grounds of cost rather than for a specific combat benefit. The number of belly guards also suggests the possibility that they were sometimes worn in pairs. Belly guards no. 1 and no. 8 in Hoffman and Raubitschek (1972, p. 77) seem to have parts of the same dedicatory inscription, suggesting they were both from the same panoply. I would suggest that the plain guard hung at the back and the decorated one at the front. Such a piece of armour might seldom have proved useful, although the same could also be said of a cuirass backplate. The belly guard hardly ever appears in art. As recently as 1965 Snodgrass (1965a, p. 89) could state that it was never shown in art, just as Benton (1940–5, p. 82) had said earlier. Jarva (1995, p. 58) has now published a photograph of a sculpture from Albania that does clearly show the belly guard. It is worn with a bell cuirass and Corinthian helmet, but is apparently from the fifth century, which is after the bell cuirass and belly guard were in use in Greece and Crete. This fact, and the complete lack of illustrations of the belly guard in mainstream Greek art, shows that it was very much restricted to Crete in the seventh and sixth centuries and to northern Greece (or north of Greece!) in the fifth. There is also some uncertain evidence in the form of a sculpture for its use in Etruria (Jarva 1995, p. 59, fig. 24). Apart from the throat, the groin and thighs formed the other vulnerable area in combat. Spear thrusts deflected downwards by the shield might go below the cuirass to injure a warrior there, and it is perhaps surprising that this belly guard was not more popular. It would have added more weight to the panoply, of course, which was perhaps not thought to justify the added protection. When pteruges were invented in the middle of the sixth century they were widely adopted, showing that the hoplite was well aware of his vulnerability in this area, but had been generally content (until the advent of pteruges) to rely on his shield for protection.

## GREAVES

Armour for protecting the limbs was also used extensively through the Archaic period, with the greave being the most popular item. This is due to the fact that the lower legs are the hardest part to protect with a shield and, although the lower legs were not very vulnerable in hand-to-hand combat, they were vulnerable to missiles. Greaves are mentioned late in the seventh century as being specifically worn for protection against missiles (Alcaeus, frag. 54 (Diehl); see Jarva 1995, p. 85). As with helmets and body armour, the greave had been invented in Mycenaean times, but evidence for continuity of use through the Dark Age is problematical (Jarva 1995, p. 85). There are European greaves,

*Opposite page:* Fig. 37: Greaves from Ruvo in Apulia, featuring gorgon heads on the knees, c. 550–500. *(Trustees of the British Museum GR 1856.12-26.615)*

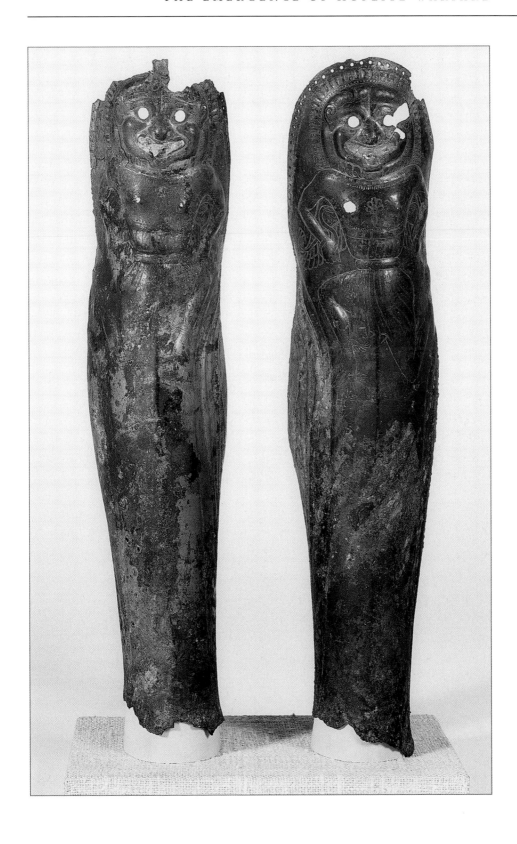

which may date from as early as 800, but the same problems of dating exist with them as for the European cuirasses (Schauer 1982, *passim*).

The earliest Greek greave is almost certainly an example from Olympia, which Kunze dates to *c.* 750 (1991, p. 5 and plate 1; but see Jarva 1995, p. 85, who suggests it is much later and non-Greek). Although not datable by context, this is an extremely simple short greave, which was laced onto the leg in a similar fashion to Late Mycenaean greaves. The most remarkable feature about it is that it has three parallel repoussé lines at the edges, and two large circle decorations with central bosses near the top. This decoration is almost identical to the best-preserved Late Mycenaean greave from Enkomi and suggests either a possible continuity, or again the resurrection of use through the discovery of examples in Mycenaean tombs, as has been suggested for cuirasses.

The Argos grave containing the cuirass and the Kegel helmet (Fig. 28) also produced some thin fragments of bronze, which were interpreted as possible greaves. Their fragmentary state in comparison with the cuirass and helmet from the same tomb is a useful reminder of how many pairs of early greaves may have corroded away for ever. Another probable early pair of greaves comes from Kavousi in Crete, although not everyone is agreed on the interpretation, some thinking they may be part of a bronze statue (Jarva 1995, p. 65). Kunze (1991) thinks they are greaves and can be dated to the late eighth century. They are short at 23.5cm, and are decorated with studs rather than repoussé lines around the edges. They could not have fitted onto the leg without lacing and, although there are edging holes for attaching a lining, there seems to be no means of attachment to the leg. The greaves are very fragmentary, however. Apart from a pair of miniature greaves from Gortyn (Yalouris 1960, p. 51) in Crete, the only other early greaves (perhaps *c.* 680) are a badly crushed pair from Praisos that are only about 20cm high (Astrom 1977, p. 46, fig. 15). Astrom sees these as one greave and one lower arm guard, matching what he found in the Dendra cuirass tomb (Astrom 1977, p. 49; Schauer 1982, p. 148), whereas Snodgrass (1965a, p. 87) thinks they are early short greaves but perhaps not a matched pair. Kunze (1991, p. 6, no. 15) thinks that they are from a bronze statue and not armour at all. In support of Kunze is the fact that they are plain pieces of bronze, whereas the early short greave from Olympia and the Kavousi greaves all have decoration of some form. However, the Kavousi greaves, which I think definitely are greaves, are quite different from the early Olympia greave, and also from the 'prototype' greaves from Olympia (see below), which begin in the last quarter of the eighth century, if not earlier. It seems there is no standard design at this early period.

Apart from these early pieces, more than two hundred greaves have been uncovered at Olympia and recently published by Kunze (1991) where they have been sorted into types and dated stylistically. Jarva (1995) has added to this by dating using the edge perforations. Most Archaic greaves had edge perforations for the attachment of a lining, and the gap between each hole narrowed over time. In the early seventh century each hole was about 25mm apart and linings seem to have been fixed with rivets (Jarva 1995, p. 65). By the time we get to c. 525, holes were less than 2mm apart and the lining was probably sewn on to the bronze through these holes (Jarva 1995, pp. 65–72 and fig. 28). Both Jarva's and Kunze's methods have exceptions, but between them they help to date approximately many otherwise undatable finds from Olympia. Jarva has divided the Archaic greaves (pre-700 to c. 500) into four groups: prototype, transitional, calf-notch and spiral. There is also a later anatomy group, which will be discussed in Chapter 4.

The prototype greaves started in around 700 according to Kunze, but could have begun as early as 750 according to Jarva (1995, pp. 85–6). Their main typological features are that they are short, 32 to 36cm, ending on or below the knee, although this made them much longer than the early greaves discussed above. They also often came with extra lacing holes to secure the greave to the leg. Most have some decoration, perhaps delineating the calf muscle and with a semi-circle or volute at the knee, and some are a little more elaborate (Jarva 1995, pp. 86–7; Kunze 1991, plates 2–9). This greave was in use until about 650/640. Jarva's transitional greave (1995, p. 88) has more of an angle with the front face at both bottom and top and is slightly longer, 34 to 39cm, sometimes covering the knee. Kunze (1991, p. 25) says that there is more elasticity in these greaves and that there is usually only one set of lacing holes near the top of the greave for holding them on. It is this greave type that features on the Chigi Vase (Fig. 27) as the sharp angle at the top of the greaves can be seen, as well as the fact that they do not cover the knees (Jarva 1995, p. 90). This type lasted until c. 600.

The third type of greave, Jarva's 'calf-notch', was the first to cover the kneecap and generally corresponds to Kunze's High Archaic greave. These average about 39cm in length, but vary between 36 and 44cm. The inner side of each greave is marked with a distinct notch outlining the calf muscle, and the greaves wrap around the back of each leg much more. Only a few of these had lacing holes, and most were held on just by the elasticity of the bronze. A few of the later greaves in this group did not have edge perforations for a lining, which must have been glued on instead. These greaves have the edges of the bronze rolled over (Furtwangler 1966, no. 988). The calf-notch group lasted from *c.* 630 to after 540, becoming more elaborate and developing into the spiral group. The spiral group saw the calf-notch develop into decorative spirals, sometimes ending in lotus heads or snake heads and with anatomically decorated kneecaps. Kunze has further divided this group, depending on a decorative feature below the kneecap, into the V variant, S variant and club variant (Kunze, 1991, p. 68; Jarva 1995, pp. 94–5). The V variant dates from *c.* 560–540, the S variant from *c.* 540–510 and the club variant from *c.* 540–525. All variants average about 42cm in height, and the bronze in the spiral group tends to be thinner than in earlier greaves (Kunze 1991, p. 66). Some elaborate greaves had engraved sides or decorated kneecaps (Fig. 37) (Jarva 1995, p. 95) and this decoration may have been enhanced by painting, as we surmised earlier for helmets and cuirasses. Spiral greaves are sometimes shown on vases of the period and correspond well with the dates formulated by Kunze and Jarva using style and perforations (Boardman 1979, no. 2.1; 1980a, no. 68).

## OTHER LIMB GUARDS

Not nearly as common as the greave, the ankle guard is nevertheless represented by over fifty finds from Olympia (Jarva 1995, p. 101), making it the commonest item of armour after helmets and greaves. The earliest example comes from Praisos and is dated to about 675/650 (Snodgrass 1965a, p. 88). There are no Mycenaean forebears, but Jarva (1995, pp. 104–5), following Furtwangler, sees a possible connection to the silver 'ankle clips' mentioned in Homer. The Greek could mean that greaves were well fitted to the ankle pieces, making the two pieces essentially two halves of a matched item. I prefer to think of the word *episphyrios* as referring to the metal lacing seen on Mycenaean greaves, especially since the earliest Olympia ankle guard dates only from *c.* 650, as might also the Praisos piece: both comfortably later than Homer.

To have had a guard for the ankle does seem strange. It is a great deal of work for a part of the body that is very unlikely to be hit in battle. I think the idea first suggested by Yalouris (1960, p. 59 n. 38), that the guard has much to do with the myth of Achilles' heel, has much to recommend it. The ankle guards are relatively simple pieces of bronze moulded to cover the back and sides of the heel, with the bronze coming over the top of the foot to be fastened by laces. There are embossed circles on each side to allow for the ankle bone. Using his perforation-dating technique, Jarva has dated examples from *c.* 650 down to about 525. The perforations allowed for a backing to be attached, but Jarva suggests they might have been attached to a sandal or shoe as fortified footwear.

There are no convincing illustrations in art. These guards are about 11–13cm in height, but there is a different group of ankle guards that are much higher at the back, up to 25cm (Jarva 1995, pp. 103–4). These appear to date from after 525 and even through the fifth century, because they have no perforations at the edges. However, they are nearly all from south Italy and Sicily (where a provenance is known), and may have been a local derivation from the earlier Greek ankle guard. Their size would have made them difficult to wear with greaves and their length would have made walking difficult, especially in a battle situation. They were perhaps decorative and for non-combat situations only (Jarva 1995, p. 104). Cavalry was being more frequently used in the fifth century, especially in south Italy and Sicily, and Jackson (personal comm.) has suggested that these long ankle guards may have been for use by cavalry. I am

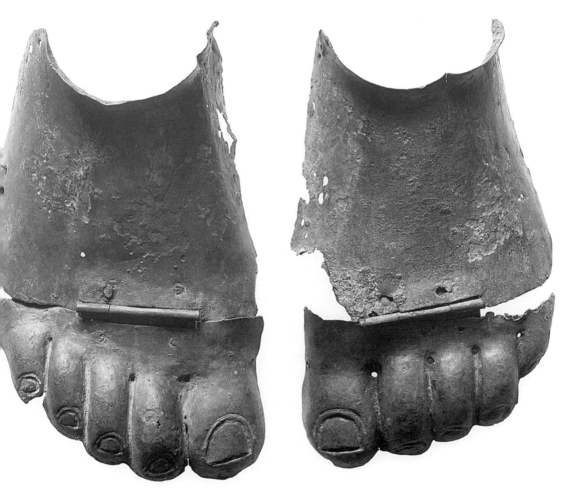

Fig. 38: Pair of hinged foot guards from Ruvo in Apulia, c. 500. (GR 1856.12-26.714)

certain that greaves were never worn by cavalry because of possible damage to the horse, and because the rider needed to be able to grip the horse with his legs. I would think that the same was true for these long ankle guards, and that parade use only is more likely.

Closely related to the ankle guards are foot guards, which covered the top of the foot and the toes. However, these are much rarer than ankle guards, with only four known examples. From Olympia we have two one-piece foot guards dating from c. 625 and c. 525. Also from Olympia is the toe section of a hinged guard dating from about 500, and finally there is the complete pair of hinged foot guards in the British Museum (Fig. 38), which come from Ruvo in south Italy and may be from as late as the fifth century. These last may be connected with the high ankle guards and be of a ceremonial nature, since they appear to date from a period long after most bronze body armour had ceased to be used in Greece. Even the earlier pieces would have been very awkward to wear, more so without the hinge at the toes, and it is hardly surprising that the item is rare. Only the earliest piece has perforations for a lining attachment, but Jarva (1995, pp. 106–7) suggests that all of them could really be parts of an armoured shoe, as he has suggested for ankle guards. Most hoplites are shown going into battle barefoot until c. 500, and I do not agree with Jarva that this is because of artistic licence portraying 'heroic nudity'. Bare feet are immensely practical on the field of battle, if you have been brought up shoeless to harden the soles. They give a far better grip than any shoes. It is interesting to note that there are several scenes from Crete of warriors wearing sandals. They are not wearing greaves, and it seems likely that the greave, and indeed the ankle and foot guard, were not as popular in Crete, possibly because of a late adoption of hoplite warfare.

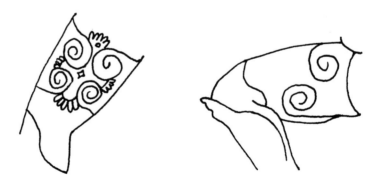

Fig. 39: Thigh guards with spiral decorations featured on black figure vases, c. 550–540.

The evidence for the use of thigh guards in Archaic Greece is almost the opposite to that for ankle guards. While they are by far the most frequently depicted limb guard in art after greaves, we have only one example, found at Olympia. Jarva (1995, pp. 79–84) organises thigh guards into five groups, which I think unnecessarily complicates the evidence. His 'Type I' is the actual example from Olympia, which pre-dates any artistic illustrations we have by about a century. It is also quite different from those illustrations. It is bronze, about 24cm high, and has the knee and thigh muscles modelled onto it. It covered the front half of the thigh and was tied on with lacing. There are lacing holes as well as the usual edge perforations on the top and sides for attaching a lining (Jarva 1995, pp. 79–80). These perforations and the artistic style date the thigh guard to *c.* 650, and Jarva compares the style to the prototype greave group. This is the short greave, which did not cover the knee, and explains why this thigh guard reaches down so far. As the greaves became longer and covered the knee, so the thigh guard moved up the leg to concentrate on protecting the thigh.

Jarva's 'Type II' is based on one relief vase from Sparta, which shows long thigh guards with lacing up the side; he sees it as possibly being a material thigh guard. The lacing is shown on the inside of one leg but on the outside of the other, indicating some artistic confusion. The relief dates from *c.* 575 (Jarva 1995, p. 80).

Jarva's 'Type III' is based on two or three pieces, which show bronze thigh guards with an early spiral pattern, and a gap on the inside of the thigh where the guard may have been laced, or just held on with the elasticity of the bronze (Boardman 1980a, no. 64.3; Jarva 1995, p. 80). These date from *c.* 650–550.

Jarva's 'Type IV' is the main group of thigh-guard illustrations which appear to be open at the back, again being laced or held on by the elasticity of the bronze. They are usually decorated with spirals, sometimes clearly enhanced by painting, and date from *c.* 550 to *c.* 500 (Fig. 39). There are also some earlier vases which do not appear to show thigh guards, but where the thighs of the hoplite are still decorated with spirals. These date from as early as *c.* 560 (Jarva 1995, p. 82). A well-known statue of a Spartan warrior of about 525, from Longa, wears a pair of these thigh guards, as well as upper and lower arm guards on the right arm (Jarva 1995, p. 27, fig. 6; Connolly 1998, p. 59; Sekunda 1999, p. 56).

It seems clear to me that all thigh guards would have been open at the back in the same way that greaves are, and that the illustrations of 'Type II' and 'Type III' are mistakes or artistic licence on the part of the illustrator. These are all clearly the same guard, becoming gradually more decorated as the century progresses, and perhaps longer (Boardman 1980a, no. 217) in order to cover the gap between thigh guard and greave. (Jarva's 'Type V' is a short, round-edged thigh guard which, although derived from the Greek, is clearly fifth-century Etruscan and does not belong in this study.) It is difficult to gauge the popularity of the thigh guard. The single example from the seventh century seems to show a rare, almost experimental item to help cover the gap between greaves and cuirass, but it did not catch on. When the thigh guard re-emerged a hundred years later, it seemed to be a useful and practical piece of equipment throughout the second half of the sixth century, yet we have no surviving examples. Given that the thigh and groin were a particularly vulnerable area, I think we must accept the vase illustrations as showing the true popularity of this item. The reason for our lack of finds at sanctuary sites is probably just an unfortunate occurrence giving us a statistical blip.

Extra armour was also used for the right arm, which was unprotected by the shield. Seventeen upper arm guards are known, fourteen from Olympia, and they seem to fall into two main types (Jarva 1995, p. 74). There are large guards that open at the back, i.e. between the arm and the torso, and that have a large shoulder piece, often decorated with palmettes or a gorgon or animal head (Fig. 40) (Jarva 1995, p. 74, figs 30–3; Connolly 1998, p. 59, no. 5). Another

Fig. 40: Upper arm guard from Olympia, late sixth century.

type has only the front of the shoulder protected and does not reach down as much to the elbow (Jarva 1995, p. 75, fig. 32). A third type listed by Jarva appears only on the left arm of an Amazon on a vase from Tarquinia. It is decorated with a spiral and stops short of the shoulder. Arm guards were not worn on the left arm in reality, because of the shield. The Amazon on the Tarquinia vase has no shield, so a shoulder guard can be put on her left arm. It is clumsily executed and I do not think we can derive a third upper arm guard type from it (Jarva 1995, p. 74 and fig. 33). Apart from one early short guard which Jarva (1995, p. 76 and fig. 32) dates to *c.* 670, all the remaining long and short guards date to the period *c.* 600 to *c.* 510. This accords well with the few artistic depictions we have, mostly from Attic vases (Boardman 1980a, no. 100). The use of the long upper arm guard would have been difficult with a bell cuirass and that is presumably why the shorter version was made as well. Although the Longa statuette appears to show otherwise, it is possible that long upper arm guards, covering the shoulder, were used only with linen cuirasses (Boardman 1980a, no. 100), which started to come into use in the middle of the sixth century (see below). The shorter pieces could be used with the bell cuirass (Jarva 1995, p. 76). The dates given by Jarva for long and short upper arm guards do not completely support this, however. There are long guards dating to 600, when we have only the bell cuirass (although see below for padded linen and scale corslets); and short upper arm guards dating to as late as *c.* 510 (where we have an example without perforated edges for a lining), at a time when the bell cuirass was becoming obsolete (Jarva 1995, p. 76). But Jarva's edge-perforation dating (1995, pp. 75–6) conflicts a great deal with Kunze's artistic dating on the upper arm guards. If we ignore Jarva's perforation rules here, and just date the pieces on artistic style, it becomes possible to date all the big shoulder piece upper arm guards to no earlier than 560, suggesting they might well all have been worn with linen cuirasses. The shorter upper arm guard goes with the bell cuirass, or perhaps just as a more comfortable option. The guards were never very popular, judging by the few examples and illustrations we have.

Less popular still was the lower arm guard, of which we have just five examples, four from Olympia (Jarva 1995, p. 77). They all appear to date from *c.* 625 to *c.* 575, judging by style and perforation. They covered the right forearm from elbow to wrist, and would not always have fitted well with an upper arm guard. They may perhaps have been used as alternatives, but the Longa statue is clearly wearing both (Jarva 1995, p. 27, fig. 6; Sekunda 1999, p. 56; see also his reconstruction on plate D, fig. 1). This statuette dates to *c.* 540 and is therefore a bit later than the originals. Apart from that, the only artistic representations are a metope from Corfu of *c*. 575 (Jarva 1995, p. 78) and a black figure vase by Lydos (Boardman 1980a, no. 68) dating to *c*. 540.

None of these limb guards, with the exception of greaves, can be proven to date from before the introduction of hoplite warfare in *c*. 650. When Greek soldiers began to fight in the cut and thrust of the tightly packed phalanx, they no longer needed mobility and so began to add further pieces of bronze so as to be completely protected. From the surviving numbers of these extra guards that we have it is clear that this was a luxury option, adopted by some hoplites if they could afford it. These extra guards all fell out of fashion by *c*. 525, just as the bell cuirass did, when hoplites were opting for much lighter equipment to cope with the changing face of the battlefield. The only exception to this general rule appears to be the hinged foot guard, which was only introduced at about this time and may have been used into the fifth century. It has more perhaps to do with decoration and parade than combat, and seems to be an Italian Greek idea.

## THE ARCHAIC SCALE CORSLET

Although the Greeks emerged from the Dark Age into the seventh century wearing bronze armour for the most part, there are hints of other forms of body armour coming into use, especially in outlying areas, and these too should be looked at. Armour made from bronze scales has been mentioned as a defence in both the Mycenaean and Dark Age periods and it is possible that Greeks in Crete, Lefkandi on Euboea, and the Dodecanese maintained contacts with Cyprus and the Near East and continued to use scale armour. With the opening up of trade links again in the eighth century, Greeks certainly had access to Near Eastern military technology, as can be seen from the use of crested helmets like the Kegelhelm. It is difficult to see why the Greeks invented the bell cuirass when the scale armour of the East was probably just as effective, protected more of the body and was easier to repair. The idea of Greeks discovering that their Mycenaean forebears had worn bronze plate armour, and wishing to emulate them, seems to be the only explanation.

Greeks in Cyprus certainly wore scale armour, as can be seen from the finds, and this is no doubt because from *c*. 700 to the late sixth century they were subject to the Assyrian Empire. The scales used were mostly of the same design as we have seen in the Mycenaean period (Fig. 20). They were *c*. 5cm by 3cm, with a central median ridge for reinforcement. If we look at contemporary Assyrian reliefs, we can see that at this period scale armour was generally worn in a jerkin that reached to the waist (Madhloom 1970, plate XLVI.2). By 700, the Assyrians had also developed lamellar armour. This is similar to scale armour but the individual scales or lamellae are longer and thinner, being about four times as long as they are wide. They also overlap each other upwards rather than downwards (as well as sideways), and are often more securely fastened to each surrounding lamella rather than just to the ones on each side as in scale armour (Madhloom 1970, plate XLVI.3; Russell Robinson 1975, p. 163, figs 171–4). This gives a much stronger if less flexible defence. The earliest known example of lamellar armour does in fact come from Amathus in Cyprus. The fragments of lamellae were found in a rich tomb of *c.* 700, and the occupier could have been Greek, Phoenician or Assyrian, as Cyprus was becoming quite a melting pot by this time. These lamellae are 3cm by 1cm, with a rounded end at the top, and are made of iron. The Assyrians started to use iron for helmets in the ninth century, but this is the earliest example of its use in body armour. Iron is a stronger metal than bronze, can take a sharper edge and had been used by Greeks since the tenth century for swords and spears. It is much harder to work into thin sheets for armour, especially without its becoming brittle, which is why iron plate armour does not appear in Greece until the fourth century. The manufacture of small scales or lamellae was easier, however, and so iron armour was soon in use in Cyprus. The Amathus lamellae have a hole near the upper, rounded end, followed by a short repoussé ridge and then another hole. They were held together with plaited leather thongs and overlapped upwards to the extent of half a scale, as well as sideways. The knots of the thongs were clearly tied on the outside of the armour because they are on the same side as the repoussé ridges. Some scraps of linen were also found attached to this side of the armour, leading the excavators to assume that the knots were on the inside of the armour to protect them from combat damage, and that the linen was a lining or padded jack (Gjerstad 1935, vol. II, p. 13). This would have been uncomfortable, and would also have had the bumps of the repoussé ridges on the inside, which is not how they are designed. It is clear that the linen was worn on the outside of the armour as a covering, probably to stop the armour overheating in the sun. This is certainly how the Persians wore scale armour later on. The scale cuirasses on the soldiers of the well-known Chinese terracotta army have knots on the outside, and these are obviously not too vulnerable to battle damage (Bishop 1989, pp. 697–705). The inside of the lamellar armour shows that it was mounted on long, horizontal leather straps in a similar way to the later Roman *Lorica Segmentata* (Russell Robinson 1975, pp. 174–86). Gjerstad has calculated (1935, vol. II, p. 13, no. 57) that if the Amathus suit reached just to the waist with short sleeves, it would still have needed about 16,000 lamellae to construct, making it a very expensive armour indeed.

Conventional scale armour continued in use on Cyprus as well as in the rest of the Near East, because it was cheaper and easier to produce than lamellar, and a virtually complete suit dating to the sixth century has been found at Idalion in Cyprus (Gjerstad 1935, vol. II, p. 538, no. 236). Like the lamellae pieces from Amathus, this suit clearly belonged to a wealthy man. Five varying designs of scale, three of bronze and two of iron, are incorporated into the suit. Two of the bronze scale designs are unusual in being rectangular with squared edges, but all the scales have the usual repoussé ridge in the middle, except for the third bronze type which has two small embossed circles instead. This scale is 3.6cm by 1.3cm, whereas the others vary from 2.6cm by 1cm to 2.8cm by 1.3cm. The iron scales are far more numerous than the bronze and they made up the effective defensive body of the armour. The bronze scales, especially of the rectangular variety, were clearly used as a decorative element for borders, or for bands across the armour, giving a two-tone effect that is again reminiscent of Agamemnon's armour. The Idalion suit ended at the waist and incorporated some 6,800 scales (Gjerstad 1935, vol. II, p. 538, no. 236). A few more iron scales from a different suit have also been found at Idalion, showing that Greek and other Cypriots continued to use scale armour after the demise of the Assyrian Empire, when the island came gradually under Persian control. A set of bronze and iron scales has also been found at Delphi, which could have been a Cypriot offering or may show occasional use by mainland Greeks (Snodgrass 1965a, p. 85). They may even have belonged to a later composite corslet, as they are not securely datable (see Chapter 4). So it seems that the Greeks in Cyprus, or at least the wealthier ones, would have used scale corslets, and this type of corslet may occasionally have been used in the islands or even on the mainland. There are no clear illustrations of its use, but a proto-Corinthian *aryballos* mentioned earlier (Fig. 26) shows a 'hoplite', with a hoplite shield, who may be wearing scale armour. It is also possible, however, to identify this as padded linen armour.

## PADDED LINEN CORSLETS

Another type of body armour which mainland and island Greeks, as well as others, did adopt from the Near East was armour made of linen. By about 500 linen armour, in the form of the stiff linen corslet, had replaced bronze as the most popular form of body armour, for reasons that will be discussed in Chapter 4.

Padded linen armour appears much earlier, but its use and form are difficult to follow because of a lack of evidence. Padded linen armour is made of two layers of linen, quilted and stuffed with a padding material. This would have been cotton wool in the East, but was more likely to have been wool or linen scraps in Greece. Padded linen might not have given as much protection as bronze, but it was certainly lighter and more comfortable to wear. The earliest evidence for linen armour is a section of layered linen from the Mycenaean Shaft Graves, and linen armour is also mentioned on a couple of occasions by Homer. He was rather disparaging about the two people who wore linen armour, the lesser Aias and Amphius, and this may have been a reason why it did not prove as popular in Greece as bronze armour in this period (750 to 525).

Some evidence for padded linen corslets does exist in the Archaic period and they were certainly worn by some warriors, although there is no evidence either way for their use through the Dark Age. There is an example of a padded linen corslet on a relief of Tiglath-Pileser III of c. 750 (Madhloom 1970, plate XLV.2). It is short, ending at the waist, but if it followed the designs of scale armour, there were no doubt other examples reaching to the thighs and worn with a waist belt. Like the crested Kegel helmet, the linen cuirass would have been copied from the Assyrians by the Greeks at this period. The only illustration of what appears to be a padded linen corslet in Greece is on an *aryballos* of c. 690–680 (Fig. 26). This shows a warrior wearing a black-and-white checked tunic reaching to his knees, which must surely be armour of some sort. It is possibly meant to represent a scale corslet, but padded linen seems more likely, with the checks representing the quilting. This type of corslet had to be worn with a waist belt, and examples and illustrations of bronze belts are well known (see below). Fragment 54 of Alcaeus, writing probably in the seventh century, mentions linen corslets and belts hanging in his house, and Snodgrass agrees (1967, p. 64) that these were to be worn together. This shows that these are padded linen corslets, since the later stiff shirts had no need of belts (but see Jarva 1995, p. 41).

Another piece of evidence which probably refers to padded linen corslets is an early seventh-century poem referring to linen-corsletted Argives (Snodgrass 1967, p. 71). The early date here probably precludes the idea that these were stiff linen corslets, and the context shows that the padded linen corslet was more popular than seventh-century art would have us believe, if the Argives, as a fighting nation, are described thus. Perhaps the padded linen corslet was preferred to the bell cuirass in Argos, for them to earn such an epithet. Jarva has found some early depictions of material corslets (1995, pp. 33–4 and fig. 9), which he thinks are forerunners of the stiff linen shirt (his shoulder-piece corslet), but they are not desperately clear, and could be padded linen or simply tunics. Most scholars would still not see the stiff linen corslet as appearing until *c.* 560, with the vases of Ezekias (Boardman 1980a, no. 100). Whether the padded linen corslet remained in use right up until the adoption of the stiff linen corslet is unknown. The evidence of Alcaeus would seem to suggest its use until at least 600.

The bronze belts mentioned by Alcaeus are worn by many early votive statuettes from Olympia and elsewhere, but they are worn on their own on an otherwise naked warrior, who may also wear a helmet (Snodgrass 1965a, plate 5). This is obviously a descendant of the Late Mycenaean waist belt mentioned by Homer, his *zoster* or *zoma*. It could therefore have been worn as a piece of armour on its own or with a padded linen corslet. Amphius, whom Homer describes as wearing a linen corslet, was killed by Aias with a spear thrust through his belt (*zoster*) (Homer, *Iliad* II, 830; V, 615). The obvious reason for a belt would be to hold a scabbard for a sword, but it may also have been used as a decorative object or even amulet. Obviously it would not give much in the way of protection on its own. There is an example from the island of Chios which is from the seventh or sixth century, made of bronze with perforations for a lining and a decorated clasp (Buchholz and Wiesner 1977, fig. 19*a*). Such belts became very popular in Sicily and Italy, where they lasted into the third century (Connolly 1998, pp. 105–12, especially p. 108, fig. 2 and p. 110, figs 3, 10).

Although the helmet, bell cuirass (and padded linen corslet) and greaves were all in use before the introduction of hoplite warfare, it seems that all the other additional guards for limbs were introduced as a direct result of that warfare, to give added protection. At the end of the period under discussion in this chapter, only the helmet and greaves remained. There is no firm evidence for the use of the padded linen corslet after *c.* 600. The bronze bell cuirass died out in *c.* 525, as did the belly guard (in Crete), the ankle guard, the foot guard, the upper arm guard and the lower arm guard. The thigh guard – probably the most useful extra piece of armour, especially before the common use of pteruges – may have continued until about 500. The reason for the lightening of the equipment will be looked at in Chapter 4.

The limited numbers found of certain items of armour also make it clear that not all hoplites were identically equipped. This is because each warrior bought his own equipment and, indeed, the ability to be able to purchase hoplite equipment was a step towards citizenship (Salmon 1977, *passim*; Jarva 1995, p. 147). Jarva has looked at the quantities of armour found at Olympia. This includes some 350 helmets, 280 shields, 225 greaves, 50 or more ankle guards, 33 cuirasses, and much smaller amounts of other limb guards (Jarva 1995, p. 111). Jarva then reconstructs a small phalanx with a front rank of eighty-eight men and a depth of four. If the better-armoured men are in the front rank, and all have shields and helmets (which are essential), then he suggests that all the hoplites only in the first two ranks wore greaves, along with half of the soldiers in the third rank. Only 55 men in the front rank would have ankle guards, 33 breastplates, 14 upper arm guards, 4 lower arm guards, 3 foot guards and only one would have a thigh guard (Jarva 1995, p. 125). As Jarva himself admits, however, the data is flawed. He has put all the finds together from before 700 until the Persian Wars. There were no hoplites as we know them for the first fifty years of this period, before the introduction of the phalanx, and for the last fifty years there were few bell cuirasses compared to the new linen corslets, which were then coming in. Also there was a great flourishing of armour dedication towards the end of the sixth century, which distorts the figures (Jarva 1995, p. 126). Shields are likely to be underrepresented, because they might have been mainly of wood and leather construction, which would not have survived. The same goes for linen corslets. Cuirasses are probably underrepresented because of the use of linen alternatives and they, along with other pieces of body armour, may have been less likely to be offered than the more personal and displayable items of helmets and shields (Jackson, in Hanson 1991, p. 230). However, even if we try to balance out these anomalies it is obvious that certain pieces of equipment were not worn by all hoplites.

A more useful piece of analysis by Jarva (1995, p. 114), because it might be more likely to show actual equipment use, is the portrayal of hoplites on black and red figure pottery. On black figure art, which covers only the second half of the sixth century, 66 per cent of hoplites wear bell cuirasses, 22 per cent the new linen cuirasses, and 100 per cent have greaves. Red figure pottery, which covers hoplites after 525 (see Chapter 4), has 66 per cent of hoplites with the new linen cuirasses and only 66 per cent with greaves. So, although Jarva suggests (1995, pp. 112–13) that as few as 10 per cent of hoplites wore the bell cuirass, it is far more likely that it was worn by nearly all hoplites from the introduction of hoplite warfare in *c.* 650 until about 550, when the linen corslet begins to replace it. Greaves were virtually universal at this time, but the other limb guards were clearly used only by a few. Jarva suggests (1995, pp. 127–8) they might have been used as an officer recognition system, as an alternative to being worn by wealthy men in the front rank. There is no real evidence for this, and it seems better to view them as extra items purchased by the few. At the other extreme, it is also clear that a few hoplites wore no body armour at all, perhaps not even greaves, especially during the seventh century. Wearers of the bell cuirass are often shown as being naked underneath (see the Chigi Vase, Fig. 27), and are sometimes shown fighting completely naked except for helmet and shield (Robertson 1979, p. 94). While this is clearly artistic licence when it occurs on vases in the fifth century, fighting naked could well have occurred in the Dark Age and may have continued into the seventh century. We know that Celtic warriors did this, so why not Greeks? Indeed, as with the Celts, it was probably the adoption of body armour that led to the more general wearing of clothes in battle, and also explains the anatomical designs adopted for the bell cuirass.

After the seventh century it is rarer to see naked warriors, or warriors naked apart from a cuirass, but we do occasionally see hoplites wearing just their *chitons*, or tunics, into battle (Jarva 1995, p. 61; Boardman 1998, no. 353). This became more common in the fifth century, as we shall see in Chapter 4.

Fig. 41: Warriors with square, Dipylon, and round shields on a Geometric vase, late eighth century. *(Joint Library of the Hellenic and Roman Societies, Slide G.0812)*

## SHIELDS

Although helmets and armour were worn by warriors before and after the introduction of hoplite warfare, it was the hoplite shield that helped to bring about the change. From the beginning of the period covered by this chapter until about 700, there was a wide variety of shields in use, judging by both archaeological finds and artistic depictions (Fig. 41). At the end of the Mycenaean period we saw that the round shield with central grip was the most common type, perhaps with larger examples being carried by foot soldiers, and smaller examples by chariot-borne infantry. An exception is a vase fragment from Iolkos in Thessaly dating from the thirteenth century, which seems to show a small shield with in-curving sides (*Bulletin de Correspondance Hellénique* 1961, p. 770, fig. 20). This is similar to contemporary Hittite shields and also to the Dipylon shield, which will be discussed later.

From 900 to 700, the single-grip round shield remained in use and came in varying sizes (Boardman 1998, p. 118, fig. 213). Much of our evidence comes from bronze shield bosses with which they were sometimes reinforced. These round bosses had a central dome protecting the handgrip, sometimes reinforced with a spike which could be used as an extra weapon at need (Snodgrass 1965a, p. 38). A major problem has been that tombs often contain round bronze objects which are not shield bosses, but cymbals, horse trappings or belt fittings. Snodgrass did admirable work in sorting out criteria to distinguish these items, which seem to show that such shield bosses lasted down to *c.* 700, but no later. The exception is Cyprus where, as we have seen in the case of helmets and armour, the Greeks there were doing their own thing and may have come to hoplite warfare rather late (Snodgrass 1965a, pp. 40 ff.). The bosses average around 15cm in diameter and are generally reconstructed as fitting onto shields of about 45–50cm in diameter. Snodgrass (1965a, p. 48) points out, however, that a round shield boss does not necessarily mean a round shield. The Kaloriziki shield from Cyprus was probably not round, and Ognenova (1952, pp. 61–81) has reconstructed round shield bosses onto 'Boeotian' shields. While that seems unlikely, round bosses could certainly have been attached to the square shields that also appear in art at this time, and perhaps even the Dipylon shields.

Graves are sometimes found with more than one boss, which Snodgrass thinks may have been mounted on the same shield (like Kaloriziki), but I disagree. I think the Kaloriziki reconstruction is incorrect, and that it is far more likely that multiple bosses equals multiple shields, especially when they are of a similar size. A grave at Mouliana had four bosses, each about 19cm across; they are all bosses to protect central handgrips and cannot be seen as decorative extra bosses. The quantity simply points to the status of the warrior. Apart from warrior burials, a large number of shield bosses have been found at Olympia (Fellman 1984). Nearly all of these fall into the 900 to 700 date bracket, although there are some from the seventh century. Fellman sees these as being dedications from further afield in Europe, where single-grip shields with bosses continued to be used. He also points out that there were some areas of Greece that did not adopt hoplite shields and warfare in the seventh century. Achaea, for example, still used rectangular shields (the *thureos*) a couple of hundred years later, and so small, single-grip shields may still have been used in 'backward' parts of Greece.

With the increased availability of bronze, shields with complete bronze facings first made their appearance in Crete in the eighth century. The idea possibly came from the Near East, where similar shields were also in use (Snodgrass 1965a, pp. 52–3). There are three types. The animal-head protome shield has a three-dimensional animal head in the centre of the shield, instead of a simple boss. Examples are known from Olympia, although they may also be Cretan. They date from the eighth century and, although Snodgrass says this may have been a Cretan idea instead of the mainland shield blazon, they did not really overlap chronologically as the animal-head protome shields were no longer in use by 700.

The second type of bronze-faced shield is also Cretan and is called the Omphalos shield, after the conical Omphalos stone at Delphi marking the centre of the world. This shield has a cylindrical or conical bulge in the middle of the bronze facing to protect the handgrip and is decorated with concentric circles. Examples from the Idaean Cave in Crete are 34.5cm and 27cm in diameter. There are no certain examples from Olympia, but fragments are difficult to distinguish from Herzsprung or later hoplite shields. It is probably another mainly Cretan shield.

The last type of bronze-faced shield is called the Herzsprung shield after a find spot in north Germany. Similar to the Omphalos shield, the bronze facing of the Herzsprung type has a V-shaped notch in the centre and no bulge covering the handgrip (Snodgrass 1965a, p. 55 and plate 24; Sekunda 1999, plate A, no. 3 for a reconstruction). This decoration was derived from an original hide construction and, after translation into bronze, the notch became smaller and more stylised, allowing for some typological dating. Examples are known from Crete and Delphi, and there are also votive miniatures from the islands. Snodgrass thinks the Herzsprung shield is Cypriot in origin, and spread from there to the Aegean by 700. It became larger than the Omphalos shield; an example from Idalion is 83cm in diameter, and is thus as large as some hoplite shields, which may have been derived from it. The Herzsprung shield spread northwards and became popular in Europe, but was supplanted by the hoplite shield in Greece by *c.* 675.

Another type of shield, probably of Cypriot invention, is the small spiked shield, which developed from the small round shields, with or without bosses. Votives of such shields dating from the seventh and sixth centuries have been found on Rhodes and Crete, but it does not seem to have been in use on the mainland (Snodgrass 1965a, p. 56). Rhodes was later famous for its slingers and Crete for its archers, and these small shields may have been used by such troops, where skirmishing warfare rather than hoplite warfare was the norm.

What appears at first to be a very strange shield type is depicted on Geometric vases in the eighth century, particularly those by the Dipylon Master and his followers at Athens from 760 onwards (Fig. 25 and Fig. 41, middle) (Coldstream 1977, pp. 109–14). Known as the Dipylon shield, it is oval in shape but with two, often very large cut-outs in each side. In the seventh and sixth centuries this shield design developed into the Boeotian shield, with much smaller cut-outs, depicted on vases showing mythical scenes, and with a hoplite grip that simply would not have worked (see below). Since this is generally considered to be an artistic invention, Snodgrass (following Webster) states that the Dipylon shield is also the result of artistic licence and does not depict a genuine shield (Snodgrass 1965a, pp. 58–9). He is quite correct in his assertion that a shield shaped like those we see on Late Geometric vases (late eighth century) is of no practical use. Such large cut-outs as are generally depicted would render the shield useless. But did the Dipylon shield really look like that? The problem is the style of Geometric art. People are drawn in a stylised way with broad shoulders and a very narrow waist, quite unlike real people. If we assume that the cut-outs are exaggerations, then we come up with a reasonable shield which could be used in combat, and had those cut-outs for a reason.

There are two much more accurate representations of this type of shield which are unaffected by artistic licence. The first is a terracotta miniature shield of the late eighth century in the British Museum (Fig. 42). Although Snodgrass (1965a, p. 60) dismisses this as a votive, Connolly (1998, p. 51) shows that it is clearly copied from a real shield. It appears to be made of wickerwork, with supporting braces on the inside. It presumably also had a central handgrip. The second accurate depiction of this shield is on the proto-Corinthian *aryballos* featuring the hoplite in possible padded linen armour (Fig. 26). The figures

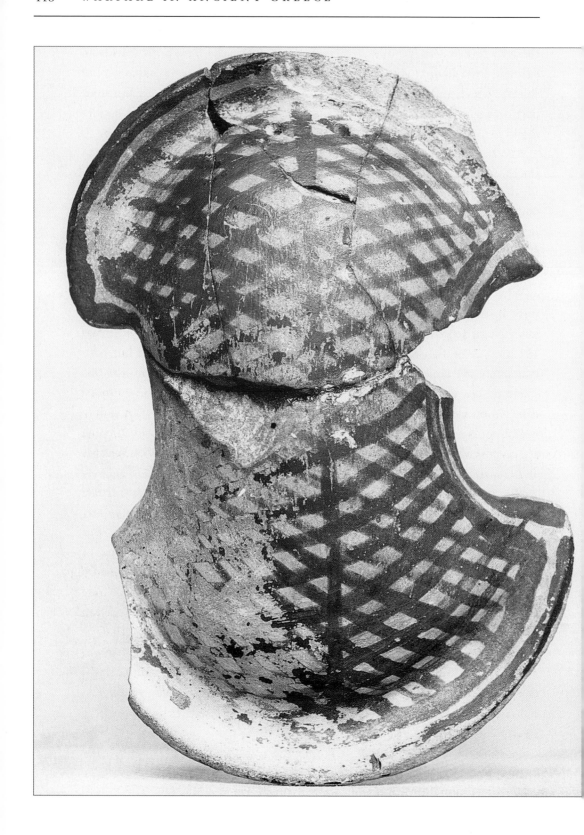

pitted against him are carrying Dipylon shields and wearing Corinthian helmets. This shows (as does the British Museum terracotta) that the shield was not flat but concave, and that the cut-outs were there to enable a second spear (or more) to be carried by the hand clutching the central grip. It also shows that the Dipylon shield lasted well into the seventh century. The *aryballos* dates to *c.* 680. It seems likely that this shield is a direct descendant of the Mycenaean figure-of-eight shield, but there is a dearth of evidence for its use in the thirteenth century, when the round shield dominated. The only exception is the Iolkos sherd mentioned above, which dates from *c.* 1300 and appears to show a shield with in-curving sides. This is not very similar to the figure-of-eight shield, and may have been separately derived from Hittite shields of the Near East, and the Dipylon shield could then have been descended from that. Then again, it may just have been a fresh Greek invention made to overcome the difficulty of wishing to carry several spears and a handgrip shield at the same time. Apart from the central handgrip, it appears that Dipylon shields usually had a shoulder strap as well, and could be worn on the back when not in use (Snodgrass 1967, plate 16). Greenhalgh (1973, pp. 67 ff.) also suggests that the cut-outs would have helped the shield to keep out of the way of the elbows when worn on the back like this. He is certainly correct when he says that it is the most popular form of shield depicted in late eighth-century art, although this may not reflect reality, especially as so much of this art is Attic. Geometric artists may have just enjoyed depicting this shape in particular.

Depictions of the Dipylon shield also vary in size, from ones almost as big as body shields to those barely reaching below the waist (Ahlberg 1971, p. 59). Something like a metre in height would seem about right to me (Sekunda 1999, plate A gets it about right).

From about 650 onwards, and particularly in the sixth and fifth centuries, a large oval shield with very small cut-outs at the sides features on vases. This is the Boeotian shield, which also features on coins of Thebes and its allies, and later as a shield blazon. It is always featured in heroic scenes, never in those of real life, and it seems to be a poor remembering of the Dipylon shield (Ahlberg 1971, p. 63). It is often shown fitted with a central elbow grip, or *porpax*, and a handgrip, or *antilabe*, at the edge, like a hoplite shield. In battle this would have brought the shield up horizontally, which is clearly incorrect. In fact there is no

*Opposite page:* Fig. 42: Terracotta model of a Dipylon shield, probably from Athens, *c.* 800–700. *(Trustees of the British Museum GR 1977.11-18.1)*

evidence for such a shield being in use at such a time, and it is generally agreed to be an artistic invention (Snodgrass 1965a, p. 58; Greenhalgh 1973, p. 64).

Another shield type which is occasionally represented in Geometric art of the eighth century is the square or slightly rectangular shield (Fig. 41, right). If the Dipylon shield is descended from the figure-of-eight shield, then Snodgrass (1965a, p. 61) suggests this square shield may be a descendant of the Mycenaean tower shield. There is even less evidence for this, however, than for the Dipylon. The square shield seems to appear only for this short period in the eighth century, and might even be considered simply as an artistic device to show two different sides in the depiction of a battle (Boardman 1998, p. 38, no. 50). However, Olympia has occasionally turned up strips of bronze with guilloche decoration which are straight, rather than curved. These may be the edging from straight-sided shields.

All these shield types were gradually ousted by the hoplite shield, which in turn led to the hoplite warfare of the phalanx (Jarva 1995, p. 122). The hoplite shield was round with an offset rim, which could rest on the shoulder to help with the weight. The main distinguishing feature is the way it was carried. It has a central arm-band, called the *porpax*, through which the left arm was passed up to the elbow. There is then a grip at the edge of the shield called the *antilabe*, which the left hand gripped (Fig. 26). When these features are shown in art, we know we are dealing with a hoplite shield; but when the shield is shown face on, it becomes harder to distinguish it from single-grip round shields like the Herzsprung. This two-handed grip system seems to have been a Greek invention, and may be behind Herodotus's story of shield grips and blazons being invented by the Carians (Herodotus I, 171). From just before 700, shield blazons are shown on some round shields. These are designs that need to be held the right way up, and it is generally accepted that this works only with the two-handed hoplite grip (Fig. 27) (Snodgrass 1965a, pp. 61–2; Jarva 1995, pp. 121–2). Far more common than these blazons at this time were circle and spiral designs, which are not subject to a right-way-up rule and which appeared as early as *c.* 750 on vases with Dipylon and square shields. A series of other non-blazon designs have recently come to light on a late eighth-century vase from Paros. This shows a line of warriors in Kegelhelms carrying large, round shields decorated with a large cross or with chequerboard designs (Zapheiropoulou 2001, p. 289). Such shields are also sometimes shown with a telamon, showing that they are single-grip-type shields.

When the first blazon shields appeared in *c.* 700, they were not shown on the same vases as spiral-patterned shields; but in the seventh century both shields were shown together and it is clear that the spiral patterns carried on to be used on hoplite shields. Ueda-Sarson (2000; see website listed in References) has compiled illustrations of dozens of shield blazons from *c.* 700 to the Macedonian period, and spiral patterns continued to be shown until about 550, while other symmetrical abstract designs continued up to the Persian Wars. Only after *c.* 500 did nearly all shields carry blazons. Spartan bronze figures carry spiral designs down to the third century, but this is probably an artistic convention (Snodgrass 1965a, p. 62).

Fig. 43: Shield interiors from the seventh, sixth and fifth centuries.

These designs were mostly painted onto the shield, which was of wood covered with leather and with a bronze rim, the latter usually decorated with a guilloche pattern. The Chigi Vase (Figs 27 and 43*a*) suggests that the earliest shields may have been of wickerwork or ply, like the Dipylon shield. Many fragments of the bronze rims have been found at Olympia, and some bronze blazons have also been found. Snodgrass illustrates (1967, plate 22) a particularly impressive winged horse and Connolly (1998, p. 54) a gorgon. A cockerel, and a right arm with clenched fist have also been discovered (*Olympia Bericht*, vol. I, plate 12 and vol. V, plate 32). Connolly (1998, p. 54) thinks that these are too delicate to have been used on shields in battle, and must have been made specially to be dedicated. Most arms and armour dedicated in sanctuaries were, however, precisely that captured from the enemy, and so I am sure these bronze blazons were used in battle (Jackson, in Hanson, 1991, p. 230). Shields completely faced with bronze have also been found at Olympia, and it would have been much easier to paint (and repaint) designs onto these. They also give us the size of hoplite shields, which usually varies from 80cm to 100cm, although one example is 120cm (Snodgrass 1965a, p. 64). Sekunda (2000, p. 10) suggests that bronze-faced shields did not appear until *c.* 500, judging by the colours used on vase paintings, but the prior existence of the Herzsprung shield shows that the Greeks were capable of producing thin bronze sheet at a much earlier period. Examples of bronze hoplite shield facings from Olympia can be dated to as early as *c.* 625 (Bol 1989, p. 683). The *antilabe* handgrip was presumably made of leather, but the *porpax* was bronze, often highly decorated, and the survival of large numbers of these, more than bronze facings or blazons, shows that most shields were just fronted with leather or some other perishable material. The interiors of the shields also seem sometimes to have been painted (Fig. 34) (Sekunda 1999, p. 53 and plate C1), and from *c.* 550 are sometimes decorated with separate tassels (Fig. 43*b*) (Boardman 1980a, nos 64.2; 73).

By *c.* 675 the hoplite shield had ousted all other shield forms in most of Greece, and its use lasted right down to the fourth century, as we shall see in the following chapters. Compared to the wickerwork Dipylon, the hoplite shield was much heavier and stronger, and this was because of the new *porpax/antilabe* grip system. This meant that more weight could be carried by the left arm. The jutting rim of the shield meant that some weight could also be carried on the left shoulder, especially when at rest. Such a heavy shield was hard to swing around in combat and was another reason, along with the heavy bronze armour, for sticking close to your fellow warriors in the heat of combat. The phalanx of hoplite warfare developed from this, with men in close order, usually eight ranks deep. This made throwing spears, which seems to have been the popular form of warfare from before 900 to 700 and later, difficult, and led to the exclusive use of the thrusting spear as outlined below.

## SPEARS AND SWORDS

Spearheads from the Dark Age and Geometric period are fairly plentiful finds in Greece; Snodgrass devoted many pages (1965a, pp. 116–32) to a listing of different types, and his list tells us that iron replaced bronze for use in spearheads in the eleventh century. An anomaly, however, is that there are many spear finds from Olympia that must be from the eighth century or later, but which are made of bronze. As has been mentioned earlier, iron is much more efficient than bronze for use as a spearhead, and it was also more readily available. It is, however, harder to work and was therefore more expensive as a finished product. Iron might also be considered less aesthetically pleasing.

Bronze spearheads seem to have retained their popularity in south Italy and Sicily until the eighth century, and in Crete for even longer; but there is a probability that bronze was reintroduced as a metal for spearheads in mainland Greece at some point in the sixth century (Snodgrass 1965a, p. 134). This may have had something to do with the expansion of hoplite forces. Where spear butts are known, these also tend to be of bronze (Fig. 44).

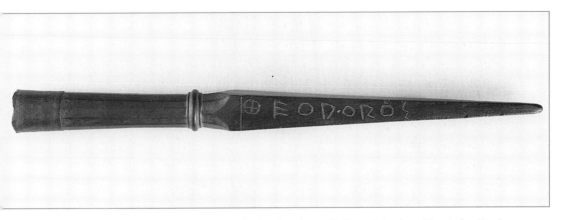

Fig. 44: Spear butt from Olympia inscribed: 'Theodoros dedicated (me) to (Zeus) the King', *c*. 500. *(Trustees of the British Museum GR 1915.7-14.1)*

The spearhead of the ninth and eighth centuries was 30cm to 50cm long but was certainly part of a throwing spear, as is depicted in Homer (Lorimer 1950, p. 257). It is difficult to find any artistic evidence of its use as a thrusting weapon (Jarva 1995, p. 123). Spears found in graves are often in pairs of the same size, and it is possible that both were thrown before close combat was joined with the sword. Late eighth-century vases frequently show pairs of spears being carried (Figs 25, 41); most warriors are also shown carrying swords. In the seventh century the sword is depicted less, and one spear was used for thrusting in the new tactics of the hoplite phalanx.

As mentioned above, a second spear for throwing was kept by these early hoplites. A 'still life' *aryballos* of *c*. 680 (Fig. 45) shows a thrusting spear paired with a throwing spear, its throwing loop clearly visible. The Chigi Vase seems to show hoplites with more than one spear and, in the arming scene to one side, two spears – one long and one short – are shown waiting to be collected for battle. An anomaly here is that both spears have throwing loops, but this is perhaps an artistic error (Snodgrass 1965a, p. 138; Jarva 1995, p. 123). Both

Fig. 45: Corinthian alabastron featuring a 'Still Life' of early hoplite equipment, c. 680. (Archäologischer Anzeiger 4, 1889, p. 93, no. 8)

these depictions make it more likely that the second spears were for thrusting, rather than being an extra throwing spear (Snodgrass 1967, pp. 57–8).

Although the use of two spears, one for throwing, seems to have died out by c. 640, there are a few later depictions. These often show warriors on horseback, and date from the middle of the sixth century. They cannot all be explained away as being 'heroic' depictions, or cavalry rather than mounted hoplites (Boardman 1979, nos 2.1, 2.2; 1998, nos 375, 464). It seems that on occasion some hoplites still carried a throwing spear into battle, but that it really did go out of use by the 520s and, in most states, probably a lot earlier. The problem with the throwing spear was that, for throwing it, a lot of space and movement was needed, which was entirely incompatible with the close phalanx formation. Once this was discovered, hoplites were encouraged more and more to rely on the single thrusting spear. With the introduction of more solid hoplite shields and bronze armour, it is likely that thrown spears were becoming less effective anyway. Tyrtaeus urged the Spartan hoplites not to stand out of the range of missiles, but to ignore them and close with the enemy (Tyrtaeus: fragment 11, in Sage 1996, p. 28).

The sword retained its importance in the ninth and eighth centuries and was invariably still the cut-and-thrust, Naue II Type sword introduced in the thirteenth century. It continued in use right through the Archaic period to *c.* 520, although later examples are rare (Snodgrass 1965a, pp. 93–4; Kilian-Dirlmeier 1993, plates 41–54). They vary from 50cm to 70cm in length and have half-moon pommels, clearly depicted in Late Geometric art where the sword is the commonest weapon shown (Fig. 25). Since we have seen that spears were thrown in this early period (900 to *c.* 650), it is natural that all warriors would also have needed a sword for hand-to-hand combat. Greenhalgh (1973, p. 73) suggests that the early phalanx in some states, such as Euboea, may have been composed of men who threw spears or javelins first and then closed with the sword in a phalanx formation. A fragment from Archilochus, who talks of javelin warfare on Naxos and Paros, mentions that Euboeans spurned the bow and sling, and fought close up with the sword, although he also calls them 'Spear-famed', indicating that they had this weapon at their disposal as well (Greenhalgh 1973, p. 90). Archilochus was writing in the seventh century, when hoplite warfare was becoming the norm, and he seems to be talking about places that were still fighting in an earlier style.

The introduction of the phalanx certainly undermined the sword's previous prestige. After 700, weapons were shorter and stubbier, but they were frequently left out of artistic depictions altogether. Some examples have been found at Olympia of a single-edged, straight slashing sword, of a type known from Macedonia, Thrace and Thessaly (Snodgrass 1965a, p. 100). These seem to be mostly from the eighth century, although the type is seen in use later (Sekunda 2002, pp. 16, 29). It was probably from this sword that the *kopis* or *machaira* developed. This is a curved sword with the sharp edge on the inside (recurved), like a Gurkha kukri – which indeed is descended from it (Snodgrass 1967, plate 50). An example dating to about 650 is known from Crete (Snodgrass 1965a, p. 100), and one is illustrated on an alabastron from Syracuse of about the same date. This geographical difference has led Sekunda (2000, p. 16) to suggest that they came from the Near East, and Connolly (1998, p. 63) to suggest that they were an Etruscan development. I think, like Snodgrass, that a Thracian origin is the most likely. They do not appear to have become common until the end of the sixth century and were not as popular as the straight sword until perhaps the fourth century.

In the eighth century, the Naue II Type was a cut-and-thrust sword, but Geometric art shows that it was more often used as a cutting weapon (Ahlberg 1971, p. 46). In the later phalanx, a shorter weapon was preferable so as to be more easily wielded, but it seems to have still been used as a cutting or slashing weapon (Connolly 1998, p. 63). The adoption of the *machaira* shows that the straight sword was seldom used for thrusting, and the *machaira*'s thicker upper edge would have made it a much stronger cutting weapon. How effective these swords were as a secondary weapon in the warfare of the phalanx is uncertain. A thrusting spear might break in the initial charge so a sword seems essential, but whether it was really effective if your immediate opponent's spear was still intact is unlikely.

## OTHER TROOP TYPES

Nearly all the evidence we have discussed in this chapter refers to infantry developing from lightly armoured skirmishers into the heavily armoured hoplite phalanx. There is, however, evidence for a few other troop types. Although Greeks for the most part abandoned the chariot for the riding horse during the tenth century, the existence of Greek cavalry is not certain before the Peloponnesian War. There are plenty of vase illustrations of armoured warriors on horseback but, as Greenhalgh shows (1973, *passim*), these are hoplites on horses, who would have dismounted to fight in battle. This is certain because the warriors carry hoplite shields, which cannot be used on a horse; and also they are invariably accompanied by a squire, who would hold the horses while the battle raged and be ready for a quick getaway if necessary. The horses were in fact being used in the same way as chariots were used earlier, as a taxi service to and from battle.

Two questions arise from this. Did all hoplites ride into battle, and did the squires fight as light troops, whether mounted or not? The first question is likely to be answered with a 'no'. It takes a lot of land and money to look after horses (and to own a squire), and so only a small percentage of hoplites could have afforded to ride to battle. We see a reminder of this when just 300 Spartans were present for the Battle of Thermopylae in 480. These men were the personal bodyguard of King Leonidas, called the Hippeis, or 'Horsemen'. They suggest the number of hoplites that might have ridden to battle in an earlier period – a small number, that could sometimes be sent on ahead as an advance unit or for small actions. The Theban Sacred Band of 300 may have had a similar origin, or may indeed be copied from the Spartans.

As for squires taking part in the battle, this is certainly what Herodotus suggests at a later period, at the Battle of Plataea in 479, when the Spartan squires (all 35,000 of them!) were supposed to have fought as light troops, along with 34,500 from the other Greek states! However, he fails to then mention any role they played in the battle itself (Herodotus IX, 29). In the sixth century there are certainly signs of light cavalry use, which may have come about from the squires of hoplites joining the fight. Greenhalgh shows many illustrations (1973, pp. 112, 114, 115, etc.), which seem to depict light cavalry fighting with javelins in battle, as opposed to hunting scenes.

Literary evidence is more scant. Athens seems to have had just ninety-six horsemen for coastal patrols organised under the reforms of Solon in 594 (Bugh 1988, p. 5). In the Persian Wars of the early fifth century, no cavalry fought on the Greek side at all, although this may be because it seemed pointless to use a small force that would be so heavily outnumbered by the Persian cavalry (Bugh 1988, pp. 10–11). Finally, we know for a fact that the Spartans did not raise a cavalry force until 424 (Bugh 1988, p. 24). In northern Greece, the situation was somewhat different. The wide plains of Macedonia, Thessaly and, to some extent, Boeotia meant that these states were provided with cavalry. Indeed, Thessalian cavalry was often used by Athens and other states as a mercenary cavalry. They seem to have used javelins and not to have been armoured at all at this period (Snodgrass 1967, p. 86). The Greeks of south Italy and Sicily also developed a true cavalry before 500, some of whom may have been armoured (Snodgrass 1967, p. 87) (see Chapter 4). There are vase illustrations of what appears to be true cavalry from c. 580 (Greenhalgh 1973, pp. 96 ff.) but, as the literary evidence shows, it was very much a small part of the military scene until the Peloponnesian War.

Similarly, the use of light troops is elusive. In the late eighth century they are clearly very common, especially archers, and appear frequently on the Late Geometric vases of the Dipylon Master and his followers (Ahlberg 1971, p. 44). This was the skirmishing warfare which preceded the hoplite phalanx and, for a brief period, the archer had a central role in warfare. Pausanias, writing much later, mentions their use by Spartans in the Messenian Wars of the eighth and seventh centuries (Snodgrass 1967, p. 81), but by the time of the introduction of the hoplite phalanx in c. 650 the archer, slinger and javelin thrower had mostly disappeared. As we have seen, the phalanx did not appear overnight, however, and there are some interesting pieces of evidence showing the transition. Greenhalgh (1973, p. 99) illustrates a vase showing early hoplites possibly fighting in a phalanx formation but, in between them, there is an archer also taking part in the battle. Tyrtaeus, a mid-seventh-century poet, after he talks about the phalanx standing shoulder to shoulder, exhorts the light-armed troops to hide behind the shields of the hoplites and then hurl their stones at the enemy (Sage 1996, p. 29). This last quote seems to refer to ordinary rocks rather than sling stones, for which the evidence is very thin at this period.

There is plenty of other evidence for archery in Greece in the seventh and sixth centuries, but much is concerned with hunting and, once the phalanx was in place, only Crete supplies evidence for the use of the bow in combat. Indeed, just as Thessalian cavalry was used by other states, so Cretan archers were used as mercenary troops.

Evidence for javelin throwers is also thin after the introduction of the phalanx, although they are again mentioned by Tyrtaeus in the mid-seventh century (Snodgrass 1967, p. 79). Otherwise they too did not resurface until the Persian Wars of the early fifth century. The widespread adoption of the phalanx seems to have developed into a semi-ritualised sort of warfare between Greek states. The heavily-armed phalanx would have been very vulnerable to missile troops, and could have been devastated (once defeated) by a cavalry force, but these troops seem to have simply not been used (Hanson 1991, p. 232). It is unfortunate that we have no reliable accounts of hoplite battles in the seventh and sixth centuries, which might have told us more about the use of missile troops.

Only when the threat of the Persian Empire grew, and the Greek states knew that they would have to fight a non-Greek enemy who had thousands of cavalry and missile troops, did they start to adapt the phalanx, and also to introduce or reintroduce cavalry and missile troops.

FOUR

# The Persian and Peloponnesian Wars, 525–400 BC

The period covered by this chapter is at last fairly fully covered by written sources, mainly Herodotus, Thucydides and Xenophon. Although they were mainly concerned with war as part of history, they do occasionally give us insights into army organisation and equipment – especially Xenophon, whose treatise *On Horsemanship* is invaluable. Athenian black and red figure vases continue to help us greatly with depictions of equipment, although during the Peloponnesian War in the later fifth century pictures of warriors became markedly less popular. Dedications of arms and armour at sanctuaries also declined, and this is thought to be related to a growing distaste for glorifying war, especially against one's fellow Greeks (Jackson, in Hanson 1991, pp. 228 ff.).

The evidence we have from these sources for the late sixth century onwards shows a great change in the warfare of the phalanx. As we have seen, many extra pieces of limb armour fell out of fashion after *c.* 525, and the bell cuirass also ceased to be used (except in Thrace and perhaps Macedonia). Lighter helmets and body armour were worn, and the phalanx became a much more mobile formation. Herodotus tells us that the Athenian phalanx at the Battle of Marathon in 490 was the first to charge at a run, although the idea that they ran for a full mile is unlikely (Herodotus VI, 114). Herodotus tells us that the Athenians were also the first Greeks to be able to look upon the Persians without flinching, as the word 'Persian' used to strike terror into all Greeks up until that point. This was no doubt because of the tremendous advances of the Persian Empire in the later sixth century. The Persians conquered Lydia in 546, closely followed by the Ionian Greeks on the coast of Asia Minor. They conquered Babylon in 538 and Egypt in 525. This threat was quite probably the reason for the change in hoplite armour, as Sekunda has suggested (1999, p. 31). The Greeks would have seen that a clash with Persia was likely, if not inevitable, and the Persians would not 'fight fair' in the way that Greek city-states had fought each other for the previous 150 years.

As has been mentioned, the heavy phalanx was very vulnerable to missile troops and cavalry, which Persia had in abundance. By lightening the armour, the phalanx would be able to advance quickly to join in hand-to-hand battle, and so negate the missiles of the Persians. Following the experience of the Persian assaults, the Greeks, particularly the Athenians, looked to improve their army by introducing their own archers and other missile troops, as well as a real cavalry arm. During the seemingly endless Peloponnesian War, the large numbers of troops used in order to gain an advantage often meant that these troops were less well equipped with armour. Conversely, perhaps especially after the excellent performance of the Sicilian cavalry in the latter stages of the war, horsemen appear to have become more heavily armoured, and perhaps reached an equal status to the hoplite phalanx. The Peloponnesian War also saw a greater use of mercenaries and the growth of the professional soldier, who previously had existed only at Sparta. Strategy and tactics became increasingly more important in the search for victory, and the old ritual of the phalanx battle disappeared. Let us examine in detail how these changes affected the equipment of Greek warriors in the late sixth and fifth centuries.

## HELMETS

The lightening of hoplite equipment manifested itself in helmets with the introduction of two new, but similar types: the Chalcidian and the 'Attic'. There is still some evidence for the use of the Illyrian helmet (Fig. 49c) from finds at Olympia (*Olympia Bericht* VIII, plates 66–71), and for the Corinthian helmet from finds and in art down to the middle of the fifth century (Fig. 46). The Illyrian helmet remained particularly popular in Macedonia, and a helmet recently discovered there is interesting in that it has a crown raised up on a repoussé ridge, like late Corinthian helmets (Savvopoulou 1990–5, p. 163). Both Corinthian and Illyrian helmets were now likely to have ear holes cut out to aid hearing, and also to have their cheek pieces hinged.

The Chalcidian helmet is a variation on the Corinthian, which had cut-outs for the ears and rounded cheek pieces, hinged on the later versions (Fig. 47). The cut-outs for the eyes were generally larger, too. The Chalcidian helmet is named after 'Chalcidian' vases of the late sixth century, when it first appeared (Pflug 1989, p. 21). These actually came from south Italy, and south Italy and Sicily have also produced about half the actual finds of Chalcidian helmets. This

Fig. 46: Late Corinthian helmet from Corinth, with raised crown above a repoussé ridge, c. 500–480. *(Trustees of the British Museum GR 1873.9-10.1)*

suggests they could have been invented there before coming to Greece (Snodgrass 1965a, p. 34). These states used cavalry in warfare to a greater extent than the Greeks of the mainland, and it could be that the Chalcidian helmet was developed from the Corinthian helmet especially for cavalry, or for infantry who were likely to face cavalry. Examples have also been found as far afield as Macedonia and the Black Sea, as well as several examples from Olympia (Snodgrass 1965a, p. 34). The Chalcidian helmet developed at about the same time as the Corinthian was having the whole crown raised on a repoussé ridge (Fig. 46), and this ridge, usually present on Chalcidian helmets, often meets in front as a brow guard.

The 'Attic' I have mentioned in inverted commas is the helmet called by that name by Snodgrass (1967, p. 70) and subsequently Connolly (1998, pp. 61–2). The term is also used by Pflug and Dintsis (q.v.). This helmet appears frequently on Athenian vases, usually being worn by Athena, and is really just another Chalcidian variation. It has a more jutting neck guard, long straight cheek pieces, which are sometimes hinged and worn vertically, and a high forehead guard or frontlet with no nose guard (Boardman 1980a, figs 98, 154, 161, 162, 188, 191, 223–5). The helmet worn by Athena on these vases may even be derived from the Ionian helmets mentioned in Chapter 3, which are of a very similar construction. Some illustrations of Athena on late sixth-century black figure vases show just a simple cap with a large crest on top (Boardman 1980a, figs 121, 145). This is obviously artistic licence in order to show Athena's face clearly, as such a helmet would never have worked and it warns us to be sceptical of all we see on vases.

By 510 there does seem to have been a common variant of the Chalcidian, which has long hinged cheek pieces, sometimes with a scalloped front edge, which could be put up into a vertical position when not in combat (Connolly 1998, p. 61, no. 19). Chalcidian cheek pieces were also frequently shaped in the form of rams' heads. The British Museum has an example, and others have been found at Olympia (*Olympia Bericht* VIII, figs 59–60). An extraordinary example, now in the St Louis City Art Museum in the USA, has a complete three-dimensional ram's head beaten out of the crown of the helmet (*Olympia Bericht* VIII, pp. 61–2). The ram is the leader of the flock and so it seems likely that such helmets, with ram's head decorations, belonged to officers. These Chalcidian (and Attic) helmets usually had only a short nose guard, or no nose guard at all.

The Attic helmet seems to be most popular in Attic vase painting, but that is perhaps because, with the cheek pieces in a vertical position, the artist could

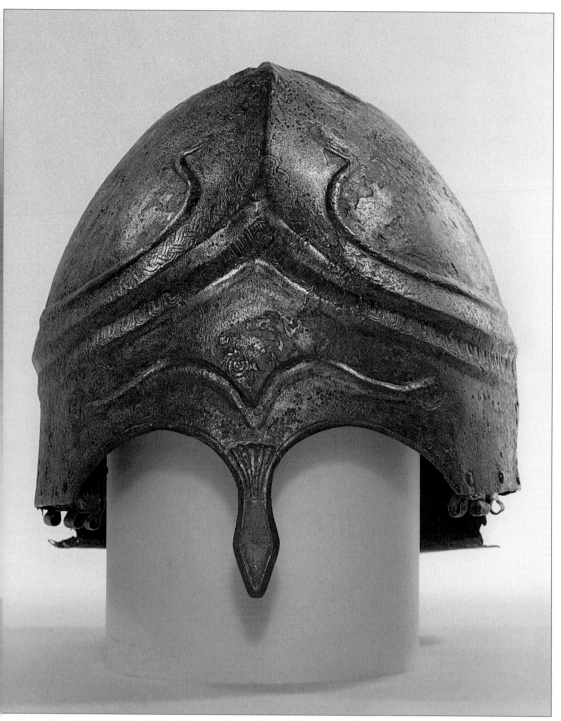

Fig. 47: Chalcidian helmet from Italy with raised crown and eyebrow decoration (missing the cheek pieces), early fifth century. *(Shefton Museum of Greek Art and Archaeology, University of Newcastle-upon-Tyne, no. 101)*

depict the soldier's facial features clearly. For the same reason, when the Corinthian helmet is depicted, it is usually pushed up on the head like a cap, so that the soldier's face can be seen. Attic helmets are much rarer in finds, but this may be because they were popular only in Athens and Attica, hence the name.

Vase paintings of this period also show us some very detailed decoration on some helmets, which is hard to explain. A vase from *c.* 490 shows dark-coloured Attic helmets with a few white studs painted on (Boardman 1979, no. 135). The well-known Douris Cup (Snodgrass 1967, plate 45; Boardman 1979, no. 28; Connolly 1998, p. 58) depicting hoplites arming shows a similar helmet with little white rings painted on, and two helmets seemingly decorated with inverted scales, like those that appear on some contemporary corslets (see below). The likeliest explanation seems to be that these helmets have been painted. We know helmets were painted at a later date, and we have already seen some evidence for the painting of armour and helmets in earlier times. There are other explanations, however. Dr Jackson suggested to me many years ago that the scale effect could be embossing. We know that Greek armourers were very skilled and at this time were certainly capable of such delicate work, but such a large amount of work seems likely to weaken the skull of the helmet and render it impractical for one that was to be used in battle. The main argument against it is lack of evidence. We have none for such embossing work on helmets. Similar decoration can be found on corslets of the period (see below), where it is quite clearly the actual attachment of scales and other reinforcing studs etc. to a material base. Sekunda (2002, pp. 18, 79–80) has taken this one step further by suggesting that these helmets are composite ones. He suggests that metal plates could have been fixed to a hardened leather cap with ornamental rivets, or that scales might have been attached to a leather cap (Sekunda 2000, plate C and p. 56). Conversely, Beazley also suggests that material could have been put over a bronze helmet to stop it getting too hot, and that is what we are looking at in the case of helmets with a checked design, which more usually appears on clothing (Anderson 1970, p. 31 and plate 16; Boardman 1979, no. 308.2). While the latter is possible, no helmets have yet been found with traces of material attached to the outside, although that is perhaps not surprising. As for Sekunda's helmet made up of separate pieces, again we have no actual evidence for this. It seems unlikely to me that the Greek armourers would go back to making helmets in separate pieces, which have weak joints, when they were capable of beating a helmet out of one piece of bronze. While I favour these patterns being painted onto helmets, there also remains the possibility that they are a fantasy by the artist, painting intricate designs to show off his skill. The otherwise apparently accurate portrayal of hoplite equipment is an argument against this.

Depictions and examples of the true Corinthian helmet ceased in about 400, although the Apulo-Corinthian and Pseudo-Corinthian helmets continued right through to the Roman period. These last two classes (so designated by Dintsis in his work on Hellenistic helmets) were helmets following a vague Corinthian outline, but designed specifically to be worn as caps on top of the head. They were particularly popular in Italy and did not really feature in Greece. The Chalcidian helmet and Attic helmet both lasted longer, to c. 300 BC and to c. AD 400 (!) respectively, but again often in Italy, after they were no longer used – or at least not used to any great extent – in Greece.

These new helmets, or helmet developments, had two main changes from the older helmets. They nearly all had a crown raised up on a repoussé ridge, which would have given more room for padding. A cup by the Sosias Painter (c. 500), featuring Achilles bandaging Patroclus (Boardman 1979, no. 50.1; Connolly 1998, p. 57, no.1), shows Patroclus apparently wearing a separate 'arming cap', put on before the helmet. The raised crown may have been developed to accommodate this, or perhaps this raised section had its own extra padding glued inside. The warriors on the Douris Cup seem to be just tying their hair up to provide padding under the helmet. Whatever the case, it is clear that hoplites felt they needed more protection and comfort from their helmets. The other main change was the exposure of the ears. The Chalcidian helmet left the ears free and most, but not all, late Illyrian and Corinthian helmets also have cut-outs for the ears. Hearing in battle had not been considered essential in the close-packed phalanx of the seventh and sixth centuries, but now hoplites had to be able to hear orders. They needed to know when to charge and when to halt, and to be told about other happenings on the battlefield, which were no longer as straightforward as they had been.

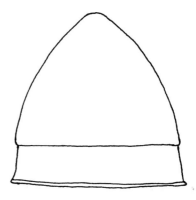

Fig. 48: Bronze Pilos helmet from Egypt, probably fourth century.

From the middle of the fifth century, in addition to the Corinthian, Chalcidian and Attic helmets, the Greeks also developed the Pilos, Boeotian and Thracian helmets, which soon supplanted the former in popularity.

The Pilos helmet derived from a felt cap called the Pilos. This simple, bell-shaped cap was quite possibly first worn as a protection underneath the helmets we have been discussing. Later Corinthian and Chalcidian helmets did not have perforations around the edges for attaching a lining and, although we have suggested that a lining might have been glued in, it is possible that a separate cap of felt was sometimes worn under this. With the movement towards lighter equipment, it seems possible that some hoplites wore their felt caps but no longer bothered with the heavy helmet (Anderson 1970, pp. 29–30). From *c.* 450, we know of examples of this cap translated into bronze – the Pilos helmet – which could of course be worn over a felt Pilos (Fig. 48) (Sekunda 1999, p. 30). This helmet was light and gave all-round vision, and seems to have been adopted by the Spartans first (Anderson 1970, p. 31). It was certainly not exclusively Spartan or Peloponnesian, as there are examples on Attic vases and on an Athenian tombstone (Anderson 1970, plate 12). The helmet was also worn by Boeotian hoplites, and depictions from Boeotia, Athens and south Italy show that the helmet could have a plume, either fore-and-aft or transverse, although such crests seem to have become less popular after 450 (Anderson 1970, pp. 32–4; Sekunda 1999, plate H). Ancient authors make specific mention of the Laconian or Arcadian Pilos as being made of felt. This, and the passage in Thucydides about the Spartan Piloi being of no use against Athenian archers at Sphacteria, suggest that Spartan hoplites may have been content with the felt Pilos, and may not have worn the bronze Pilos helmet at this time (Thucydides IV, 34.3). That other hoplites wore only felt hats is clear from the tombstone of a Megarian carved at Athens, who is clearly clutching a felt Pilos, rather than a Pilos helmet (Anderson 1970, p. 31). This helmet was probably the one worn by most of the 'Ten Thousand' mercenaries on their expedition to Persia in 400 (Xenophon, *Anabasis*), and continued to be used throughout the Classical and Hellenistic periods. Compared to earlier helmets, the Pilos is of a very simple construction and must have been very cheap to make. As the fifth century progressed, city-states recruited more people from lower social classes into their armies, and this helmet – or perhaps just the felt cap – may have been the only sort they could afford.

Another helmet derived from ordinary headgear, in around 450, was the Boeotian helmet (Fig. 49*b*). This derived from a Boeotian riding(?) hat, similar to a Pilos but with a brim and chin straps. These chin straps were attached to

Fig. 49: A selection of Classical and Hellenistic helmets. *(a)* Cone helmet, late fourth or third century. *(b)* Boeotian helmet, late fourth or third century. *(c)* Illyrian helmet, sixth century. *(d)* Corinthian helmet, sixth century. *(Ashmolean Museum, Oxford)*

either side of the cap and bent the rim down into two folds when they were fastened. This shape was then translated into bronze, giving the Boeotian helmet its crinkly rim (Sekunda 2000, p. 59). The helmet is known as Boeotian because of the number of depictions from there, and because Xenophon, in his treatise *On Horsemanship* (XII, 3) mentions the Boeotian helmet. He recommended it as a good cavalry helmet, because it gave all-round vision. Xenophon's description therefore fits with the helmet modern scholars call 'Boeotian' and, as with the Corinthian, the nomenclature is almost certainly correct in this case (Snodgrass 1967, pp. 94–5). As with the Pilos, the Boeotian helmet lasted right through the Classical and Hellenistic periods. It is often depicted being worn by cavalrymen as Xenophon suggests, but it was certainly worn by some Theban and Boeotian hoplites as their version of the Pilos. Demosthenes mentions a painting of the Battle of Marathon, in which the Plataean hoplites can be distinguished from the Athenians by their Boeotian helmets (Demosthenes LIX, 94, in Snodgrass 1967, p. 94). The Boeotian helmet had not actually been invented at the time of the Battle of Marathon in 490, but

Fig. 50: Red figure vase by the Achilles Painter, showing a hoplite in a Thracian helmet, linen corslet and greaves, *c. 450–440. (Trustees of the British Museum GR 1843.11-3.1)*

this painting was showing hoplites armoured as they would have been in Demosthenes' time, in the fourth century.

In about 460, another new helmet appeared on Attic vases. This is generally known as the Thracian, because of later examples discovered there, but it is clearly a derivation from the Attic helmet, and was probably developed in Athens shortly after the Persian Wars. Pflug continues to call this new development an Attic helmet, whereas Dintsis settles for Pseudo-Attic (Dintsis 1986, Helmet type 7; Pflug 1989, p. 24). The old Attic helmet, which continued in use, often omitted a nose guard and was quite close-fitting to the head. The new 'Thracian' helmet had a forward-projecting rim at the front and sides, giving greater protection from downward blows (Fig. 50). There was also sometimes a frontlet of reinforced repoussé work on the brow. So that the cheek pieces continued to fit close to the wearer's face, they were now attached by leather hinges to the inside of the helmet. This also protected the join from damage. The cheek pieces were often elongated to give good protection to the face, and the design seems to be at odds with the more widespread lightening of equipment (Boardman 1989, nos 1, 10, 80.1). The helmet is rarely depicted and is usually shown with the muscle cuirass or an elaborate composite corslet, indicating a wealthy hoplite (Boardman 1979, no. 361). Also, it is often highly decorated with embossing and/or painting (Boardman 1979, no. 331; 1989, no. 80.1). The helmet was perhaps, then, a statement of wealth, separating its wearer from those who could afford only a Pilos type. We tend to have a cluster of illustrations from around 460–450, when the transition was being made from heavier to lighter helmets, and then not much until the fourth century, so it is possible that it did not see much action in the Peloponnesian War. The illustrations we have usually have the fore-and-aft crest, but one has additional side plumes or feathers (Boardman 1979, no. 331); and an example from c. 425 shows the new style of crest which was to become popular in the fourth century. This is the simple plume of horsehair rising from a central knob, which replaced the fore-and-aft stiff horsehair crest at this time, although most helmets seem not to have bothered with crests at all (Boardman 1989, no. 219). Later Thracian helmets often had a fore-and-aft ridge of bronze in place of the old crest, giving more protection to the crown (Pflug 1989, p. 26; Connolly 1998, p. 61, no. 20). Despite its heavier appearance and protective features, the Thracian helmet still left the ears clear so that the soldier knew what was happening on the battlefield. The gradual disappearance of fore-and-aft horsehair crests from nearly all helmets after c. 450 had probably to do with expense. More hoplites were opting for basic equipment as all they could afford, and by the end of the fifth century most city-states were supplying equipment to soldiers, rather than soldiers having to purchase their own arms. The simple, flowing horsehair that was starting to be introduced would have been a much easier and cheaper option.

## BODY ARMOUR

As mentioned in the introduction to this chapter, the bell cuirass went out of use towards the end of the sixth century, almost certainly in an effort to make the hoplite phalanx less slow and cumbersome in the face of the Persian threat. Lighter armour was generally adopted in the form of the linen or composite corslet discussed below, but the bronze cuirass also survived by being developed into the muscle cuirass, which Jarva calls Type III (1995, pp. 30–2). The collapse in the market for the bell cuirass must have hit bronze workers hard, but they seem to have adapted to the situation well. Instead of making large numbers of bell cuirasses for the majority of hoplites who no longer wanted them, they spent much more time and effort making elaborate muscle cuirasses which could have been afforded only by the wealthiest of hoplites. The basic structure of the cuirass remained the same, but a lot more anatomical detail was painstakingly hammered out of the bronze sheet (Fig. 51).

The statue from Longa, which has been discussed before (Jarva 1995, p. 27, fig. 6; Connolly 1998, p. 59) and which dates to *c.* 525, shows a halfway stage between the bell and the muscle cuirass. It has the bell shape, chest spirals and an omega curve showing the outline of the ribcage, but it also has fully detailed stomach muscles over the abdominal area. By *c.* 490, the fully developed muscle cuirass is seen on red figure vases. An early example shows the front edge of the cuirass dipping to cover the lower belly area, which was to become a feature of this cuirass, replacing the bell curve or jutting flange of the bell cuirass (Arias 1962, fig. 144). As well as the stomach muscles, the chest muscles (pectorals) are outlined, as are the lower chest or serratus magnus muscles to the side. There are spirals on the chest, which continued to be a feature of most fifth-century muscle cuirasses and which may have been painted on as well as embossed. The strange twist in the cuirass is caused by the artist trying to put the hoplite into an action pose, and not quite managing it. This may also show that it was an early attempt by the artist to show this form of cuirass. An early fragment of a

*Opposite page:* Fig. 51: Bronze muscle cuirass with silver nipples from Ruvo in south Italy, fifth century. *(Trustees of the British Museum GR 1856.12-26.614)*

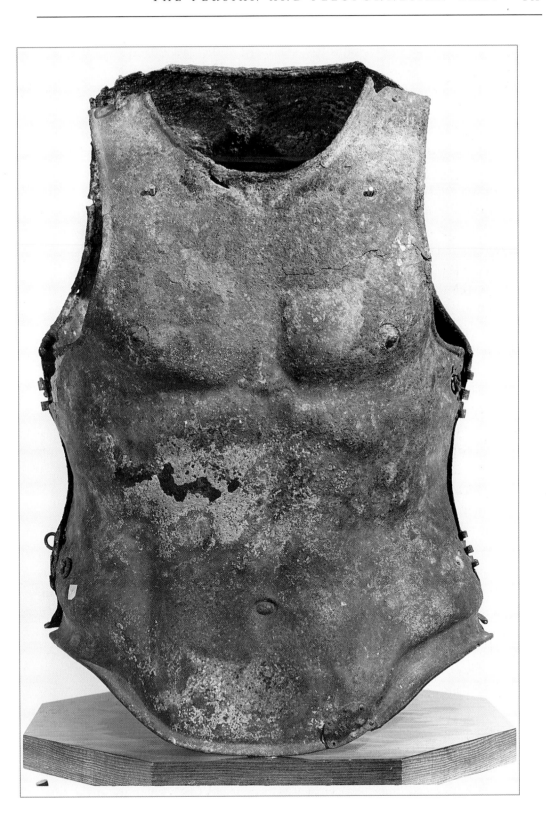

muscle cuirass from Olympia has been dated to the early fifth century, and so it seems that this form of cuirass was available for the Persian Wars. Sekunda (1999, p. 28) suggests that it was particularly popular in Sparta, judging by bronze statue finds from there, although he admits the evidence is thin. The amount of work which went into the construction of this cuirass meant that it was always a rare item, as is borne out by the relatively few illustrations of it in Attic art. I cannot see, as Sekunda does, whole phalanxes wearing the muscle cuirass even if they are Spartans (Sekunda 1999, plates E and F). There is even a possibility that the muscle cuirass was known as 'Attic' and originated from there (Jarva 1995, p. 32). If that is the case, and our earliest depictions are *c.* 490 and from Athens, it is possible that only a few rich Athenian hoplites would have had access to this form of body armour during the Persian Wars.

Illustrations became a little more frequent after the Persian Wars in the 470s and 460s, when the cuirass reached an early peak of artistic development. An example from south Italy in the British Museum (Fig. 51) is deeply curving at the front to guard the abdomen, a curve which is matched to an extent at the back of the cuirass. There is a high degree of anatomical detail here, including the serratus magnus muscles and the navel. The nipples are inlaid in silver. Vase illustrations from the middle of the fifth century (Snodgrass 1967, plate 43) often still show spiral and tendril decoration on the chest area, which, as suggested earlier, was probably a painted addition that does not survive on the archaeological finds.

These cuirasses were fastened by fully developed hinges, rather than the primitive tube-and-pin hinges used on most bell cuirasses. There were usually two hinges on either side of the cuirass, one under the armpit and one at the waist, and a hinge at each shoulder. On either side of the hinge were bronze rings for a strap and buckle, and these were used to pull the two halves of the cuirass together before the hinge pin was inserted (Connolly 1998, p. 54). An apparently later cuirass from Italy has a full-length hinge running from armpit to waist on the left-hand side, which must have had the long hinge pin inserted before the cuirass was put on (Connolly 1998, p. 56). Some other, perhaps later, cuirasses have no hinges and make do with bronze rings and straps (Walters 1899, nos 2848, 2850).

A cuirass illustrated by Snodgrass (1967, plate 43) shows a line of holes at the neck, and armholes for the attachment of a padded lining, and it seems clear that the earliest muscle cuirasses were made in this way. From about 470, muscle cuirasses appear with pteruges to protect the thighs (Fig. 52), an idea probably copied from the linen and leather corslets that were in use at the time

(Anderson, p. 22). Hoplites are sometimes depicted with a skirt or kilt of an apparently heavy material (see below), and it seems most likely to me that these pteruges were also a separate skirt worn below the muscle cuirass. It is also possible that such pteruges were attached to the bottom of the cuirass permanently, which would have made putting on the ensemble somewhat quicker, but we have no real evidence. A final system was to incorporate pteruges with some sort of arming jack that was put on first, followed by the two halves of the bronze cuirass, which would then no longer have needed to be separately padded. This certainly seems to be how the armour was worn in Hellenistic times (see Chapter 5), and there is evidence that seems to show that such a jack, called a *spolas*, was in use by the end of the fifth century. This will be examined in the next section dealing with composite or shoulder-piece corslets.

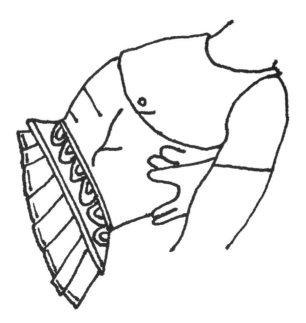

Fig. 52: Short muscle cuirass with waist flange, illustrated on an Athenian *lekythos, c.* 425.

As with other pieces of armour, illustrations of the muscle cuirass are rarer in the later fifth century, due to a decline in demand for warlike subjects during the Peloponnesian War. One of the best is on a funeral *lekythos* (vase) of *c.* 425, depicting a fallen warrior being borne away from battle (Fig. 52). His cuirass seems to have good anatomical detail although the paint has faded somewhat, but instead of a deep curve covering the abdomen this example stops at the waist, where there is a wide, decorated flange. Beneath this is a short set of pteruges. The Peloponnesian War, which was raging at this time, saw cavalry being used in an increasingly important role by Athens and other Greek states, and it seems likely that we have here a depiction of an aristocratic cavalryman. This would explain the short cuirass, enabling the wearer to sit on a horse: men who could afford to own horses, and therefore qualify as cavalrymen, could certainly afford muscle cuirasses. A fourth-century muscle cuirass from Bari in southern Italy shows another method of adapting the muscle cuirass to cavalry use. It has the abdominal dip at the front of the cuirass (which is matched at the back) but it is made very broad in the hips from front to back, so that the wearer could certainly sit on a horse (Connolly 1998, p. 56).

Although many of our finds of the muscle cuirass are from Magna Graecia (south Italy and Sicily), which has led some to suggest that the muscle cuirass was developed there (Jarva 1995, p. 32), the same used to be said of ankle and arm guards, for example. The reason is probably just that the Greeks (and local Italians) in Magna Graecia were wont to bury warriors with arms occasionally, and these have been excavated. This did not usually happen in mainland Greece after *c.* 700, and so our arms finds come from the sanctuary sites. Recent publications of these finds from Olympia and elsewhere have redressed the balance somewhat, and the perceived popularity of bronze armour in Magna Graecia compared to mainland Greece is probably illusory.

I have mentioned the expense of the muscle cuirass, which can be guessed from the extra labour needed for all the repoussé work. Another related reason is the way in which the shape affected the weight and comfort of the armour. One bell cuirass was pretty much the same as another and could be worn by a variety of men, with the weight of the cuirass resting almost solely on the warrior's shoulders. The muscle cuirass, however, was moulded to the individual's torso, so that the weight was more evenly distributed. This is made clear in a passage from Xenophon's *Memorabilia* (III, 13), where Socrates has a discussion with Pistias the armourer:

> The good fit is less heavy to wear than the misfit, though both are of the same weight. For the misfit, hanging entirely from the shoulders, or pressing on some other part of the body, proves uncomfortable and irksome; but the good fit, with its weight distributed over the collar-bone and shoulder blades, the shoulders, chest, back and belly, may almost be called an accessory rather than an encumbrance.

It is clear that Pistias is here talking of a muscle cuirass, and that a man ordering such a cuirass would have to be measured and fitted many times during its manufacture, to ensure this good fit. Such a fit, distributing the weight across much of the upper body, would have made the cuirass much easier to wear than the bell, and would have enabled the few wealthy hoplites who owned one to keep pace with the majority of their compatriots, who wore linen or leather corslets. The protection offered by the muscle cuirass was similar to the bell, with the curved bronze surfaces offering protection against glancing blows, but probably not against a well-aimed direct thrust, or an arrow. It certainly seems to have been a prestigious piece of equipment. In the later fifth century, the muscle cuirass may have been used more by cavalry, who were becoming more frequently employed and more heavily armoured, and it is probably this form of cuirass that Xenophon recommends (see below). It was also probably the muscle cuirass that was awarded, as part of a complete panoply, as a military decoration in Athens at this time (Plutarch, *Alcibiades* 7, 3–5).

## THE SHOULDER-PIECE CORSLET

The alternative to the muscle cuirass, and the form of body armour which was most used by hoplites from *c.* 525 to the end of the fifth century and beyond, was the shoulder-piece corslet, a term coined by Jarva (1995, p. 33) who also calls it his Type IV (Fig. 50). These are often referred to as linen corslets, especially in the early period when that material seemed to dominate; but later corslets were made of leather, and could have metal scales attached as extra protection. This type of shoulder-piece corslet is usually known as a composite corslet. Greeks had used corslets made of padded linen in earlier times of course, but the new corslet, which appears definitely for the first time on Attic vases of *c.* 560, is a stiff shirt. It has a U-shaped shoulder guard, which stood up vertically behind the warrior before the flaps were fastened down onto the chest (Connolly 1998, p. 58). Jarva (1995, p. 35) suggests that such a shirt may have been in use from the Geometric period, but the illustrations are not convincing and the literary material, principally Alcaeus, seems to suggest padded linen corslets at this earlier time, as mentioned in Chapter 3.

We know that a linen corslet was given by the Egyptian Pharaoh Amasis to the Spartans, at some time between 569 (when he became pharaoh) and 547 (when the Samians stole it), and that he gave a similar one to Lindos (Herodotus III, 47; II, 182). Herodotus's description of the Spartan example shows that it was not of the quilted/padded type as Snodgrass (1967, p. 90) suggests, but was woven into a stiff linen shirt of the new design. This evidence, then, points to Egypt as the place of origin for this new corslet, where it may well have been in use since shortly after 1000, with the invention of the treadle loom (Barnes 1985, p. 16). This allowed for an even stress to be placed on the warp threads, which would make the production of the thicker cloth needed for corslets easier to achieve. In 664 some Ionians and Carians made an expedition to Egypt (Herodotus II, 152), and this has often been noted as the time when the Greeks first came across the linen corslet and brought the idea back to Greece. The archaeology appears to tell a different story, however. The middle of the seventh century is just when the bell cuirass is flourishing and is frequently depicted in art although, as with padded linen corslets, it is possible that the stiff linen shirt was used but not depicted for artistic reasons. Perhaps it was a rare item at the time. The alternative date for the introduction of the linen shoulder-piece corslet is the middle of the sixth century, when it appears in Attic black figure art and elsewhere. The depictions of the new corslet increased rapidly, while those of the bell cuirass declined. This seems a much likelier date for the introduction of the linen corslet, given the general lightening of helmets and reduction of limb armour that also occurred at this time or a little later.

Amasis redefined the port of Naucratis as a Greek trading centre in *c.* 550 and kept a Greek bodyguard (Boardman 1980b, p. 117; Herodotus III, 3). Trade between Egypt and Greece increased, and gifts of corslets were given to Greek sanctuaries. All this helps to support an introduction date of *c.* 550 for the linen shoulder-piece corslet.

By *c.* 500, the new corslet and its derivatives had ousted the old bell cuirass from use. This is understandable when one considers its advantages. Connolly (1998, p. 58) has made a reproduction corslet which weighs only 3.6kg, as compared with the 6kg or more for a bell cuirass. This lighter weight allowed for greater distances to be covered on campaign, as well as faster movement in battle (Snodgrass 1967, pp. 91–2). Linen was more comfortable to wear, as it was more flexible and much cooler than bronze under the Mediterranean sun. It was also more easily repaired. Above all it was cheaper, allowing many more men of the hoplite class, who had previously relied entirely on their shield for personal protection, to invest in body armour as well. Even the richer hoplites turned away from the bell and adopted the new linen and composite corslets for these many advantages: although, as we have seen, some of the richest persisted with bronze in the form of the muscle cuirass. As far as protection goes, the main advantage of bronze was a surface which deflected glancing blows. A direct hit would punch through bronze, but might be held up by the padding underneath. These new linen corslets would not deflect glancing blows, but would be as effective as bronze against any major thrust. This protection, then, was slightly less than that of bronze, but the advantages of comfort and weight overrode that consideration.

The stiffness of this new corslet is clear from vase illustrations, as I have said, but with no surviving examples from the archaeological record, its construction is still debatable. Snodgrass and Connolly both suggest that the linen corslet was constructed from several thin layers of linen. Snodgrass (1967, p. 90) quotes Amasis's corslet as being of many layers quilted together, presumably like a padded linen corslet but without the padding. Connolly (1998, p. 58) thinks construction was of layers of linen glued together. There are instances of layers of linen forming protective armour – perhaps even an example from the Shaft Graves – but nothing from Archaic or Classical Greece. On the other hand we do have Herodotus's written description of Amasis's linen corslet, and it seems that this mentions neither glue nor layers of linen. It apparently says that each fine thread of the corslet was made up of 360 individual strands of linen, not that the corslet is 360 layers of linen thick. A strand of linen is about 0.2mm in diameter, and 360 such strands twisted together would form a cord of about 1–1.5cm in diameter, which was then woven conventionally – although perhaps with some difficulty – to form a stiff linen shirt. A problem here is that Herodotus calls this cord a 'fine thread' (*aspedoni lepti*) (Herodotus III, 47). However, *aspedoni* in itself does not necessarily mean a thin thread, and *lepti* can be interpreted as the alternative meaning of the English word 'fine', i.e. delicate, well made or splendid, rather than thin. As Herodotus is describing a linen corslet of the pharaoh of Egypt, then this is appropriate enough. Herodotus finds the number of strands forming the cord a 'wonder to behold', and it would appear from this that the more ordinary Greek corslet had rather fewer strands giving an overall thickness of only 0.5cm, which would nevertheless be adequate.

Another feature of all shoulder-piece corslets is the skirt of strips at the lower edge known as pteruges, which are essential for ease of movement once the length of the corslet reaches below the waist (Fig. 53). The pteruges were formed by cutting, or perhaps originally weaving, the linen into strips from the waist down to the upper thigh. Vase illustrations show us that the number of pteruges was 12–15 until about 500 BC, but after that the number increased to 15–20. The increase in number meant these later pteruges were narrower, and they also tended to become longer, reaching down to the middle thigh to give more protection. After 500, it seems that more of these shoulder-piece corslets were being made out of leather (Jarva 1995, p. 44), and it may be that this

Fig. 53: Composite corslet worn by Achilles from the name vase of the Achilles Painter, c. 450.

material made it easier to make longer and thinner pteruges. Only a few corslets are shown with a single set of pteruges, because the slits obviously left gaps, and so a second set of pteruges was added underneath to cover these gaps (Connolly 1998, p. 58). It is possible that this was an original Egyptian idea. It seems that this second set of pteruges was made in one piece with a waistband, before being attached to the inside of the body of the corslet. It may also have been possible for the second set of pteruges to have been woven in one piece with the rest of the corslet, each pteruge being half the thickness of the body of the corslet.

The method of fastening these corslets also varied. The central figure in the arming scene on the Douris Cup (Connolly 1998, p. 58) wears a corslet that clearly fastens down the middle, although the method is unclear. Achilles, on the name vase of the Achilles Painter, has the fastening on the front of the left side (Fig. 53). There are two sets of bronze (?) studs attached to the front and side sections of the corslet, which would have been tied with laces. This would appear to be a more secure area for a fastening because, as with the earlier bell cuirasses, the fastening would have been protected to an extent by the shield. Fastenings on the right side are also sometimes shown (Anderson 1970, p. 22; Jarva 1995, p. 33) but, along with the central fastening, these may have come in only later, when such joins were frequently protected by scales in the composite version of the shoulder-piece corslet. After the corslet body had been secured, the warrior fastened the shoulder flaps down onto the chest. These flaps were probably originally simple extensions from the back of the corslet, but certainly by the time they were illustrated in Greek art, they were made from a separately woven piece of stiff linen. This was U-shaped and attached to the back of the corslet. The two arms of the U formed the wide shoulder guards. There were narrow extensions on the end of these which had laces or leather thongs attached, and these were then tied to bronze studs or rings on the chest of the corslet. These small fittings are the only elements which have occasionally survived today (Snodgrass 1967, p. 91). There are two good reasons for this form of shoulder protection. First, the front part of the shoulders, which was a vulnerable area to an overhead spear thrust, was now protected by a double thickness of linen. Second, these shoulder pieces were the most likely to suffer battle damage, and they could be replaced without having to replace the whole corslet.

Although these corslets could be plain (Boardman 1979, no. 29), the vast majority had varying amounts of decoration on them. If we return to the corslet of Amasis as described by Herodotus (III, 47), we see that it was decorated in two ways. Figures of animals were actually woven into the cloth and, when the corslet was finished, separate embroidered decoration of gold and cotton thread was also used. Heavy decoration such as this is rare on Greek illustrations, but a vase of Exekias showing Achilles and Ajax at play, made in c. 535, does show two such decorated corslets – probably embroidery, judging by the fine nature of it (Snodgrass 1967, plate 37; Boardman 1980a, no. 100). The commonest form of decoration seen on these corslets is a horizontal band, usually of the well-known 'Greek key' pattern, either at the back of the corslet covering the join between the body of the corslet and the shoulder piece, or at the waist just above the pteruges. This appears to have been a separate piece of material sewn on as an extra reinforcement, although Jarva (1995, pp. 33, 37, fig. 11) sees it as a belt which could also tighten the corslet at the waist. This might have been the case with leather shoulder-piece corslets, but not with stiff linen. The stele of Aristion, dating to *c.* 510, has such a band (Snodgrass 1967, plate 39) and other details which were originally painted on can be traced (Boardman 1978, p. 122, fig. 235). The body of the corslet appears to have been blue, with two red bands at the waist just above the pteruges and around the middle, covering the base of the shoulder guard. It also had a star or sunburst design on the wide part of the shoulder guard. This early linen corslet also shows the short pteruges in use at the time. The colouring of the main body of the corslet is particularly interesting because it shows that the entire body of a corslet could be woven from linen which had already been dyed, and not left in the natural white.

On black figure vases, linen corslets are often distinguished by being separately painted white (Boardman 1979, nos 141, 237), but on red figure vases these corslets are nearly all left in the natural red/orange colour. This gives us less idea of what colour the corslets actually were, and indeed whether they were still being made of linen. Later composite corslets like those on the Douris Cup used both black and red, so it seems likely that different colours were a feature. Other simple decoration on these corslets consisted of coloured bands and, sometimes, small stars added to the pteruges, the bands perhaps being woven in, the stars embroidered (Boardman 1979, no. 135). Animal heads such as pumas, or gorgon heads, were also sometimes added to the front or back of the shoulder guards, and these remind us of the animals on Amasis's corslet. Large stars and sunbursts, such as that featured on the front shoulder pad of Aristion's corslet, also feature in vase illustrations (Figs 53, 54). Because of the nature of the vase painting at this time, it is impossible to know what colours were being suggested, but we do have useful evidence from contemporary or slightly later Etruscan wall paintings. Corslets depicted on them are often red, contrasted with dark blue or black, which are the same colours as on Aristion's stele (Connolly 1998, p. 57). Apart from weaving colours and designs into the body of the corslet and embroidering them on afterwards, it is also possible that some designs may have been painted on, although this becomes less likely as linen was replaced with leather.

Despite the advantages of cost, weight and general ease of movement, it seems that some of the Greeks felt vulnerable in their linen corslets for, almost immediately after their introduction, we find that bronze reinforcements were added in the form of armour scales (Fig. 54). As well as added protection and security for the hoplite, who was perhaps unsure whether this new corslet was as

Fig. 54: Duelling hoplites in composite corslets from a vase by the Tyszkiewicz Painter, *c.* 480.

effective as a bronze cuirass, scales seem also to have been used as just another form of decoration, or perhaps of status. These corslets are known as composite corslets, because of the combination of materials used in their construction. Anderson (1970 p. 267, no. 38) has drawn up a chart of shoulder-piece corslets as depicted on Attic red figure vases showing that the plain corslets, whether of linen or leather, outnumber the more elaborate composite corslets by about two to one. The composite corslet is a much more interesting item to depict than a plain one, and so it is possible that this ratio puts too high an emphasis on the composite corslet. In reality, the proportion of composite corslets to plain shoulder-piece models may have been as low as one in five or even one in ten. This shows that the extra metal additions were an added luxury, and certainly were not thought of as essential.

I have mentioned the increasing use of leather for these corslets, which Anderson suggests (1970, p. 23) happened because it was a cheaper alternative to linen and more easily accessible. That the earliest of these corslets were linen seems clear from the artistic and literary mentions, but red figure art of the fifth century is less clear, and black figure art of the later sixth century seems to suggest corslets of either linen or leather (Jarva 1995, p. 44).

Certainly by the time of the *Anabasis* of Xenophon in 400 (Xenophon's journey with ten thousand mercenaries, from the depths of the Persian Empire to safety on the Black Sea coast), there was a corslet called a *spolas* which was made of leather, although this may have been a somewhat different item. When we consider the composite corslets, with their additional bronze scales attached, I must agree with Snodgrass (1967, p. 91) that this would be very difficult to do with stiff linen, and that the use of leather here seems assured. Such attachment of scales was a well-established practice in Cyprus and the Near East, whereas attaching them to 0.5cm thick linen would have been far more difficult. It is possible that leather was introduced as a cheaper alternative to linen, but that its lesser protection then led to the addition of scales to the armour. Leather on its own gives very little defence unless it is boiled or treated with vinegar to make it hard, but neither of these practices are known to have occurred before the late Roman period (Russell Robinson 1975, p. 147; Jarva 1995, p. 42). Most corslets still seemed to have at least the shoulder piece made from linen, as this is shown standing up stiffly even when the body of the corslet is scaled and so, presumably, is made of leather. This seems to suggest that composite corslets could be made out of all these materials in combination. Jarva tries to distinguish between leather and linen corslets in vase paintings by considering the attitudes of the soldiers. If they are bending with ease, he suggests a linen corslet; whereas if the opposite is the case, he suggests a stiff leather corslet. While the exercise is possible, the interpretation disagrees with what I have said about the construction of these corslets. It seems to me that the stiff linen corslets would be the ones difficult to move in, and the leather ones easy, because I am assuming the leather was soft; whereas Jarva (1995, p. 44) stiffens it with vinegar – a Byzantine practice which is not known to date from this early period.

Returning to the scales used on the composite versions of the shoulder-piece corslet, the types of scale used and their location vary considerably.

Fig. 55: Small section of scales from a composite corslet from Olympia, fifth century.

A chronological pattern is difficult to see, because so many styles were in use concurrently. However, as a generalisation, the earliest designs protected a large part of the body of the corslet (Fig. 54), whereas later designs restricted themselves to protecting specific areas, notably the sides of the corslet (Fig. 53). As far as the individual scales go, conventional scales of the type going back to Mycenaean times were used at first, but after *c.* 500 square or rectangular scales appeared, as well as round-ended scales embossed with a repoussé circle in the lower half (Fig. 55). One early example of a composite cuirass (Boardman 1980a, no. 86), shows scales in use only on the shoulder guard, the front flaps of which reach down an extraordinarily long way to be tied at the waist rather than on the chest. As mentioned before, the shoulder guards were a vulnerable area and this downward extension, as well as the addition of scales, would have offered a great deal of extra protection. The well-known plate featuring Achilles bandaging Patroclus (Jarva 1995, p. 39; Connolly 1998, p. 57, no. 1) from *c.* 500 demonstrates that fully scaled composite corslets were in use by this time, with even the short pteruges of Patroclus having scales on them. The upper chest area of Patroclus' corslet seems to be only some sort of padded linen, but this would have been covered when the shoulder flaps were down. His scales are of conventional style, whereas those of Achilles lack the usual median ridge.

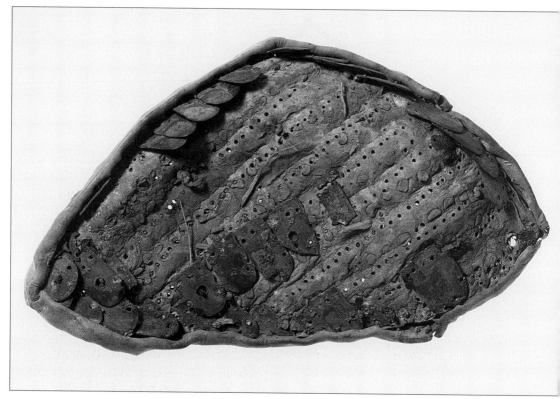

Fig. 56: Shoulder piece of scale armour from a composite corslet from the Crimea, *c.* 400. (*Ashmolean Museum, Oxford*)

The Ashmolean Museum has a group of similar scales, probably a shoulder piece of a composite corslet from the Crimea dating to the late fifth century (Fig. 56). This has recently been fully published, and we now know that the scales were sewn onto sheep- or goatskin leather, and edged with calf hide (Vickers 2002, p. 46, plate 17). The leather is two layers thick. It seems that the corslet also had a large, bronze, elk's-head plaque attached to the chest (Vickers 2002, pp. 44–5), which is of distinctly Scythian manufacture. The reconstruction on the front of Vickers's book suggests that this was simply a decorative element, but it is also reminiscent of the gorgon's head on the front of Achilles' cuirass in Fig. 53, and could have been a protective plate covering the ends of the shoulder ties. Despite the Scythian influences, the other finds from the graves in this part of the Crimea are overwhelmingly Greek and, if these are not part of a Greek corslet, then they are a close Scythian copy.

A more usual form of scale protection is shown in a vase painting of *c.* 480 (Fig. 54), and is also worn by most of the warriors on the Douris Cup (Boardman 1979, nos 57.2, 281; Connolly 1998, p. 58, fig. 1). This has just the body of the corslet protected by scales, with the pteruges and shoulder guards plain. The scales of the warriors on the Douris Cup are those with a small circle at the lower end. A small group of five scales of this type has been found at Olympia (Fig. 55) (Furtwangler 1966, p. 158, no. 984, plate 60). They would have formed part of a splendid suit, as they were originally of silver-plated bronze; their design is certainly Greek, since we have the parallels of the Douris Cup, and they do not come from a captured Persian suit. With other odd scales it can be harder to tell (Snodgrass 1965a, p. 85). There is another find of scales datable to the fifth century from the sanctuary at Delphi, consisting of alternate bronze and iron scales which, as Snodgrass points out (1965a, pp. 83, 238), is an Egyptian decorative idea. This does not necessarily mean that these scales are from there, however, as we have already seen that this style was used in Cyprus and of course on Agamemnon's corslet in the *Iliad* (Homer, *Iliad* XI, 24). The interesting feature about the Delphi find is that the scales are attached to a thin, bronze backing sheet. This would have given a corslet that was a far cry from the flexibility of earlier designs, where the scales were just sewn onto the leather backing. Such a system would have given a very stiff cuirass indeed if it was used all over, as it would be virtually a return to the bronze cuirass. A possible example of a corslet like this is illustrated on a vase of *c.* 420, where a hoplite in a shoulder-piece corslet has his torso area decorated with what look like inverted scales (Boardman 1989, no. 289.2). The torso edges also appear to be made of sheet bronze rather than material.

Sekunda (2000, plate A and p. 51) proposes a similar corslet made of thin bronze sheets covered with material, and indeed seems to be suggesting that most – or at least some – shoulder-piece corslets were made from metal covered in material, and not linen or leather at all. This idea is derived mainly from the cuirass of Philip II of Macedon, which was of iron covered in material, but of the same shape and style as a shoulder-piece corslet (see Chapter 5). There is, however, no evidence that this form of cuirass existed before Philip II, and so it must remain speculation.

Apart from scales, there was what appears to be a further type of metal protection in the form of bronze rings attached to the corslet (Fig. 57). This 'ring-armour' usually only appeared on the U-shaped shoulder guard, but one of the warriors on the Douris Cup has rings attached to the upper part of the corslet body as well. These rings appear to be 2–3cm in diameter, but the

Fig. 57: Back of a composite corslet from a vase by Myson, showing 'ring armour', *c.* 490.

shoulder guards have four large rings with a diameter of 5–6cm. The very simplicity of these designs argues for their being a metallic reinforcement, rather than weaving or embroidery. In discussing the attachment of scales to these corslets, I suggested that scales were perhaps fastened only to leather armour, but that shoulder guards were clearly still made of stiff linen. These large rings may well have been the Greek answer to the problem of attaching metal reinforcements of some sort to stiff linen.

From about 480, another type of scale appears in Greek art. This is the rectangular scale, sewn lengthways onto the corslet in rows (Fig. 54, right) (Boardman 1979, no. 186). These scales are apparently quite large, though no actual examples have been found, and they do not overlap each other sideways like conventional scales. This meant that they were not as protective as conventional scales, but the lack of horizontal overlapping probably meant fewer holes in each scale and a simpler fastening system. They would also have been easier to manufacture and replace.

Lamellar armour does not seem to have been used often on these corslets, although there is a possible example on a statue of Hercules dating to the fifth century (Lullies 1957, plate 87; Boardman 1978, p. 188, fig. 206.6). This shows Hercules wearing a composite corslet with an interesting detail of a fastening below the left arm. Below this, and presumably helping to protect the join, is a block of twenty squares, laid out four vertically and five horizontally. These are obviously metal scales, but they have the longer side in the vertical and do not appear to show any overlapping. This appears to be similar, then, to the armour worn by the Chinese terracotta soldiers discussed in Chapter 3, with rectangular scales attached to those on each side as well as those above and below, forming a rigid lamellar defence. There remains the possibility, of course, that the sculptor was trying to show conventional rectangular scales using the difficult medium of stone.

Small sections of padded or quilted linen also appear on some of these corslets, as has been mentioned with the armour of Patroclus above. Vases sometimes show parts of corslets that have a chequer or rhomboid-pattern design (like Fig. 58, left), and this seems to be best explained by padded linen – although they could be other scale forms, or merely artistic liberties taken with scale forms (Boardman 1979, nos 268, 315). After the Persian Wars, and perhaps owing to battle experience, we often come across extra scale protection, specifically at the sides of the corslets rather than all over (Fig. 53). This could have protected a side fastening, and the left side was also particularly vulnerable in battle, being the side facing the enemy. The right side would have been covered in scales for purposes of symmetry.

It is clear from the above descriptions that the composite corslet was a far more complicated piece of armour than the simple shoulder-piece corslet made of either linen or leather. The separate materials of linen shoulder piece, leather body, metal scales and pteruges may all have been made by separate craftsmen, and then assembled by a master armourer. Connolly (1998, p. 58) suggests that the pteruges may have been detachable, but there seems to be no reason for this in a shoulder-piece corslet. There are certainly no illustrations of shoulder-piece corslets without pteruges to my knowledge. The pteruges design certainly inspired the bronze armourers to fit them to the late bell cuirasses and to the new muscle cuirasses that were coming in, and these could well have been separate skirts (Anderson 1970, p. 22). The thighs remained a vulnerable area below the shield and above the greave, and pteruges offered a modicum of protection.

This vulnerability of the thighs, as opposed to the torso which was routinely protected by the shield, seems to have led to a heavy, kilt-like piece of armour,

Fig. 58: Heavy 'kilts' shown on vases by the Foundry Painter, c. 480 (left), and the Kleophon Painter, c. 440 (right).

which is sometimes worn under the pteruges but more frequently on its own (Fig. 58) (Boardman 1979, nos 166, 274). It is interesting that some hoplites should have favoured equipping themselves with this piece of armour rather than a corslet, presumably because the latter was better protected by the shield (Anderson 1970, p. 25). This 'kilt' armour, possibly called a *perizoma*, appears after the Persian Wars, but seems to have fallen out of favour before the Peloponnesian War if we can rely on the few illustrations we have (Sekunda 2000, p. 57).

The shoulder-piece corslet, whether of linen, leather or metal-reinforced composite, seems to have lasted until the end of the fifth century as a piece of hoplite equipment, and there is also some evidence for its use by cavalry (see below). We have already noted that leather probably became more popular than linen after c. 500, and may have been the only material used during the Peloponnesian War. It seems likely that metal reinforcements also died out before or during the Peloponnesian War, especially for hoplites. Our principal evidence for this is Xenophon's *Anabasis*, where he often tells us about the equipment of the 10,000 Greek mercenaries hired by Cyrus for the campaign of 400, when he hoped to win the Persian crown. The only time Xenophon mentions linen corslets is when he is referring to Persian equipment; they were never worn by the Greeks. Indeed, when Cyrus inspected his hoplites, Xenophon tells us that they were wearing helmets and greaves, but no body armour (*Anabasis* I, 2, 15–16). It seems possible that many hoplites no longer bothered with corslets by the end of the fifth century, relying on their shields for the main defence (Sekunda 2000, p. 58 and plate F). This might have been especially true of mercenaries about to undertake a long campaign in Persia but, later on in the expedition, Xenophon makes it clear that some of the hoplites did wear the leather body armour called a *spolas*. Although infantrymen in the *Anabasis* wore this as their only armour, when a cavalry force was being put together they were issued with the *spolas* and the *thorax*, which is the more usual word for a cuirass or corslet. This seems to suggest that the *spolas* was an arming tunic or jack, worn under a muscle cuirass or other metal cuirass to prevent chafing. This method of wearing metal armour, rather than attaching padding to the inside of the cuirass, was a simple system that was certainly in use during the Hellenistic period. It would seem that hoplites who might have worn leather shoulder-piece corslets earlier now wore this *spolas*, or arming jack, on its own as an equivalent – if they bothered to wear armour at all. The increasing use of equipment supplied by the state, rather than being purchased by individuals, may also have led to the demise of more expensive equipment. By the end of the fifth century the muscle cuirass, for example, seems to have been restricted to officers and cavalry, while composite corslets had disappeared.

## GREAVES

The other main piece of body armour that continued to be worn was the greave. From *c.* 500 these followed the design of the new muscle cuirass in being strictly anatomically detailed (Kunze 1991, pp. 76–9; Jarva 1995, pp. 96–7). They also followed the helmets, in that edge perforations for a lining were superseded soon after 500 by rolled-over bronze edges. Jarva has shown (see Chapter 3) that in the sixth century these holes were also used to help fasten the greave to the leg. Previously it had been thought that greaves were held onto the leg simply by the elasticity of the bronze. That was perhaps the case only from *c.* 500 onwards, when the edges were rolled over and a lining glued in. There almost certainly were linings to the greaves for extra protection, just like other pieces of armour. Sekunda (1986, p. 8; 2000, p. 52, no. 16) has also noticed that, at about the same time, some vase illustrations suggest a roll of cloth at the ankle to stop the greave from slipping down. This roll of cloth is not easy to illustrate on a vase and can easily be confused with a rolled-over lower edge of bronze, but it seems likely to me that all fifth-century greaves had this feature. Even if the greave's elasticity could have held it around the leg, there is something to be said for a roll of cloth to prevent it from slipping downwards.

Fig. 59: Various *pelta* shields, as drawn by the Geneva Painter, *c.* 460.

These fifth-century greaves are also lighter than those of the seventh and sixth centuries. They average 0.67kg each, whereas the older greaves approached or sometimes exceeded 1kg. Despite this it seems that some hoplites stopped using greaves altogether. Only two of the seven hoplites on the Douris Cup have greaves, although they are still in the process of arming, and other illustrations suggest that perhaps only about half of hoplites bothered with greaves after *c.* 450 (Fig. 54). Nevertheless, returning to Xenophon's Ten Thousand: when they were drawn up for parade in 400, they were all apparently equipped with greaves.

## PELTASTS

The lightening of hoplite armour, which had begun probably as a response to the Persian threat, continued throughout the Peloponnesian War, as a result of the successful use of light troops against hoplites. Peltasts, named after their crescent-shaped shield called a *pelta* (Fig. 59), were the main troop type of Thrace, and their style of warfare was adopted by Athens and other Greek states. Initially, actual Thracian peltasts were hired as mercenaries, but later, native Greek troops were armed in the Thracian style. Peltasts dressed in Thracian fashion, with high boots instead of greaves, and distinctive fox-fur hats. Apart from the shield they had no armour and were armed with javelins. They could attack hoplites and then retreat before the hoplites could catch them. The most notable feat of peltasts in the Peloponnesian War was the capture of an elite Spartan hoplite force by Athenian peltasts (and archers) on the island of Sphacteria near Pylos in 425 (Thucydides IV, 31–40). The Spartans were outnumbered two to one, but the capture of 292 hoplites – including 120 Spartiates, the cream of the army – by light troops and not even by other hoplites was still a great shock to both sides and, indeed, to interested spectators.

Instances such as this led to lightly armed hoplites called *ekdromoi*, who could rush out of a phalanx and keep peltasts and other light troops away from the hoplite phalanx (Sekunda 1986, pp. 13–14). Peltasts were still mainly used in scouting and siege operations, ambushes and the like, and pitched battles in the late fifth and early fourth centuries were still fought mainly between hoplite phalanxes, although cavalry also made its appearance (see below).

## SHIELDS AND WEAPONS

The construction of the hoplite shield remained the same throughout the fifth century, though bronze blazons disappeared. Sekunda (1999, p. 26; 2000, p. 10) suggests that all hoplite shields now had a thin bronze covering over the entire surface, and that the bowl shape may have become somewhat deeper after 500. Both may be true. A bronze covering would certainly have helped to deflect missiles, although it was the wooden core of the shield that was its main strength. A deepening of the bowl might have made the shield heavier and stronger, possibly to act as a counterbalance against the lightening of other armour, but the idea is based on some artistic illustrations and there is no archaeology to back it up. There were nearly always tassels now on the inside of hoplite shields, and these were usually joined to each other by a cord going around the inside of the rim (Figs 43c, 54). They appear to have served no purpose other than decoration, and do not appear to be connected to the *antilabe* (rim handle). There is one illustration which shows the cord being used as a sort of telamon (Sekunda 2000, p. 51), but it seems very impractical and the cords generally do not appear strong enough to support the weight of the shield in this way.

Fig. 60: Shield apron from a vase of *c.* 470–460 in the British Museum.

A change that is clear from some artistic illustrations was the addition of a 'shield apron' to the bottom of some hoplite shields (Fig. 60) (Boardman 1979, no. 280.2; 1989, nos 6, 17, 54). This was a square of cloth, attached to the bottom of the shield to give further protection to the legs. It appeared in *c.* 475, and so may have been a response to Persian archery, but it only ever appeared on a small number of shields, mostly in the middle of the fifth century. These aprons were usually decorated with an eye to ward off incoming attacks. There is at least one late example dating to *c.* 400 (Boardman 1989, no. 309), so it may have featured in the Peloponnesian War, but it does not seem to have been very popular.

Another major change to the hoplite shield was the blazon. From *c.* 525 to the later fifth century, these continued to be the individual choices of the hoplites, but vase paintings show a gradual move away from complicated to more simple designs, including the warding eye that appears on most shield aprons (Ueda-Sarson 2000, *passim*). At the Battle of Delium in 424, Athenians attacked Athenians when they failed to recognise each other, and this sort of problem led to most Greek states, it seems, decorating their shields with a national emblem – like the club for Thebes – or with a letter, such as lambda (Λ) for Lacedaemonia (Sparta). The latter was certainly in use by 412 (Sekunda 1999, p. 28), and maybe as early as 422 (Anderson 1970, p. 18), although evidence for other states is often not available until the fourth century. What this also tells us is that Greeks were not always providing their own equipment by this stage. Uniformly decorated shields suggest that they are being issued by the state, and in the late fourth century Athens would provide hoplites with both shield and spear on completion of training (Snodgrass 1967, p. 59). Other equipment was to be provided by the hoplite himself, and the larger numbers of poorer troops being used towards the end of the fifth century may be another reason for the lightening and lessening of equipment.

The shield used by peltasts, the *pelta*, seems to have usually been a crescent-shaped shield, although other shapes, such as a small circular shield, are also mentioned by sources (Fig. 59) (Anderson 1970, p. 112). Vase paintings show it with either a central handgrip, or a double grip similar to that used on the hoplite shield. Either would have been practical. Sometimes the shields were also equipped with a shoulder strap for carrying them on the back (Connolly 1998, p. 48). Vase illustrations also show us that the *pelta* was a wickerwork shield and therefore quite light, although Xenophon suggests that it could sometimes have a bronze sheet facing. Shields were certainly sometimes decorated in a similar manner to hoplite shields, suggesting a facing of some sort (Ueda-Sarson 2000, *passim*). This type of shield design probably stemmed from the variety of equipment and the tactics used by peltasts. Although they were certainly 'light' troops compared to hoplites, and they wore no body armour, they were sometimes armed with spears instead of javelins and could be used in close combat. This might account for the hoplite-grip shields and the bronze facing. By the end of the fifth century, many peltasts were available for hire as mercenaries, both Thracians and Greeks, and Sparta used them a great deal in its early fourth-century campaigns against Persia (Anderson 1970, pp. 120–1).

The spear used by hoplites, and the occasional peltast, did not change from the preceding century (Fig. 61), with some spearheads (as well as butts) still being made of bronze, and there is very little evidence for the sword. What

Fig. 61: Spear heads in the British Museum, fifth century. *(Trustees of the British Museum GR 1865.7-20.53, 54, 55)*

there is suggests that swords were getting shorter, especially in Sparta, and that the single-edged chopping sword, the *kopis* or *machaira*, was becoming more popular (Fig. 54) (Sekunda 1999, p. 31).

## CAVALRY

Thessaly and Macedonia were still the only Greek states to have had a large amount of cavalry in the first half of the fifth century although, as we have seen, Athens seems to have had a small force. Athens often used mercenary Thessalian cavalry, but this changed in 458/7 when, at the Battle of Tanagra, the Thessalians changed sides and inflicted heavy casualties on the Athenians. Athens also used Macedonian cavalry in 432 at Potidaea, but realised that they needed to raise and use their own cavalry if they were to combat future threats; they raised a force in stages, which eventually reached 1,000 men (Bugh 1988, pp. 41 ff.). This seems to have been a lightly armed skirmishing force, armed with javelins, and was not considered to be a very important force initially. After all, when Athens sent its great expedition to Sicily in 415, it sent only thirty horses to accompany a 7,000-strong army. The Athenian army suffered considerably at the hands of the Syracusan cavalry because of this, and by various methods they quickly managed to raise a force of 600 cavalry to help. Other Greek states also built up cavalry forces. The Boeotians were able to field 1,000 cavalry at Delium in 424, and Sparta formed a small force. In Sicily and Italy the Greek states tended to have larger cavalry forces, but these were often recruited from native Sicels and Italians. For example, in 404 Dionysius, tyrant of Syracuse, had a force of 1,200 Campanian cavalry. These were probably lightly armed 'Tarentines', who became very popular in the fourth century (see Chapter 5).

During the Peloponnesian War, while the infantry were wearing less and less armour, it seems that cavalry soldiers began to adopt it. By the war's end they were being used as combat soldiers to a greater extent than before, whereas previously they had been mostly scouts and messengers. Armour was less of an encumbrance to them since the horse, or a servant, carried the load. We have already seen how some of the muscle cuirasses that exist today were shaped for a man to sit on a horse, and the shoulder-piece corslet with its pteruges could easily be worn on horseback. Several of the horsemen on the Parthenon sculptures are wearing such corslets with Attic helmets or the broad-brimmed *petasos* hat (Bugh 1988, figs 4*a*, 4*b*). The *petasos* may even be a helmet, as a bronze helmet of exactly this shape has been discovered in Athens (Alexandre

1973, *passim*). Alexandre, the excavator, describes it as a Boeotian helmet (and is followed by Dintsis), but it really is quite distinctively similar to the Thessalian *petasos* and should be classed as such (Sekunda 1994b, plate 200c).

Our best evidence for the equipment used by cavalry is the treatise *On Horsemanship* by Xenophon, which was written in the early fourth century and so collects on all the experience of the Peloponnesian War, and various Greek exploits against the Persians in which Xenophon participated. Firstly, he recommends a Boeotian helmet (Fig. 49b) to give good all-round vision. He does not mention the *spolas* here but only pteruges, which were presumably worn as a separate skirt. He recommends a metal cuirass, which must be of the muscle type since he stresses the need for a perfect fit, distributing the weight as evenly as possible. He suggests the right armhole should be cut away to help in the throwing of javelins. He also suggests the use of a separate neck guard, resting on the breastplate and covering the rider's face up to the nose. The language he uses suggests this was his own idea, and no such guards have been found dating to this period. The description is very reminiscent of the Dendra neck guard from Mycenaean times, but such a guard was always going to be awkward and uncomfortable to use. To guard the left arm, Xenophon recommends a piece of armour called 'The Hand', a segmented arm guard reaching from the shoulder to the hand, of a type undoubtedly similar to those depicted on the Hellenistic Pergamum altar reliefs some 200 years later (see Chapter 5). Xenophon also recommends a guard for the right upper arm, which appears to have snapped into place like the greaves and was presumably similar to upper arm guards of the seventh and sixth centuries. Xenophon stresses the vulnerability of the armpit, especially when the arm is raised, and recommends a piece of metal or calfskin to cover the gap. He suggests no means of attachment, and may be theorising rather than describing a well-known piece of equipment.

For the legs, Xenophon recommends thigh guards for the horse, which would also protect the rider's thighs; but it is inconceivable that one piece of armour could have protected the thighs of the rider and the thighs of the horse, as seems to be suggested. It must be that the armour was a piece of horse armour called the thigh guard (*parameridia*) because it protected the rider's thighs, and not in relation to the anatomy of the horse. Head (1982, p. 87) suggests two varieties of armour to which Xenophon could be referring. The first, from a fifth-century Lycian tomb painting, is a stiff guard curving out from the saddle cloth to protect the fronts of the thighs. The second, also Lycian, is rather like a pair of cowboy chaps, covered with scales that protect the whole of the rider's leg and part of the horse's flank as well. The latter seems closer to Xenophon's description, but perhaps reaching only as far as the knee. Finally Xenophon recommends knee-high boots. Greaves were almost certainly impractical for cavalry, because they might have damaged the horse and would have affected the rider's grip. Before saddles, much of a cavalryman's control was exerted through his legs, which needed to be able to grip the horse's sides.

The shield was not used by horsemen at all at this time. Xenophon recommends the use of javelins rather than the spear, which suggests that some cavalry did use spears at this time, although evidence is hard to come by. The main uses for cavalry were still as a skirmishing force and for protecting the hoplite phalanx, especially the flanks, as it formed for battle. Cavalry would also be used in the pursuit after a victory. This was still the case as late as the Battles of Leuctra in 371 and Mantinea in 362. We have mentioned Athenian cavalry becoming a force to be reckoned with before the Peloponnesian War, and Theban/Boeotian cavalry was known even earlier; but Sparta and other Peloponnesian states did not invest in cavalry until after 425, and Spartan cavalry had a particularly poor reputation (Spence 1993, pp. 60–5). As the fourth century progressed, however, cavalry was to become the dominant force in Greek warfare under the auspices of Macedonia.

Fig. 62: Lamellar arm guard from the same Crimean grave that produced the composite corslet shoulder guard shown in Fig. 56, c. 400. (Ashmolean Museum, Oxford)

## MISSILE TROOPS

As far as missile weapons go, Athens again led the way with the hiring of Cretan mercenary archers to man ships at the Battle of Salamis in 480 (Snodgrass 1967, p. 98). By the middle of the fifth century Athens had its own corps of archers, and possibly even mounted archers; it was Athenian archers, along with peltasts, who won the victory over the Spartans at Sphacteria in 425. After this defeat, Sparta too hired mercenary archers and other states followed suit (Snodgrass 1967, p. 98). Mercenary archers tended to be Scythian or Cretan. Revisiting the grave from the Crimea, which produced a scale shoulder guard (Fig. 56) and chest decoration from a composite corslet, we find that the grave also contained a bronze lamellar armour guard (Fig. 62). This is published as a greave, but given the Scythian connections of the grave it seems much more likely that it is an arm guard (Vickers 2002, p. 46, plate 17). At 20.4cm long it seems much too short for a greave, and it might well be an arm guard for an archer, to protect the left arm when the bow was shot. Scythian archers used very small arrowheads, but Cretan archers used large, heavy heads, which could do more damage but had a shorter range, perhaps 150 metres. The Ten Thousand Greeks in Xenophon's *Anabasis* found their archers were outranged by the Persians, who used the Scythian bow, and they had to muster a force of slingers to counteract them. Sling bullets of 20–50g had a range of perhaps 300 metres, and could certainly shoot further than arrows (Connolly 1998, pp. 48–9). These bullets were often decorated with slogans such as '*DEXA*', which means 'Take that' (Connolly 1998, p. 49, no. 5), or with the name of the general who issued them. Fig. 63 shows a sling bullet from Boeotia, probably dating to *c.* 400. One side has an ox-head, and on the other side is written '*KLEANDRO*', 'of Kleandros' (retrograde). Sling bullets are also known from the fourth century inscribed with 'PHILIPPOU', 'of Philip' – meaning Philip II of Macedonia – showing again how the state was responsible for supplying all necessary military equipment.

Mercenary slingers were often hired from Rhodes and, to recruit his slingers, Xenophon asked which of his hoplites were Rhodian, as they would be bound to be able to use the sling. He mustered 200 slingers as a result (Anderson 1970, p. 115).

Archers and slingers were, like peltasts, often hired as mercenaries. When the Athenians attacked Sicily in 415 their force contained 480 archers, of whom 80 were Cretan mercenaries, and 700 mercenary slingers from Rhodes. This hiring of troops, along with payments already made for the shields and spears of hoplites, had evolved by the fourth century into states supplying all the

Fig. 63: Lead sling bullet inscribed with an ox-head on one side, and 'KLEANDROU' in retrograde on the other, fifth or fourth century. (Shefton Museum of Greek Art and Archaeology, University of Newcastle-upon-Tyne, no. 719)

equipment needed by their forces. Men no longer needed to buy their own weapons or armour, although no doubt the wealthiest continued to upgrade or add to these basic supplies.

While hoplite warfare had remained unchanged from *c.* 650 to *c.* 525, a period of 125 years, the next 125 years saw profound changes to the troops and equipment being used. The phalanx remained, but we have followed the adoption of lighter and lighter helmets and armour – possibly affected by economics, but mainly in the search for greater mobility and battlefield awareness. To counteract the Persian archers and cavalry, the Greek hoplites sought battlefield mobility, so that they could move quickly around the battlefield to fight an enemy not versed in the tradition of hoplite warfare. By the time of the Peloponnesian War, less armour became popular, with the need for long campaigns over great distances, followed finally by the need to hire large numbers of mercenaries as cheaply as possible. The actual combat of the phalanx, once battle was joined, remained the same, using the spear, shield and sword.

The other major change in the fifth century was that the fundamental weakness of the phalanx was recognised: and that was its vulnerability to cavalry and missile troops. Especially in the case of Athens, we see the introduction and use of cavalry and archers and slingers on a much greater scale than before. Most other Greek states followed, but because there was often little tradition of these other troop types, the mercenary soldier came to be used more in battle. With the devastation of the Peloponnesian War and a surge in population growth, mercenary hoplites – as well as specialist missile troops – became available in large numbers. This led to some standardisation and simplification of equipment, as we will see in Chapter 5.

FIVE

# The Hellenistic Period, 400–150 BC

This final chapter follows the great changes in Greek warfare that occurred in the fourth century under the influence of Iphicrates of Athens, Epaminondas of Thebes, and Philip II and Alexander the Great of Macedonia. These led to the hoplite and peltast being replaced by infantry wielding a two-handed pike called a *sarissa*, and to the greater use of heavy cavalry. The third century saw the rise and fall of the use of elephants and, to a much lesser extent, the use of chariots again. Finally, the second century marked the rise of Rome and the demise of the Greek kingdoms as an effective military force. The same period also saw the development of siege artillery (catapults), which will be touched on.

The evidence for this period is widespread across the three spheres of artistic representations, archaeological artefacts and literary evidence, but there are still major problems with interpretation. Rather than the vase painting of the Archaic and Classical periods, it is sculpture and, to a lesser extent, coinage that provide the best artistic evidence for the period. These start with Athenian funerary monuments and the Alexander Sarcophagus, and end with the great Hellenistic monuments such as the Artemision at Magnesia-on-the-Meander and the altar friezes at Pergamum.

Of the archaeological finds, pride of place must go to the ones from the royal tombs at Vergina in Macedonia; but there have also been outstanding finds of an iron muscle cuirass from Thesprotia in north-west Greece, and cataphract armour from Ai Khanum in Afghanistan.

As for literature, we have good secondary sources in Diodorus and Arrian for the earlier period, and an excellent primary source in Polybius for the later period. There are also an increasing number of useful contemporary inscriptions, like that from Amphipolis referring to military equipment under Philip V.

Another difference in this period is the geographical coverage. Apart from Greece and the islands, this chapter includes Macedonia in north Greece to a much greater extent. Philip II of Macedonia conquered the rest of Greece and then his son, Alexander the Great, conquered the Persian Empire, including Egypt, and pushed on to India. After his death, various generals – the Successors – quarrelled over the spoils. These disputes eventually settled down into new kingdoms: Macedonia itself, the Ptolemaic Empire of Egypt, the Seleucid Empire of Syria and the East, and several smaller kingdoms that came and went. The Greek states of mainland Greece obtained varying degrees of freedom, but were generally under the Macedonian yoke. This means that much of the evidence for later Greek warfare comes from Egypt, Asia Minor, the Near East and the Far East – even as far as Afghanistan. These Hellenistic kingdoms used the same troop types as one another, with minor differences. Mainland Greece tended to continue with peltast and hoplite warfare using the ordinary spear, but most changed eventually to the *sarissa* and Macedonian-style warfare. After Alexander they played a small part in warfare, which was dominated by the larger Hellenistic states.

## THE REFORMS OF IPHICRATES

We have seen how light troops called peltasts had been effective against the Spartans at Sphacteria in the Peloponnesian War. The Athenians repeated the feat in 390 when Iphicrates defeated a unit of Spartan hoplites in the field with a force of peltasts (Connolly 1998, p. 49). He later campaigned with his peltasts in Egypt and, after returning from there in 373, he apparently instituted some military reforms. We do not have a contemporary source for this fact, but only the later reports of Diodorus Siculus (Diodorus XV, 44, 2–4) and Cornelius Nepos (*Life of Iphicrates* XI), which are so similar that they must have copied the same earlier source. The following is Best's translation of Diodorus (Best 1969, pp. 102 ff.):

> Soldiers who used to carry the *aspis* (hoplite shield) and were called hoplites, now carried the *pelta* and were called peltasts. Their new spears were half as long again or even twice as long as before. Sword length was doubled. He introduced a new type of boot called the Iphicratid, and linen corslets replaced the bronze cuirass.

The original author of this can have known nothing of the military practices of the early fourth century as it is full of errors, leaving interpretation difficult. The first clear misconception is that hoplites became peltasts. We have seen that these two infantry types had co-existed since the Peloponnesian War. The other misconception concerns the corslet. Linen corslets had replaced bronze cuirasses for most hoplites at the end of the sixth century. By 400, if not earlier, it seems that the leather *spolas* was the main body armour of choice, apart from cavalry and officers who wore a bronze cuirass as well. It may be that Iphicrates had come across linen corslets on his campaign in Egypt, where the material originated, and brought back some to give body armour to peltasts for the first time, but there is no other corroborating evidence for this. Parke (1993) accepted these reforms as a bringing together of hoplites and peltasts to form one infantry type, with peltasts adopting the spear instead of javelins, and hoplites adopting the lighter shield of the peltast. Best (1969, plates 3, 4) has shown, however, that a thrusting spear was sometimes used by peltasts in the fifth century, although perhaps Iphicrates made it more common. Both Parke and Best accept the idea of hoplites discarding bronze cuirasses for linen, which we have shown to be incorrect and which is a problem in the original source. Many peltasts were mercenaries from Thrace, and Thracian hoplites did still wear bronze cuirasses throughout the fifth century (see below). It is possible, then, that Iphicrates took a force of Thracian hoplites as well as peltasts to Egypt, or perhaps he was put in charge of some on his return, and it was they who discarded bronze cuirasses for linen corslets and became peltasts. The Iphicratid boot sounds very much like the high boots often worn by peltasts as early as the fifth century, and there is no reason why it should not have been worn instead of greaves. It may have been adopted from the cavalry boot mentioned by Xenophon. The lengthening of the spear suggests a forerunner of the Macedonian *sarissa*, or pike, and this will be looked into when we examine infantry weapons.

The main infantry body of troops, the phalanx, continued to be made up of soldiers called hoplites throughout the rest of the fourth century, and it is uncertain whether these new peltasts existed outside one or two campaigns of Iphicrates. Some of the ideas certainly stuck, however, and we shall be examining those as they occur. The main body of this chapter concerns the armies of Macedonia and the successor Hellenistic kingdoms, which consisted of many different troop types. We will look at the infantry first.

## THE *SARISSA*

Hoplite spears seem to have been about 7 or 8ft in length from the limited evidence we have (Anderson, in Hanson 1991, pp. 22–3), so the doubling by Iphicrates would give a length of 14 – 16ft. This approaches the length of the later Macedonian *sarissas* and makes the spear a two-handed weapon. Whether Iphicrates' peltasts ever used a two-handed pike like this is doubtful. It would have removed the mobility of the soldier. It is possible that our late sources are exaggerating the lengthening of the spear and that Iphicrates did lengthen it, but not by so much. Spears up to about 13–14ft long can be managed with one hand, especially if used underarm.

In 371 BC the Thebans defeated the Spartans at the Battle of Leuctra, much to everyone's surprise. The main reason for their victory was that they had a phalanx that was fifty men deep instead of the usual eight to twelve, and they put their crack troops, the Sacred Band, on their left wing. This put them opposite the Spartan king and his bodyguard, and the depth of the Theban phalanx simply steamrollered the Spartans. The rest of the Spartan army (made up of allies) melted away. It is possible that an additional reason for this victory was that the Thebans were using longer spears, of the Iphicratid model. It seems most likely that the hoplite phalanx charged with the spear underarm, and a longer spear would have presented more spear points to the enemy (Hanson 1989, p. 162). A possible argument against this is that in 377 the Thebans were certainly still using normal hoplite spears, as they threw some at the Spartans like javelins (Anderson, in Hanson 1991, p. 20). The main argument in favour is that Philip II of Macedonia, in north Greece, was a hostage at Thebes at the time of their victories after Leuctra, and when he returned to Macedonia he built up an army which eventually included the two-handed *sarissa*. It seems likely that he got the idea from the Thebans, or developed it from what they had already achieved. It is still not certain that the *sarissa* in Philip and Alexander the Great's time was two-handed, but given the fact that both men used the phalanx – now generally sixteen men deep – as a holding force while attacking with cavalry, it does seem likely (Sekunda 1984, p. 27).

The length of the *sarissa* has caused much academic argument over the years. Theophrastus, writing in the late fourth century, mentions that the Cornelian cherry tree, whose wood was commonly used for spears, grew to a height of 12 cubits, the length of the longest Macedonian *sarissa* (Theophrastus 3.12.2). Polybius, writing in the second century, states that the *sarissa* was 14 cubits long. Ten of these cubits projected in front of the soldier, and the spears of the first five ranks projected in front of the phalanx (Polybius XVIII, 29, 2–30, 4). Twelve and 14 cubits are commonly translated as 18 and 21ft, as the cubit is to be regarded as the Attic cubit, a standard measurement. Tarn (1930, pp. 15–16) argued that the measurements were shorter Macedonian cubits, giving a Theophrastan length of only 13ft. He suggested this because the *sarissa* was used by cavalry under Alexander, as well as by the infantry, and 18ft would have been an impractical length. However, it is unlikely that an author like Theophrastus would use anything other than the standard Attic cubit, as he was writing for an Athenian audience. Also, it seems likely that the cavalry *sarissa* was a different weapon, the word *sarissa* simply meaning 'a long spear' (see below). Studies of the *sarissa* have also been hampered by Markle's reconstructions (1977 and 1978) in the 1970s. Connolly (2000, pp. 105–8) has shown that the *sarissa* head used by Markle is in fact a heavy butt end, and that *sarissas* had much lighter heads to aid balance. He has also shown that the *sarissa* was not of uniform thickness all along its length, but tapered from butt to point, also as an aid to balance. Using these criteria, Connolly has reconstructed 12-cubit *sarissas* weighing only just over 4kg, about two-thirds that of Markle's reconstruction. We still have to consider the difference between the lengths given by Theophrastus and Polybius. This seems entirely chronological, as Polybius himself says that *sarissas* were longer in earlier times (Polybius XVIII, 29). So we might suggest that the *sarissa* used by Philip and Alexander was 18ft long; in the third century it grew to perhaps 24ft, the longest manageable pike; and that by Polybius's time in the third century, it had reduced again to 21ft. It seems likely that the earliest *sarissas* were of Cornelian cherrywood, which is hinted at by Theophrastus, but that later examples – too long to be easily obtained from that tree – were much more likely to be made of ash, like sixteenth- and seventeenth-century pikes. Ash has the added advantage of being a lighter wood, and so longer *sarissas* could be made which were no heavier than the shorter cherrywood ones (Lumpkin 1975, p. 197).

The Macedonian phalanx was organised into units of 256 men, called *syntagmas* or *speiras* (Connolly 1998, p. 76). These were generally arranged in blocks of sixteen by sixteen, although at Magnesia in 190 Antiochus III arranged his phalanx to a depth of thirty-two men. The overall size of the phalanx was also larger, as Philip II had more men at his disposal. Philip's phalanx was usually 20,000 men, supported by 2,000–3,000 horse. Alexander would invade Persia with a phalanx of 32,000 and 5,100 horsemen. As was mentioned earlier, the points of the *sarissas* of the first five ranks projected in front of the phalanx. The other men held their *sarissas* upright to avoid spearing their own men, and this also helped to break up missile attacks. This new style of phalanx was much more unwieldy than the hoplite phalanx had been, and Connolly (2000, p. 111) has demonstrated the difficulties of manoeuvring it into position. With its *sarissas* lowered the phalanx was a formidable fighting machine, which held up the Persian armies with ease while Alexander won his victories with the cavalry. Later Hellenistic battles, such as Ipsus in 301 and Raphia in 217, had huge phalanxes locked in combat almost to no avail, while the battles were won and lost by cavalry encounters. The Battle of Ipsus, when Antigonus fought Seleucus and Lysimachus, featured a staggering clash of 70,000 men in each phalanx, supported by 10,000 cavalry. It was the Romans who finally showed the weakness of this type of phalanx. Because of the need for cohesion, battles tended to be fought on flat ground, where the phalanxes could manoeuvre carefully. The flexible Roman legionaries could fight anywhere and, when they drew the Macedonian phalanx onto rough ground at the Battle of Pydna in 168, they annihilated it and put an end to the Macedonian kingdom. In his campaigns in Italy in the 270s, Pyrrhus tried to add flexibility to his phalanx by inserting bodies of Italian light troops in between each phalanx block, which seems to have been fairly effective but was not copied elsewhere. At the Battle of Magnesia in 190, Antiochus III inserted elephants and their light troop guards in between phalanx blocks, but that became a disaster when

Fig 64: Macedonian cast bronze spear butt, engraved with 'M A K', late fourth century. *(Shefton Museum of Greek Art and Archaeology, University of Newcastle-upon-Tyne, no. 111)*

the Romans attacked the elephants with archers and javelin men and panicked them. They then routed and broke up the Greek phalanx.

Apart from the phalanx, Alexander the Great also had a body of men called the *hypaspists* (shield-bearers). These men were often used for scouting manoeuvres and usually formed up in battle between the cavalry and the phalanx. They were apparently lightly armoured, therefore, although the name suggests they carried substantial shields. The warriors on the Alexander Sarcophagus (which dates to the late fourth century, and was the tomb for King Abdalonymus of Sidon) carry large hoplite shields of *c.* 85–90cm and must therefore have been using a spear rather than a *sarissa* (Fig. 65). It is possible that these men are meant to be hypaspists (Sekunda 1984, pp. 28–30)

Newcastle University has a bronze spear butt in its collection, which is marked 'MAK', showing it was an official Macedonian issue (Fig. 64). It must be from a spear rather than a *sarissa*, and may therefore be from one of those used by the hypaspists. There is also the possibility that it comes from a cavalry spear. The Macedonian army was issued with all its equipment by the state, though this is the only known marked item apart from sling bullets and ballista bolts marked with Philip's name (see below).

## SWORDS

In the reforms of Iphicrates mentioned by Diodorus and Nepos, swords were also apparently doubled in length. However, there appears to be no real archaeological evidence for this, and the two types of hoplite sword – the straight sword and the recurved *machaira* or *kopis* – continued in use. By the second century the latter sword was certainly the more popular, and Polybius mentions that the Romans reinforced their shields with iron to withstand them. Most surviving *machairas* are 35 to 70cm long, although the example from the cuirass tomb in Thesprotia (see below) is 77cm (Choremis 1980, pp. 15–16). These longer examples are almost certainly cavalry versions, and a sword length of under 50cm for infantry seems more likely. At their widest point these blades measure about 5cm, and the bone or wood handles are usually in the form of animal heads. Examples on the Pergamum frieze have elaborate scabbards decorated with tassels (Jaeckel 1965, figs 5–7). The straight sword is also featured on the Pergamum reliefs and on the tomb paintings of Lyson and Kallikles (Hatzopoulos and Loukopoulos 1980, pp. 60–1), dating to the early second century BC. The latter have sword handles of a Celtic style, no doubt adopted following the Celtic invasions of the early third century.

## INFANTRY SHIELDS

The Macedonian shield has been studied at length by Liampi (1998). The adoption of the two-handed *sarissa* by the infantry obviously necessitated a change in the shield, as the left hand now needed to be able to protrude beyond the shield rim to grasp the *sarissa*. Surviving shields seem to suggest a diameter of *c.* 65–75cm. At the top end of this range they may have been cavalry shields, but Connolly (2000, pp. 109–10) has successfully used 63cm shields in a reconstructed phalanx, and the pictures suggest that larger shields of up to 70cm would not have been a problem. The shield seems to have had a shoulder strap, which would also have taken some of the weight of the *sarissa* in the lowered position, while it also enabled the shield to be carried on the back, leaving both hands free to manoeuvre the pike. A hoplite grip was still employed, with the hand also slipping through the handgrip to grasp the *sarissa*. This also meant that, should the *sarissa* be lost or broken, the grip could be used like a hoplite grip and the sword drawn, as is shown on the second-century Aemilius Paullus monument (Kahler 1965, plate 12).

Third-century depictions of this shield show it to have been very convex and there must have been quite a lot of padding behind the metallic face, which cannot all have been a wooden core. The bronze facings that survive, and the literary mentions of 'bronze-shields' and 'silver-shields', show that these shields cannot have been wicker peltast ones, as suggested by Plutarch at the Battle of Pydna. He also mentions small daggers as compared to Roman swords, and is clearly indulging in literary exaggeration. By far the commonest designs on Macedonian shields are geometric. A small shield from Olympia, and the paintings in the tomb of Lyson and Kallikles (Liampi 1998, plates 1, 3), show a large central circle and smaller circles around the edge. These were all embossed onto the bronze sheet. Occasionally the shields feature a central Macedonian star or head of a god or, on one occasion, an eagle (Liampi 1998, plates 2, 14); but what is most remarkable is the uniformity of design from 300 down until 150. The Lyson and Kallikles paintings show us that, apart from the embossing, these shields were painted as well. Sometimes different regiments, or wings of the phalanx, were distinguished by their shields. Livy describes the two halves of the Macedonian phalanx as 'bronze-shields' and 'white-shields'. The phalanx of Antiochus III, the Seleucid king in the late third and early second centuries, all had bronze shields, although he had a separate guard unit called the 'silver-shields', a name which had been used for a corps of elite troops since Alexander the Great's time. In 167 at the Daphne parade (Polybius XXX, 35.3),

Fig. 65: Foot guard or *hypaspist* from the Alexander Sarcophagus, *c.* 300.

Antiochus IV showed off a phalanx of 20,000. Part of this, or possibly in addition to this, was a unit of 5,000 'bronze-shields', some (5,000?) 'silver-shields', and perhaps some 'gold-shields', although there are difficulties with the text (Sekunda 1994b, pp. 14–15).

The shields of the *hypaspists* shown on the Alexander Sarcophagus (Fig. 65) have very elaborate portraits of gods and goddesses painted on, and one has an apparent portrait of Alexander the Great as King of Persia (although these have all virtually completely faded away now). Although Sekunda suggests these are regimental devices, I cannot see such devices being applied to the army in general, owing to the time and expense of applying such decoration. I think they are far more likely to be elaborate pictures dreamed up by the artist of the sarcophagus (Sekunda 1984, plates F, G, H). The shield from the tomb of Philip II is a highly elaborate affair covered in gold and ivory, although the basic structure was of wood covered with leather. It tells us little about the decoration of combat shields (Vokotopoulou 1995, pp. 157–8).

## HELMETS

The soldiers of the phalanx had a wide variety of helmets to choose from, and these same helmets were also worn by the heavy cavalry, and so they will all be discussed here following the designations and order given by Dintsis. The Boeotian helmet was mentioned in Chapter 4 (Fig. 49*b*), and it continued to be worn throughout the period: indeed, until about 50 BC. Usually thought of as a cavalry helmet, it was possibly worn by infantry from the third century onwards. Later versions are shown on coins and sculpture with cheek pieces and horsehair crests coming from a central knob. Alexander's companion cavalry almost certainly wore this helmet (Sekunda 1984, plates A, C, D).

The Phrygian helmet appeared from about 400 and lasted until *c.* 100. It is similar to the Thracian helmet, but its most conspicuous feature is a high crown very similar to a Phrygian cap (Fig. 65). It usually has a peak, cheek pieces, and sometimes an extra brow guard. An example in the Ioannina Museum in north Greece shows tubes at the sides and at the top of the crest to hold plumes (Sekunda 1984, p. 26). Other examples from Thrace are decorated with silver appliqués (Webber 2001, pp. 11, 23, figs 2, 4). Nearly all the infantry on the Alexander Sarcophagus are wearing this type of helmet, and it also seems to have been the favoured cavalry helmet under Philip II (Sekunda 1984, plate D). It is being worn by soldiers on the Pergamum frieze, too.

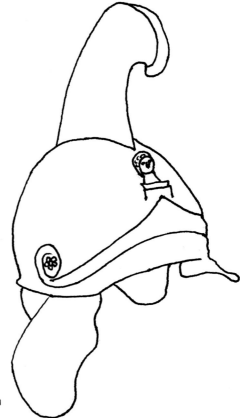

Fig. 66: The iron helmet of Philip II from Vergina, *c.* 340.

The tomb of Philip II produced an iron helmet of this type, where the crest is a raised, flat piece of iron rather than the hollow crest of the bronze Phrygian helmets, and this is no doubt because of the difficulties in working in iron. The reinforcement crests on the front of these and other Hellenistic helmets seem to appear first in the third century, and Connolly (1998, p. 80) has suggested that this was a response to the Celtic invasions of that time. The Celts wielded long slashing swords, and extra reinforcement would have been a useful addition.

The Pilos helmet (Fig. 48) also continued in use until about 150. After Alexander, this helmet incorporated the wavy lower edge of the Boeotian helmet, and is called a 'Cone' helmet by Dintsis. There is a fine example of this type in the Ashmolean Museum (Fig. 49*a*). An example with a Celtic-style crest knob is shown being worn by an officer, possibly from the cavalry, on the Artemision at Magnesia-on-the-Meander dating from the early second century BC (Fig. 67).

Fig. 67: Cavalry (?) officer from the Artemision at Magnesia-on-the-Meander, late second century.

The Corinthian helmet, which by 400 had degenerated into a cap called by Connolly (1998, p. 110, no. 5) an Italo-Corinthian helmet, seems to have remained popular in Sicily and south Italy, but not among the Hellenistic states, although there is one example on the Pergamum frieze (Jaeckel 1965, fig. 25). Cheek pieces also appeared later with this type of helmet, and it sometimes had a fore-and-aft crest or a metal ridge in place of a crest.

The Attic helmet also continued throughout this period. It features on the Alexander Sarcophagus, and developed into Dintsis's Pseudo-Attic helmet, which is generally called Thracian by other modern writers. A good number of examples are known from Thrace, but it does seem to be an Attic derivative and not to have derived from Thrace (Fig. 50). This helmet has a peak and cheek pieces, and third-century and later examples have a brow protector. Instead of a crest it usually has a fore-and-aft ridge for added protection. An example from Thrace is of the usual bronze, but originally it had iron cheek pieces (Webber 2001, p. 24), and two wonderful iron specimens are known from a cuirass tomb at Prodromi in Thesprotia near Epirus (Choremis 1980, pp. 13–14). These are both very similar in design, but one has been completely sheathed in silver, and so it seems that we have here examples of a battlefield helmet and a parade helmet. They date from about 330. The warrior in this tomb was certainly an officer and probably a cavalryman, but Thracian helmets are also seen being worn by infantry soldiers on the tomb of Antiochus II, dating to 246 (Head 1981, figs 8–10).

A final item of headgear that warrants a brief mention is the *kausia*. This is a traditional Macedonian hat rather like a beret. It features on the Alexander mosaic at Pompeii, being worn by a light infantryman who may be a hypaspist (Sekunda 1984, p. 30). A *kausia* is also pictured on the victory frieze at Pergamum, but I think it unlikely that it was used as a regular item of protective headgear for the phalanx, since we have so many references to the use of helmets. It was possibly worn off duty, like an army forage cap, and was clearly a very popular item. Kings of the Greek Kingdom of Bactria, in what are modern-day Pakistan and Afghanistan, are often shown wearing the *kausia* on coins as late as 100 BC.

Helmets were also frequently painted, and the tomb of Lyson and Kallikles is our best evidence for this. One helmet is coloured red with a black peak, yellow cheek pieces and crest, whereas the other is yellow with a black and a red stripe, silver peak and cheek pieces and a large orange plume. I would suggest that the yellow paint on these helmet pictures shows the original bronze, with the rest being painted additions on the helmets.

We have already mentioned the use of iron helmets, of which that from the tomb of Philip II (Fig. 66) is the earliest known. The expense of these meant that they were unlikely to have been used for the general rank and file, but could have been purchased by wealthy officers, perhaps especially among the cavalry. They would certainly have been stronger helmets, if rather heavier than bronze. The Roman army did not equip their legionaries with iron helmets until the time of Marius or Caesar (first century BC), and it is unlikely that any of the Hellenistic kingdoms could have been more generous. There are ambiguities with a couple of sculptures, which use blue paint. The soldiers on the Alexander Sarcophagus have blue helmets, which Sekunda (1984, plates F, G) interprets as having been painted blue, but there is a slim chance that they are meant to be iron helmets. There is also a third-century grave stele from Ptolemaic Egypt showing an officer with a helmet and a muscle cuirass both painted blue, which Head (1981, p. 24) has interpreted as representing iron. The fact that we are dealing with an officer here, both items are painted blue, and we are fifty or so years later in date, all make this a far more likely candidate for the use of iron armour.

## THRACIAN BODY ARMOUR

As with helmets, the body armour in use at this period was not generally specific to either infantry or cavalry, so both cuirasses and corslets will be discussed here. While most scholars agree that Alexander's Companion cavalry and later Hellenistic cavalry wore cuirasses, there remains some doubt as to what was worn by the infantry, and whether that changed over time.

We will look at metal cuirasses first. Macedonia and Thrace were somewhat backward compared to southern Greece in the Classical period, but in the later sixth century they adopted bronze armour in the form of the bell cuirass and the Illyrian and Corinthian helmets, just as these forms were dying out in the south. Because Thracians often buried their warriors with their armour, we have a series of nine cuirasses from *c.* 500 to *c.* 350 that throw light on the metal working of northern Greece of the fifth and fourth centuries (Ognenova 1961, *passim*). The bell cuirasses of the early fifth century have simple lines with wide bottom flanges and a minimum of anatomical decoration, but it is the cuirasses of the later fifth and early fourth centuries that are most interesting. The cuirass from Dalboki, now in the Ashmolean Museum (Fig. 68), has been dated to the early fifth century by Vickers (2002, p. 62), although the tomb it comes from is clearly after 430. Ognenova dates the cuirass to *c.* 400 and the similar 'Basova

Fig. 68: Bronze cuirass with, originally, iron neck and armholes, from Dalboki in Thrace, late fifth century. *(Ashmolean Museum, Oxford)*

Mogila' cuirass to *c.* 380, and this seems more likely to me. Unlike the earlier Thracian cuirasses, these have no high collar but a large semi-circular neck opening instead, and also much larger armholes. The edges are also not rolled over bronze wire, but consist of a flattened border over 1cm wide, marked every 2–3cm by an iron nail. At first sight it seems that these borders may have been for the folding over of a linen or leather lining, but the wide neck hole seems very vulnerable and Ognenova (1961, pp. 528, 533; see also Webber 2001, plate E) suggests this was covered by an iron pectoral. Ognenova herself points out, however, that iron pectorals are sometimes found without a bronze cuirass, and vice versa. The example from Dalboki had a gold pectoral with traces of iron on the back, so this may have been an example of the pectoral as iron armour. Traces of iron at the neck and armholes of the Dalboki cuirass, and especially on the 'Basova Mogila' cuirass, do not appear to be from pectorals, however. They seem to me to suggest that these bell cuirasses were half bronze and half iron. The bronze survives better and we are missing an iron collar, iron-reinforced armholes and an iron flange at the bottom. This is reminiscent of the bronze Thracian helmet with iron cheek pieces mentioned above, and shows that Thracians were working in iron fifty years before the first pieces of armour completely made of iron appeared. However, it is important to note that this evidence exists mainly because of Thracian burial customs. It seems highly likely that other areas in Greece experimented with bronze and iron cuirasses, and helmets in the later fourth century, but there just isn't the evidence because such pieces were hardly ever buried. If they were offered at sanctuaries they would have rusted away before disposal, and sanctuary offerings were severely on the decline by then. The three Greek iron helmets and two iron cuirasses we have come from two tombs: that of Philip II and the cuirass tomb from Prodromi in Thesprotia.

## THE MUSCLE CUIRASS

The muscle cuirass continued to be used as the most elaborate piece of body armour available to wealthier officers (Fig. 51). It was presumably this type of cuirass that Epaminondas was wearing when he was injured 'through the breastplate' at Mantinea in 362 (Diodorus XV, 87.1). On the Nereid monument from Lycia, which dates to about 400 and is now in the British Museum, over 80 per cent of the soldiers are wearing simple material corslets, with only officers in muscle cuirasses. These cuirasses have the abdominal dip of the earlier cuirasses and are now depicted with anatomically correct pectoral muscles, rather than the spiral designs seen in the previous century. These Lycian models also appear without pteruges or shoulder flaps and must have had a fitted padded lining.

In the later fourth century there was an increase in the depiction of the muscle cuirass on the funerary monuments of Athens, which is thought to have been caused by the muscle cuirass having been reintroduced after a period when not much armour was worn. Sekunda suggested this might have been as a result of the defeat of Chaeronea in 338, when Athens and Thebes and their allies lost to the Macedonians, who were using the new *sarissa*-armed phalanx and heavy cavalry. However, several of the monuments can now be dated to before this. Sekunda (2000, p. 62 and plate J) still sees this as a general rearmament, and suggests that whole armies of Athenian hoplites and indeed Macedonian pikemen were equipped with the muscle cuirass. I think this is highly unlikely. We have seen that this form of cuirass was an expensive item and that at this time arms and armour were provided by the state. I do not see how either Athens or indeed Philip II of Macedon could have afforded large numbers of this form of cuirass for the ordinary soldier. This state funding, for Athens, probably began after Chaeronea and we know it consisted of just a shield, cloak and spear (Sekunda 1986, p. 57). The few stelai we have that feature this cuirass can easily be accounted for by officers, who could personally afford the cuirass (and indeed the grave stele).

These mid- to late-fourth-century cuirasses had separate shoulder pieces giving a double thickness of bronze (or iron) at this point, which now became a standard feature of the muscle cuirass. They were obviously copied from linen and leather shoulder-piece corslets. An example of a bronze-plated iron cuirass of this type was found in Tomb II at Amathus in Cyprus, but may be of Roman date (Gjerstad *et al.* 1935, vol. II, p. 14, no. 77). The British Museum has a pair of bronze shoulder guards, from Siris in Italy, which are very elaborately decorated. They are probably from the fourth century and so Greek rather than Roman. The only complete surviving muscle cuirass of this type from this period was found in 1978 at Prodromi, near Thesprotia in southern Epirus (Fig. 69). The two iron helmets found in this tomb have already been mentioned, and the cuirass is also of iron, dating from about 330. The contemporary iron cuirass from the tomb of Philip II (Fig. 70), which is discussed below, is made up of fairly manageable flat plates except at the shoulders, and it is this Prodromi cuirass which shows the real skill in iron working that the Greeks were now attaining. Iron is much harder to work than bronze, but it is a much stronger defence. The drawback is that it is also much heavier, especially because it was hard to work into thin

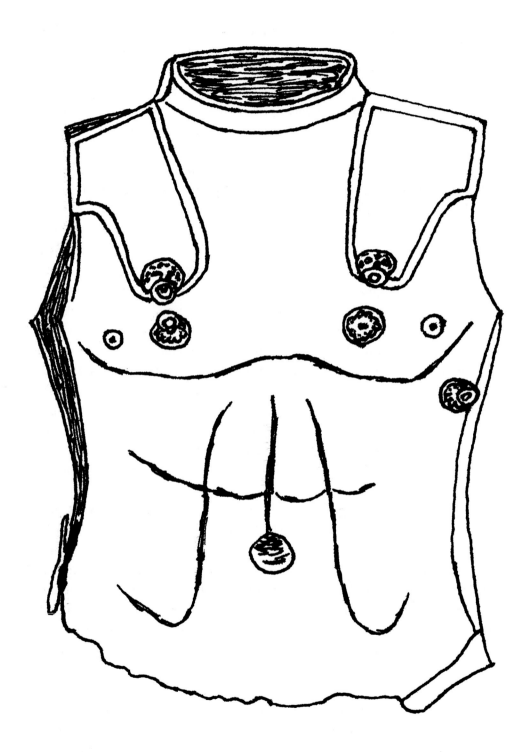

Fig. 69: Iron muscle cuirass from Prodromi in Thesprotia, *c.* 330.

sheets. No width measurements are given for the Prodromi cuirass in its original publication (Choremis 1980, pp. 10–12), but the cuirass of Philip II is 5mm thick compared to the usual 1–2mm for bronze cuirasses.

The Prodromi cuirass clearly reached down at the front to protect the belly, although some of it has broken away here. The edges at the neck and armholes are rolled over for added strength and the cuirass is hinged on the right side and at the shoulders. Straps passing through gold loops fastened the left side. The nipples are marked out in gold and next to these are gold rosettes with loops. Gold lion heads and loops on the shoulder flaps show that this is where the shoulder flaps were fastened down; the lion heads are identical to those on Philip II's cuirass. The cuirass is very wide in the hips to allow the wearer to ride a horse, and the length of his *machaira*, 78cm, shows that this man was a cavalry officer. Another proof for this was the absence of greaves from the tomb, although they were not always a prerequisite for infantry at this time, as we have seen. It is an unusual, isolated tomb and Choremis, the excavator, has suggested it was possibly a battlefield burial.

Nothing remained of the pteruges in the Prodromi tomb, and we must return to the Athenian funerary monuments such as the tomb of Aristonautes (Snodgrass 1967, plate 56) and another well-known example from Eleusis (Sekunda 2000, p. 62). Both these monuments show three sets of pteruges protruding from the bottom of the cuirass, rather than the two sets that are more usual in fifth-century depictions. These fourth-century pteruges are also much shorter than earlier ones, barely covering the groin, let alone the thighs. Later illustrations, such as those on the Alexander Sarcophagus and the Alexander mosaic, show two sets of pteruges, one short and one long, frequently with pteruges at the armholes as well. These are material corslets, probably made in one piece, although they are perhaps evidence for a separate arming tunic that could be worn under a cuirass, like Xenophon's *spolas*. Russell Robinson (1975, p. 148) illustrates a similar doublet, with one set of short and one set of long pteruges. As he explains, the upper short set of pteruges would have had to be carefully cut if they were to follow the curving, lower abdominal dip of a muscle cuirass, and this might have been a later Roman development. The fourth-century Athenian representations have no pteruges at the armholes, which seems to suggest that the three short rows of pteruges were attached directly to the cuirass or, to be more exact, to its lining. In this case one might have thought that two rows would have been sufficient, one covering the gaps in the other. The lower two rows seem to conform to this pattern but the upper row is generally much shorter, and I would suggest that only this row was attached to the cuirass. The lower two rows are more likely to have been part of an arming tunic, to help cushion the weight of the cuirass, rather than having the cuirass itself padded. Evidence for this (apart from Xenophon and his *spolas*) comes from the Amphipolis inscription dating from the time of Philip V, *c*. 200. This has a list of fines for soldiers and officers who needed replacement equipment, which is further evidence for the supply of equipment by the state. Here, ordinary soldiers were issued with a *kotthubos* for body armour, while officers received a cuirass or 'half-cuirass' as well as a *kotthubos*, suggesting that the two could be worn together. This suggests that the *kotthubos* was some sort of leather armour like the *spolas*, over which a metal cuirass could be worn.

There is little pictorial evidence for the use of the muscle cuirass under Philip II and Alexander. One is being worn by a warrior on the Alexander Sarcophagus, but Sekunda (1984, p. 33 and plate H) has shown that he is an allied Greek, not a Macedonian. It is an interesting example, since it has no pteruges and no shoulder guards and so is somewhat old-fashioned. Maybe the sculptor was using an old prop. It seems likely, however, that some of Philip II and Alexander's soldiers did wear the muscle cuirass, especially the Companion cavalry. The muscle cuirass persisted in art through the third and second centuries and it is clear that wealthier Greeks and Macedonians continued to wear it. The victory frieze at Pergamum, which is now generally dated to *c*. 170 and celebrates the victory of Eumenes and the Romans over Antiochus III at Magnesia in 190, illustrates captured Seleucid and Galatian armour, and the scenes include three muscle cuirasses. Two are similar to the Prodromi cuirass apart from the shoulders. Instead of being tied down to the chest, the shoulder flaps have a central hole which passes over a stud or loop on the chest through which a securing thong is tied (Jaeckel 1965, pp. 103–4). Both cuirasses have two rows of pteruges at the waist, but only one has shoulder flaps. These are bordered and tasselled, and seem to be made of leather covered with fabric. The third muscle cuirass is shown without pteruges, which may be further evidence for their having been attached to a separate jerkin at this time: or perhaps we are again dealing with an old-fashioned cuirass, since it has no shoulder flaps. A Macedonian officer on the Aemilius Paullus monument also wears a muscle cuirass (Kahler 1965, plate 12), and there are at least four shown on the Artemision at Magnesia. This dates from after 150, and is a little confusing in that all the soldiers, not just those in muscle cuirasses, seem to be wearing officers' sashes around the waist. Although these soldiers are shown on foot, one at least is clearly wearing boots and may therefore be a cavalry officer (Yaylali 1976, p. 106 and fig. 26.1).

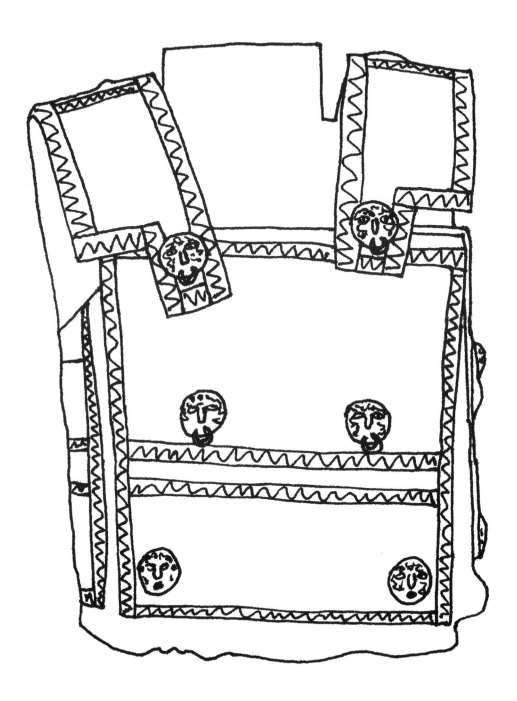

Fig. 70: The iron cuirass of Philip II from Vergina, *c.* 340.

These muscle cuirasses all have clean, unadorned lines (apart from the Siris shoulder flaps), but later Roman muscle cuirasses are often highly embossed. Indeed, some of the relief work is so high that it seems to consist of separate pieces of bronze sculpture, soldered onto the body and shoulder flaps of the cuirass (Russell Robinson 1975, pp. 149–52). This work was probably still further enhanced by painting. The Siris bronzes and a cuirassed statue from Pergamum (*Journal of Hellenic Studies*, 1985, pp. 77–8) suggest that these elaborate embossings may have begun in the Hellenistic period, but most of our evidence is Roman.

## THE CUIRASS OF PHILIP II

The cuirass from the royal tomb at Vergina, which is almost certainly that of Philip II, merits a section on its own, because it is an iron cuirass but in the shape of a material shoulder-piece corslet (Fig. 70). It has not been fully published yet, but has been well illustrated in several books (Andronikos 1977, pp. 26–7; Hatzopoulos and Loukopoulos 1980, p. 225, plate 127; Vokotopoulou 1995, pp. 156–7; Connolly 1998, p. 58). It is made of plates of iron, four forming the body, and two hinged, curved plates coming over the shoulders from the backplate, which itself curves outwards to allow space for the broadening upper back. The iron is 5mm thick, a good deal thicker than was usual for bronze cuirasses, and would have given a good deal of protection, perhaps even being catapult-proof (Plutarch, *Life of Demetrius* 21). The cuirass is decorated with gold bands around the borders of each piece, and a wide gold band around the body of the cuirass. Decorative gold panels are attached to each side, and there are six gold lion heads on the front of the cuirass. The middle pair and the top two, which are on the shoulder guards, hold gold rings in their mouths, through which straps fastened down the shoulder flaps. The pteruges no longer survive, but they were covered with gold strips which do, showing that there were originally fifty-six of them in two rows. Remains of cloth were found on the inside of the cuirass, which came from the padding or an arming jack, but more interesting was the fact that remains of material were found on the outside of the cuirass, adhering to the iron. It is clear that the outside of the iron was covered with decorative cloth, making it difficult to distinguish this cuirass from the linen and leather corslets also in use at this time.

This suddenly opens up the possibilities mentioned in the last chapter: that artistic depictions of shoulder-piece corslets may show iron or bronze cuirasses covered with cloth, rather than the material corslets most people accept them for.

Sekunda advanced this thesis in *Greek Hoplite* (2000), but there really is no evidence in the form of other surviving metal plates. I think, given the evidence of the Philip II cuirass, that we must accept that such cuirasses may have existed in the Hellenistic period – unless the Philip II cuirass really is a 'one-off'; but I don't think we can backdate the idea to the fifth century.

## HELLENISTIC MATERIAL CORSLETS

Information regarding material corslets comes mainly from sculptures, in which cuirasses of a shoulder-piece variety are often shown being worn (Figs 65, 67). These were always generally assumed to be linen, or more likely leather, just like those of the fifth century, but the cuirass of Philip II shows us that some examples may be metal.

For the end of the fourth century the main source is the Alexander Sarcophagus, which shows several infantry soldiers and one cavalryman. The flexible positions of the infantry show that the shoulder-piece corslets they are wearing are surely leather (Fig. 65). These corslets have two sets of pteruges, one perhaps attached to the corslet, the other a separate skirt, and were originally coloured purple and gold – although to what extent these reflect actual uniforms is uncertain (Sekunda 1984, plates E, F, G). In contrast, the cuirass of the cavalryman is plain white so may be linen, but could also be a material-covered metal cuirass (Schefold 1968, plate 51). Before the Battle of Chaeronea Philip II equipped both infantry and cavalry with cuirasses, but of what sort is unknown. The cavalry were the main strike force of the army and were more likely to be issued with metal cuirasses, especially as they would be less of an encumbrance for horsemen. When Alexander the Great and his army reached India, the phalanx corslets had worn out and 25,000 new sets were issued. The old corslets were burned (Sekunda 1984, p. 27). All these facts – that the corslets had worn out, that Alexander could get hold of 25,000 replacement sets almost immediately, and that the old sets were burnt – strongly suggest that the original infantry corslets were leather ones.

Further evidence for the use of material-and-metal corslets and metal cuirasses comes from an inscription from Amphipolis dating from the period of Philip V at the end of the third century (Feyel 1935, *passim*). This inscription concerns military regulations for the Macedonian garrison at Amphipolis and includes a list of fines for lost equipment. Soldiers were fined three obols for the loss of a *sarissa* or sword, one drachma for the loss of a shield, and two obols for the loss of greaves, a helmet or a *kotthubos*. Officers were fined double the amount for these items, either because they were supposed to be more careful or because their equipment was of better quality. Also, officers were fined one drachma for a half-cuirass and two drachmas for a cuirass.

This leads one to the assumption that only officers wore cuirasses; but what then are ordinary soldiers wearing when they are pictured in shoulder-piece corslets on various monuments? We must assume that it is the *kotthubos*. This word was interpreted by Feyel as being a set of pteruges, and it is true that the officers had them in addition to the cuirass (or half-cuirass), but the word equates with *kossimbos*, a shepherd's leather coat, and could have meant a leather shoulder-piece corslet and pteruges. This could still have been worn by officers, as well as the cuirass, since it would have acted as an arming jack, and it equates much better with the sculptural representations that we have.

The cuirass mentioned in the Amphipolis inscription is generally assumed to be the muscle cuirass, with the half-cuirass being perhaps a breastplate only, which is certainly feasible. The number of officers to be so equipped is unclear but, if we count officers as file leaders and above, then we are looking at about 1,000 cuirasses and half-cuirasses for a phalanx of 16,000 such as Philip V had at the Battle of Cynoscephelae. I still think 1,000 is too great a number of muscle cuirasses to be state supplied and that we must be looking at a simpler type of cuirass. The alternative, of course, is provided by the cuirass of Philip II. A cuirass like that, made up of simple plates covered with material, could be supplied by the state in quantity. The designations of cuirass and half-cuirass may refer to the amount of each cuirass reinforced with metal. The cuirass worn by Alexander on the Alexander mosaic appears to show an iron plate on the upper part of the body, with the lower part protected by scales. Varieties such as these could easily have been known as half-cuirasses. The Artemision at Magnesia shows men in what are clearly material cuirasses, and some officers in muscle cuirasses; but it also shows some officers (with officer's sashes) who wear shoulder-piece cuirasses, which are clearly made of metal (Fig. 67). They have large armholes and the figures are shown in stiffer positions. Similarly, several of the shoulder-piece corslets on the Pergamum friezes could be metal-plated cuirasses. These are all depicted with officer's sashes attached. Such adjustable corslets remind us of the fifth-century composite corslets, with their mixture of material and metal defences. Removing all the detailed work of the muscle cuirass meant that simple metal cuirasses, covered with material, could be afforded by many more soldiers – although I am personally tempted to connect such a corslet to the 'half-cuirass' of the Amphipolis inscription, and see its use restricted to cavalry and officers. I am sure that phalanx troops, and perhaps the *hypaspists*, only wore the leather shoulder-piece corslet for body armour.

## GREAVES

The popularity of greaves continued to decline under Philip II and Alexander, when the introduction of state-supplied equipment seems to have taken its toll on this optional item. The tomb of Philip II contained three pairs of bronze greaves, and a further pair of gilded bronze greaves was placed in the antechamber; but the Athenian funerary stelai of the same period, which show muscle cuirasses, show no greaves. Two of the soldiers on the Alexander Sarcophagus are wearing greaves (Fig. 65) and both originally had feathers in their helmets, indicating that they were officers. Sekunda (1984, pp. 38–9) suggests that the soldier in bronze greaves is a half-file leader, whereas the other, who wears silvered greaves (possibly iron), is of a higher rank. These greaves, like those from Philip II's tomb, show little anatomical detailing and are purely functional. Those on the Alexander Sarcophagus have a red lining and a red strap going right around the greave just below the knee, to help secure the greave to the leg. This evidence seems to suggest that only officers wore greaves; but the Amphipolis inscription of the late third century mentions fines for soldiers for lost greaves, showing that the phalanx of Philip V was equipped with greaves, though not necessarily in its entirety. A collection of lead tokens from Athens, which seem to be concerned with the state supply of equipment, suggest that Athens also supplied greaves to her heavy infantry (Kroll 1977, *passim*). The soldiers shown on the tomb of Antiochus II (third century) are not wearing greaves, and neither are the soldiers on the Artemision at Magnesia. Some 15 per cent of the soldiers on this latter monument are wearing high boots, but it is likely that they are dismounted cavalry. The frieze at Pergamum dating from the early second century shows just one pair of greaves which have two straps, one below the knee and one near the ankle (Jaeckel 1965, fig. 40). With the possible exception of the Macedonian phalanx of Philip V (and the new Achaean, *sarissa*-armed phalanx of *c.* 200), the evidence does seem to show that greaves were restricted to officers throughout the Hellenistic period. Since armour was then provided by the state, greaves were seen perhaps as too expensive a luxury for everyone to have. There is no certain evidence for greaves ever having been worn by the cavalry, who wore the high boot as recommended by Xenophon.

## LIGHT INFANTRY

Nearly all the light infantry who fought for the Hellenistic kingdoms were mercenaries, although under Alexander some may have been allied contingents, like his Cretan archers. At Raphia 5,000 Greeks fought for Antiochus III and they were probably peltasts, since they fought with the other light troops. After the Celtic invasion of Greece and the subsequent removal of some Celts (the Galatians) to Asia Minor in the 270s, Greek light troops seem to have stopped using the *pelta*, and adopted instead the large, oval Celtic shield with a central spine. This shield was called in Greek the *thureos*, and so the soldiers are often called *thureophoroi*. Mercenary Greeks armed with this shield, and javelins or spears, also fought at Magnesia in 190. Some parts of Greece, especially in the North Peloponnese, had never adopted hoplite warfare because of the terrain; they always fought as peltasts and, later, as *thureophoroi*. Plutarch tells us that the Achaeans fought like this until shortly before 200, when they decided to adopt the *sarissa*, helmets, greaves, the Macedonian shield and Macedonian tactics (Plutarch, *Philopoemen* 9.1–5).

We are fortunate to have a surviving *thureos* from late second-century Egypt. Although both Connolly (1998, p. 131) and Sekunda (2001, pp. 81–2) suggest that this shield is Roman, and the excavator thought it was Celtic (belonging to a Celtic mercenary), there really is no problem, since both Roman shield and *thureos* were derived from the Celtic long shield. The Egyptian example cannot be Roman, as Romans did not reach Egypt for another 100 years. Sekunda's explanation is that late Ptolemaic (and Seleucid) armies adopted Roman equipment. This will be discussed later. The *thureos* from Egypt is about halfway between a rectangle and an oval, and is 128cm high and 63.5cm wide with a slight concavity. It is made up of three layers of wooden laths each 2–3mm thick, constructed in a form similar to plywood for extra strength. It has a central handgrip, protected by a boss with a long vertical spine, and the outside was originally covered with felt. It would have given much greater protection to light troops than the smaller *pelta* did, especially now that missile weapons were far more common on the battlefield. There is little evidence about whether these *thureophoroi* wore helmets or not. It is probably a case of yes, if they bought them themselves or picked them up after a battle. They were probably not issued with them. They certainly seem to have worn no other body armour.

Northern Greece also provided javelineers and slingers called Agrianians (Polybius V, 79, 6). These men may have continued to use the small *pelta* shield, and there is an example from Olympia of a small 'Macedonian' shield, only

33.8cm in diameter, which could have been used by such troops (Liampi 1998, p. 51, plate 1.1). At the Battle of Raphia in 217 Antiochus III had 5,000 light troops, 2,000 Agrianian and Persian archers and slingers, and 2,000 Thracians. Thracians armed with the *rhomphaia*, a large, single-edged cutting weapon (Webber 2001, p. 39), were used by Perseus at the Battle of Pydna in 168 (Plutarch, *Aemilius Paullus* XVIII, 3) and a novel weapon, also used in this war by Perseus, was the *cestrus*. This was rather like a catapult bolt, or large arrow, but was fired from a special type of sling (Polybius XXVII, 1; Livy XLII, 65, 9).

As mentioned above, Agrianian archers featured at the Battle of Raphia in 217, but most archers continued to be supplied by Crete. Both Cretans and Neo-Cretans fought at Raphia. Neo-Cretans were probably 'newly armed' Cretans, rather than 'newly recruited' or 'newly arrived' (Griffith 1935, p. 144), and so it may have been at this time, rather than under Alexander, that Cretan archers were armed with a small shield and sword for close combat (Sekunda 1984, pp. 35–6). Antiochus III also had 2,500 Mysian archers at Raphia, and in general the Seleucids had much greater access to native missile and other light troops from their cosmopolitan empire.

## CAVALRY WEAPONS

Cavalry played a much more important part in Greek warfare in the fourth century and later. Philip II and Alexander the Great used large squadrons of heavy cavalry to break the enemy line while the phalanx held them up. In the later Hellenistic kingdoms the infantry had more of a role in both Macedonia and Ptolemaic Egypt. This was because Macedonia had not the funds any more to equip a large force, whereas Egypt did not have the breeding grounds. Only in the Seleucid Empire, and later the empire of Pergamum, did cavalry form a high percentage of the army as a whole.

Nearly all this cavalry fought with the spear, but there was a unit of cavalry under Alexander called *sarissophoroi*, who obviously used the *sarissa* as an offensive weapon. This cannot possibly have been the infantry *sarissa* of 18ft in length, because that would have required two hands to wield it, which was not an option in a period before decent saddles had been devised. Connolly (2000, pp. 107–9) has reconstructed a cavalry *sarissa* 16ft long, weighing just over 3.5kg, which in trials was successfully used both underarm and overarm with one hand. There are no later mentions of *sarissophoroi*, and it is likely that all later Hellenistic cavalry used the *xyston*, a spear about 9ft long. As a sidearm, the cavalryman used the single-edged, recurved sword, the *machaira* or *kopis*.

This was recommended by Xenophon for cavalry use, and several surviving examples — generally the longer ones — have horse-head handles implying cavalry use. Cleitus cut off the arm of Spithridates the Persian at the Battle of the Granicus with his *machaira*, during a cavalry engagement (Arrian 1.15.8), and all the wounds received by Alexander in cavalry fights were caused by swords. It seems likely that the cavalry spear often broke following the initial charge, and so the sword was certainly a vital second weapon to have.

## CAVALRY: SHIELDS AND ARMOUR

Cavalry played a much more important part in Greek warfare after 400. We have already noted the amount of armour recommended by Xenophon for cavalry use, and heavily armoured cavalry became the new force in warfare, in addition to the light cavalry that was still used. Philip II of Macedon had a force of 3,000 Macedonian and allied Thessalian cavalry when he conquered the rest of Greece, and Alexander took 5,100 horse to conquer Persia. The early battles of the Successors in the late fourth century feature anything from 6,000 to 11,000 cavalry per side. While 5,000–6,000 is the norm through most of the third century (at least where we have any information about numbers), Antiochus III was able to raise a large force of over 12,000 for the Battle of Magnesia in 190. Much of this was due to the consolidating campaigns Antiochus had carried out in the east of his empire. These enabled him to field 1,200 Dahae mounted archers and other native troops, as well as to afford Galatian mercenaries and call in other allies. While light cavalry was used for scouting and skirmishing, the armoured cavalry was used for attack, especially on the flank of the opposing phalanx. The men of this heavy cavalry wore helmets and cuirasses, and used the spear.

It is almost certain that the cavalrymen of Alexander did not carry shields, despite occasional references to them by later authors who are confusing them with later Hellenistic cavalry (Plutarch, *Alexander of Macedon* XVI, 4). Cavalry shields are not shown on the Alexander mosaic or on the Alexander Sarcophagus, as the rider needed his left hand to hold the reins and also to help him to stay on the horse — not easy with a primitive saddle and no stirrups. Cavalry shields first appeared with the arrival of the Celts in Greece and Asia Minor in 275. Celtic horsemen carried their round shields with a central handgrip, and must have controlled their horses entirely by leg movements. They could have taught Greek cavalrymen to do the same, and they probably also introduced the much more effective Celtic saddle, which had pommels at the four corners to help keep the rider on his mount (Connolly 1998, p. 236). Greek cavalry then adopted the round Celtic shield, but seem to have added a Greek grip with a central armband and a handle at the rim, and made the shield slightly concave rather than flat (Jaeckel 1965, figs 44–7). One example on the Pergamum frieze has the barleycorn boss, like the *thureos* from Egypt; this may have been a Celtic (Galatian) shield, since this monument shows arms of Antiochus III's Galatian allies as well as Greek equipment. A Macedonian cavalryman on the Aemilius Paullus monument also has this type of shield boss, however, and so it is clear that the Greeks used Celtic shields, as well as those of their own design (Coussin 1932, plate 40; Liampi 1998, fig. 11.3).

Macedonian cavalry-shield designs were similar to the infantry, consisting of geometric circle and half-circle patterns (Head 1982, p. 113). These feature on both the Pergamum frieze and the Aemilius Paullus monument, and appear to be about 70 to 75cm in diameter (Liampi 1998, pp. 53–6 and fig. 11.1).

The various helmets available to the cavalry have been mentioned in the infantry section. No helmets seem to have been specific for one branch or the other, but the monuments we have been discussing seem to suggest that Hellenistic cavalry preferred open-faced helmets like the Boeotian and Cone helmets (Fig. 49*a*, *b*). Similarly, all the body-armour types have been mentioned in the section dealing with infantry. The information put forward there, and the use to which heavy cavalry was put, strongly suggest that they were armoured with metal breastplates. Cavalrymen were generally drawn from the wealthier aristocracy (men who could ride!) and so were able to provide themselves with equipment to supplement any provided by the state. It is significant that the latest muscle cuirasses from south Italy, and the example from Prodromi, are all made so that the wearer could ride a horse – either by being made with a wide flange at the bottom or by being short and ending at the waist (Connolly 1998, p. 56).

Apart from the muscle cuirass, shoulder-piece corslets made of metal – like that from the tomb of Philip II – also seem to have been worn, most notably by Alexander on the Alexander mosaic. However, it is also true that some of Alexander's cavalry made do with linen corslets, as he did himself at the Battle of Gaugamela, although this was a Persian corslet and was perhaps worn for that reason. As noted above, greaves seem never to have been worn by cavalry. They would have interfered too much with the horseman's grip, especially once the shield had been adopted. Other pieces of body armour seem to have been used only by cataphract cavalry and perhaps chariot drivers, and will be discussed below; the only notable exception is a throat guard that Alexander also wore at Gaugamela.

## LIGHT CAVALRY AND CATAPHRACTS

Light cavalry of the Hellenistic period were generally mercenaries, called Tarentines. Although originally from Taras in south Italy, the name came to mean just a type of light cavalry armed with javelins and a small shield (Head 1982, pp. 115–16). The small shield of Macedonian style from Olympia, mentioned in connection with Cretan archers, could equally have been used by a Tarentine cavalryman. It is a moot point as to whether they wore helmets. We might presume that those who could buy their own helmet would have done so, but that they were not essential. Apart from battles, these soldiers were used chiefly for scouting by all the Hellenistic kingdoms and many Greek states.

A final type of cavalryman, who appears to have been used only by the Seleucid and Bactrian kingdoms, is the cataphract. This was a very heavily armoured cavalryman, who was covered from head to foot with armour, and who rode a horse that was also armoured. They were probably developed by the Parthians, and adopted by the Seleucids and Bactrians, the Greek kingdoms to their west and east in the later third century. Antiochus III had none at the Battle of Raphia in 217, but he did have 6,000 at the Battle of Magnesia in 190. He probably first recruited them following his travels through the eastern provinces in the late third century. There are no clear illustrations of cataphracts from this period, but there are illustrations of their armour on the Pergamum friezes, and an important find of actual armour has been made in Afghanistan (Bernard *et al.* 1980, *passim*).

The cuirass for the cataphract could have been of any of the metal types we have already looked at, no doubt fitted with pteruges, but the example from Ai Khanum in Afghanistan, which dates to the second century, is most unusual in

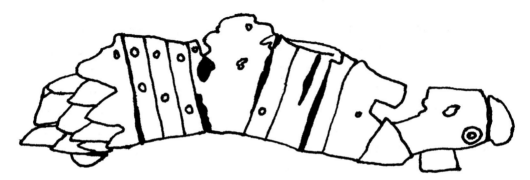

Fig. 71: Iron shoulder guard from a scale cuirass (cataphract armour) from Ai Khanum in Afghanistan, second century.

that it is made of iron scales. The surviving shoulder piece (Fig. 71) is made of iron lamellar strips and came down onto the chest with a stud attachment, just like earlier shoulder-piece corslets and the Prodromi cuirass, to be secured with a thong. Various pieces of leather, linen and felt seem to have formed a separate arming jack, and were not directly attached to the cuirass as has been surmised for other metal cuirasses (Bernard *et al.* 1980, p. 61).

As for helmets, it seems that cataphracts wore a masked helmet which completely encased the head. An example is shown on the Pergamum frieze, and a possible Hellenistic example is in Belgrade's Archaeological Museum (Russell Robinson 1975, pp. 107, 112). Such helmets were also apparently worn by chariot drivers (Sekunda 1994b, plates 4–5). Whoever wore them, they must have restricted vision dreadfully.

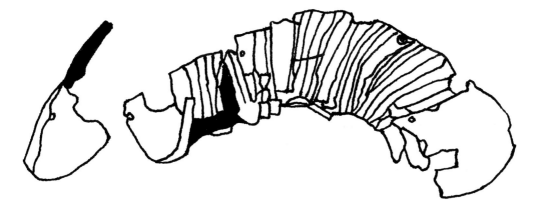

Fig. 72: Iron cataphract leg armour from Ai Khanum in Afghanistan, second century.

For arm and leg protection, tubular laminated guards were worn. These arm guards are depicted on the Pergamum friezes, and the Ai Khanum find has produced a leg guard made of iron (Fig. 72). This guard was for a left leg, with the strips of iron overlapping upwards for greater flexibility like later Roman guards (Russell Robinson 1975, plates 502–4). The topmost part of the thigh was protected by a semi-circular plate, and there was a further plate covering the foot. Earlier arm and leg guards could well have been made of bronze. A small statuette from Syria also exists, which seems to show both arm and leg guards of this style (Sekunda 1994b, figs 32–3).

The Pergamum reliefs also show horse armour in the form of a *chamfron* (face guard) and *plastron* (chest guard) and these too are likely to have been for cataphracts, or perhaps for scythed chariots (Sekunda 1994b, fig. 54, plates 4–5). A further piece of armour from Ai Khanum, made up of very thin iron lamellae in a rough square shape, appears to be a horse plastron, although the excavator thought it might be a *parameridion* or thigh guard (Bernard *et al.* 1980, p. 61). Given the fact that the rider's legs were already protected by the tubular leg guards and possibly pteruges, I think a plastron is more likely. It is highly unlikely that cataphracts used a shield as well as all this armour, and most probably they were armed with a spear for frontal assault. The Battle of Magnesia saw the cavalry and cataphracts of Antiochus III's right wing break through the Roman line and pursue the fugitives to the camp. They were unable to return in time to salvage the collapse of the infantry phalanx, and one reason must surely have been that the cataphract horses would have been exhausted after one charge. The weight of armour, especially if much of it was in iron (not necessarily the case until well after Magnesia), would have protected rider and horse from missiles, and made them a formidable strike force, but must also have exhausted the cataphracts very quickly. The timing of their charge needed to be exact, as they probably could not have been manoeuvred again for any further action.

## CHARIOTS

The chariot had gone out of use among the Greeks when horses had been bred that were big enough and strong enough to be ridden as cavalry. The same had happened in Persia, where chariots no doubt continued in use for ceremonial purposes; but, sometime before 400, the chariot made a comeback as a weapon of war. This new chariot was very different from those of former times. It was a four-horse chariot, whose horses and drivers were heavily armoured. The chariot itself was covered with scythes, and was designed to smash through enemy formations. Scythes projected in front of the chariot from the yoke poles, and also sideways from the yoke, one pointing horizontally, the other downwards. Two more scythes were attached to the axle, again horizontally, and pointing downwards. This latter probably revolved with the wheel to catch both 'duckers' and 'jumpers' (Livy XXXVII, 41). Persian chariots mentioned by Xenophon in his *Anabasis* had scythes projecting from under the box of the chariot, but these are not mentioned by Livy describing the Seleucid version and may have been dropped by then. It seems likely that they would have often got caught in the ground if the surface was at all uneven, and that may have been the main reason why Darius III had to level the ground for his chariots before the Battle of

Gaugamela. It seems that the horses and drivers of these chariots were armed in much the same way as cataphracts.

Scythed chariots have usually been dismissed as a gimmick that did not work. Livy (XXXVII, 41) describes them at the Battle of Magnesia as 'farcical', but they remained in use by Persian and Seleucid armies for over 200 years. Their first known appearance at Cunaxa in 400 failed against disciplined Greek hoplites, who moved aside to let them pass, but in 395 at Dascyleum they scored a victory against hoplites who were panicked by the sight of them. Alexander the Great managed to break up the Persian chariot attack at Gaugamela with light troops, and this became the standard defence. Molon, a Seleucid rebel, used them against Antiochus III in 220, but Antiochus himself never used them against other Greek armies because he thought they could be easily countered. Against Rome at the Battle of Magnesia he thought the element of surprise would count in his favour, but Eumenes, King of Pergamum, was on the Roman side and told them how to deal with the chariots. They were again broken up using light troops. At the Daphne parade in 166, Antiochus IV had 100 six-horse scythed chariots and only 40 four-horse versions, so it is possible he was trying to make them more effective by increasing their size. It is difficult to be sure because this was a parade and not a battle (Sekunda 1994b, p. 26). Chariots continued to be used by the Seleucids until after 150, but are unlikely to have lasted into the first century BC, when the Seleucid Empire had been reduced to a Syrian rump. There is no evidence for scythe-chariot use by other Greek states. Livy (XXXVII, 41) states that Eumenes of Pergamum knew about how they worked in war, but does not suggest that he actually had any himself. There is a slight possibility that they were used by the Bactrian kingdoms in the east, but the terrain there is not really suitable for chariotry.

## ELEPHANTS

Elephants were used by the Indian army of Porus, which fought Alexander the Great in 326. Although Alexander was victorious, the elephants had caused heavy casualties among his men. It was rumours of larger elephant armies in India that caused the army's revolt soon after. Alexander saw the advantages of the elephant, and began to recruit an elephant corps into the Macedonian army. Originally the elephant itself was the weapon, and it was made as imposing as possible. The elephants of Eumenes and Antiochus III had purple trappings, and Antiochus decorated his elephants with gold and silver and awarded them medals for bravery (Scullard 1974, pp. 238–9). If elephants were wounded they had an unfortunate tendency to run amok so, as well as the driver, a soldier or two was mounted astride the elephant's back, armed with missiles to help protect it.

Later on, elephants were issued with armour, consisting of head pieces like horse chamfrons and leg armour similar to that worn by cataphract troops, although perhaps leather rather than metallic (Sekunda 1994b, plate 7). Livy (XXXVII, 40, 4) mentions headpieces with crests on them. Scale body armour for elephants was also used and features on a damaged statuette of uncertain provenance (Sekunda 1994b, figs 52–3). For offensive purposes the elephants' tusks could be sheathed in iron (Arrian, *Punica* IX, 581–3).

As well as breaking up elephant charges with light troops and missile weapons, elephants could be disrupted by weapons placed in front of them. The elephants of Polyperchon (regent in Macedonia after the death of Antipater in 319) were once disrupted with planks lying on the ground, with nails pushed through them from underneath (Scullard 1974, p. 248). Ptolemy improved on this at the Battle of Gaza in 312 by attaching a series of caltrops (sets of spikes) to chains. These could then be quickly moved to where an elephant attack might come.

The best tactic was to make sure you had more and bigger elephants than the enemy. At Magnesia in 190 the Romans had sixteen elephants, but did not bother to use them as Antiochus III had fifty-four. Ptolemy's elephants at Raphia in 217 were defeated because he had only 75 to Antiochus's 102, although Ptolemy won the battle in the end. Ptolemy's elephants were also defeated because they were African bush elephants, which are much smaller than the Indian elephants used by Antiochus. (Connolly 1998, p. 75). After Raphia, Ptolemy captured some Indian elephants, which he used in his army, and in 145 Demetrius II of Syria captured some African elephants from Egypt, which he also used in his army. Generally, however, early Hellenistic kingdoms – including Pyrrhus of Epirus – used the Indian elephant; only the Ptolemies of Egypt, cut off from supply by the Seleucid Empire, were forced to rely on smaller African elephants.

The idea of defensive troops sitting on elephants' backs was enhanced in the early third century by placing small wooden towers on the animals' backs. These enabled more men to be carried, and gave those men greater protection. As well as elephant defence, these men now became part of the offensive capability of the elephant. The mahout, or elephant driver, still had to sit outside the tower, astride the elephant's neck. The earliest representations of towers are both from about 275. A plate from south Italy shows an Indian elephant with a tower containing two soldiers and may represent one of Pyrrhus's elephants (Connolly 1998, p. 75, fig. 2). A statue of similar date shows an elephant attacking a Celt, and has been dated to the 'elephant victory' of the Seleucids against invading Celts in 273. The towers may well have been first used by Pyrrhus at the Battle of Heraclea in 280, but were soon adopted by other Hellenistic kingdoms (Scullard 1974, p. 104).

There are two basic types of tower: the original large tower for the Indian elephant, and a smaller type devised by Ptolemy IV for his African elephants. The Indian-elephant tower, as used by Antiochus III at Raphia in 217 and Magnesia in 190, is as wide as it is high and has three merlons per side in the crenellations. The early plate, sculpture, and an elephant medallion in the Hermitage all show this (Connolly 1998, p. 75, fig. 3). The African-elephant tower has a much smaller base to enable it to sit on the smaller elephant, but is twice as high as it is wide, to make up for the lesser height of the elephant, and it has only two merlons per side (Connolly 1998, p. 75, fig. 1). Livy (XXXVII, 40, 4) states that the elephants at Magnesia had four men in each tower and this is supported by the 'elephant victory' statuette, which has two shields attached to each side of the tower. Four armed men in a wooden tower is certainly possible, but was probably the maximum allowed. The statuette of the African elephant shown by Connolly has only one shield each side and suggests a crew of only two.

Ptolemy's elephant crew at Raphia were armed with *sarissas* to poke at the opposition, but Antiochus III's elephant crew probably had two *sarissa* men and two archers or javelineers. Large amounts of missile weapons could certainly be stored in the tower (Scullard 1974, p. 240). Fear was the elephants' strongest weapon, but they did have other uses. Perdiccas used his elephants to assault the Camel fort of Ptolemy where they tore up palisades and threw down parapets (Diodorus, XVIII, 34, 2), but they were ineffective against stonework. Horses could not stand the sight or smell of elephants unless they were specially trained. After Demetrius the Besieger had been victorious with his cavalry on the right wing at the Battle of Ipsus in 301, he found himself cut off by Seleucus's screen of elephants and unable to return to the battle (Diodorus XX, 113–XXI, 2). At the Battle of Magnesia, Antiochus had his horses trained to work with elephants, and each cavalry wing was supported by sixteen of them. To try and prevent light troops from getting close to an elephant and hamstringing it, each elephant was provided with a guard of forty to fifty men, usually archers or slingers (Polybius XVI, 18, 7). Also at Magnesia pairs of elephants and their guards were stationed in between blocks of the pike phalanx, to try and add some flexibility to this formation and to protect the flanks.

After Magnesia, Antiochus III was required to have all his elephants destroyed, but at the Daphne parade in 166 Antiochus IV still had thirty-six elephants equipped for war, as well as a four-elephant chariot and a two-elephant chariot – these last two items surely for parade purposes only (Sekunda 1994a, p. 27). Whether the Romans had not got around to making sure the elephants were destroyed, or whether Antiochus IV had been able to obtain more from Demetrius of Bactria, is uncertain. In 162 Gnaeus Octavius was sent out by Rome and he did destroy the elephants, although it cost him his life at the hands of an outraged elephant lover (Green 1990, p. 437). Further elephants do continue to appear in the sources, although some sources are unreliable. It seems unlikely that either the Seleucid or Ptolemaic Empires used them after *c.* 140. By then Parthia had blocked off supplies from India, and the African bush elephant was on its way to extinction. Pyrrhus of Epirus had famously used elephants against the Romans in the 270s, but there is no evidence for Epirote use after this time, and none for their use by Macedonia, Pergamum or any of the southern Greek states. It is almost certain that the Greek states of Bactria and India used them throughout their period of existence (down to perhaps AD 10), but their coins show only elephants, elephant heads and elephant scalps on helmets. They do not show elephants with towers or soldiers, which would prove the case.

As has been said earlier, surprise and the fear they caused were the greatest weapons of the elephant. These were the main factors in the elephant victories of the early third century. But when soldiers knew how to deal with them, they were easily managed and became an expensive liability. Once enraged or wounded, they were just as likely to inflict heavy casualties upon their own side as on the enemy. Neither the Romans nor indeed the Parthians ever really bothered with them.

## ARTILLERY

Nearly all of our evidence for Hellenistic artillery – that is, bolt-throwers and stone-throwers – is literary. We have surviving Hellenistic manuals and descriptions in Arrian, Polybius, Livy, etc., of the equipment in action at the various sieges. Parts of some catapults have been found, mostly dating to the Roman period, and these also help with reconstructions. The main archaeological finds are the projectiles. At Rhodes and in other places, round boulders of specific weights, fired from catapults, have been found, and catapult bolts inscribed with Philip II's name are also known (Connolly 1998, pp. 282–3).

According to Diodorus, the catapult was invented in 399 for Dionysius I of Syracuse (Campbell 2003, p. 3). Unfortunately, we don't know quite what this machine was. The forerunner of the earliest catapult was the *gastraphetes* or 'belly-bow' devised by Ctesibius, probably towards the end of the fifth century. This was a large, composite bow mounted sideways on a stock, rather like a large crossbow. The arrow or bolt rested on a slider, which moved up and down the stock. The slider was pushed forward until a catch on it was fastened onto the bow string. The end of the slider was then rested on the ground, and the operator pushed with his stomach into the crescent-shaped end of the stock, using his weight to force the slider back, thus drawing the bow. An arrow could then be fitted and the catch released to fire it. It was a very slow and cumbersome effort.

The machines probably presented to Dionysius were similar but mounted in a base, with the slider being drawn back by a winch system. Biton describes four of these machines in his treatise, the first two designed by Zopyrus. The first, still called a *gastraphetes*, had a 9ft-long bow, and fired two 6ft bolts simultaneously. The second was a smaller version for easy transport to sieges and was called the mountain *gastraphetes*. The third machine was a stone-thrower, designed by Charon of Magnesia, which could fire a 5lb stone. The last, by Isidorus of Thessalonika, could fire a 40lb stone, using a 15ft bow. These stone-throwers had a sling fitted with a pouch, instead of the normal bowstring. All four machines were mounted on the base by a universal joint, which allowed the machine to be traversed, depressed and elevated with relative ease by one man.

These bow catapults, or ballistas, developed during the first half of the fourth century into the torsion catapult. In this design the bow was replaced by two wooden frames on either side of the stock, each containing twisted bundles of hair or sinew. A wooden arm was inserted into each bundle, and these formed the arms of the bow. After a few shots the elasticity of the bundles slackened, and iron levers were inserted top and bottom in order to retighten them (Marsden 1969, p. 81). It seems that machines of this type, capable of throwing stones, were not developed until the time of Alexander the Great. The last development seems to have been the use of curved arms for extra springiness. The first evidence for this is on the Pergamum frieze, so an introduction date of *c.* 200 seems likely. The earlier bow catapults continued to be used down until about 240.

The range of bolt-throwing catapults was about 500 yards, with the bolts being 2–5ft long, but they were really accurate only up to about 100 yards.

Stone-throwers had a range of about 300 yards – perhaps only 200 yards for the largest – and came in a variety of sizes. The most popular engines seem to have been ten minas (4.4kg), thirty minas (13.1kg) and one talent (26.2kg) machines, these weights being the weight of the projectiles. Stones larger than that have occasionally been found, but they were probably for lifting and dropping by cranes, as Archimedes did at Syracuse in 212 (Polybius VIII, 5). Further developments, mentioned in the treatises we have, never seem to have got off the drawing board. Ctesibius mentioned a catapult with bronze springs, which did not slacken like the sinew or hair in the torsion catapults, but they seem to have proved to be too expensive to manufacture. He also designed a catapult operated by compressed-air-powered springs. This was fine on the drawing board, but could not be accurately manufactured with the techniques available at the time. The final invention in this field was a repeating catapult designed by Demetrius of Alexandria, but this machine was a failure because it was too accurate; all the bolts hit the same target and did not disperse. Its range was also somewhat limited.

Although these machines were designed principally for attack and defence during sieges, they were occasionally deployed on the battlefield. At Mantinea in 207 Machanidas the Spartan stationed catapults, probably bolt-shooters, all along his line in an experiment to counter greater Achaean numbers. Philopoemen and the Achaeans charged the catapults as soon as they saw them and, since they were difficult to move, they were almost immediately destroyed or overrun and played no further part in the battle. In 198 and 191 Philip V and Antiochus III, respectively, used catapults in defensive positions against the Romans at the Aous Gorge and at Thermopylae. In both cases, the Romans found it hard to approach these defences from the front, but they were easily outflanked and captured. These would have been expensive losses, since the price for these machines appears to have been about 500–2,500 drachmas each (Philon 62, 15). For the most part the machines were installed in fortifications for defensive purposes, and could also be used in attack against such fortifications. The best-known Greek attack was that by Demetrius the Besieger against Rhodes in 305–4, at which he used a huge tower filled with catapults and ballistas of all sizes (Connolly 1998, pp. 281–5). The best-known defence was that of Archimedes at Syracuse in 213. Apart from a vast array of bolt-throwers and stone-throwers, Archimedes also had cranes which dropped huge boulders on the attacking Romans, and giant grappling hooks which pulled Roman ships out of the water and then dropped them (Connolly 1998, p. 294).

## THE REFORMS OF THE 160S

The Hellenistic warfare we have been describing in this chapter, principally the pike phalanx and the heavy cavalry, was an effective form of warfare that lasted successfully until 168. In that year, the Romans annihilated the army of Perseus, King of Macedon, at the Battle of Pydna. The legionary army proved itself more effective on the day, and this has led Sekunda (1994b, 1995, 2001) to suggest that the remaining Ptolemaic and Seleucid kingdoms in Egypt and Syria remodelled their armies on Roman lines. The evidence for this is actually slim.

A stele from Hermopolis describes new ranks and names for formations, which Sekunda (2001, p. 21) argues is the adoption of the Roman maniple or double century, but the top and bottom of the stele are broken and we do not know what sort of soldiers these are. The *semeia* which is mentioned could simply be a new word adopted for the *syntagma* or *speira*, words previously used to describe a phalanx block of 256 men. The later tacticians like Asclepiodotus and Aeneas use the word *semeia*, but they are still describing a Hellenistic pike phalanx. The use of the word *semeia* does suggest, however, the use of standards, so it may be that military standards were introduced into the Ptolemaic army at this time.

Further evidence for this 'reform' is provided by the Kasr-el-Harit shield and various stelai from Sidon. The Egyptian shield has already been mentioned by me as a descendant of the Greek *thureos*, and the soldiers depicted on the stelai are also mercenary *thureophoroi*, who have no relation to the regular Hellenistic phalanx (Sekunda 2001, pp. 65, 80).

The evidence for the Seleucid Kingdom is almost entirely contained in a sentence of Polybius (XXX, 25, 3), where he is describing the Daphne parade of 166. Here he says that there were 5,000 men equipped in the Roman manner with chain mail. These marched separately from the 20,000 men of the phalanx, and were clearly a different unit. Some commentators have suggested these men were just a bit of a gimmick, like the elephant chariots that also featured in the parade, but Sekunda is surely right when he states that they were a genuine military component. They were not armed as Roman legionaries, however. Apart from the chain mail, there was nothing to suggest that these men used the Roman *pilum* or shield, or fought in maniples. A unit of 5,000 men could easily be part of the phalanx, but the fact that they were placed at the front of the parade with other obviously mercenary troops – Mysians, Thracians and Galatians – suggests that these men were mercenary *thureophoroi*, armed with the *thureos* shield and spears.

A final pointer which seems to confirm that the Seleucid and Ptolemaic kingdoms did not reform along Roman lines was that the Macedonian-style pike phalanx continued to be used, both in the later campaigns by the Seleucids against the Jews and in Mithridates of Pontus's campaigns against Rome. Mithridates did arm half his army in Roman fashion, but he also seems to have been the last man to employ the Hellenistic pike phalanx.

## CHAIN MAIL

Further mention should be made of chain mail as a form of body armour, as it was clearly used by some soldiers in the Seleucid Kingdom. Apart from the Daphne parade mentioned above, some or all of the Seleucid phalanx was armoured with chain mail at the Battle of Beth-Zacharia in 162 (Maccabees I, 6.35). Appian (*Syrian Wars* 30–6) also suggests that cataphracts may have worn chain mail at Magnesia in 190, but he seems to confuse Celtic cavalry with cataphracts, so this idea is perhaps best ignored.) One of the stelai from Sidon mentioned above also has a soldier in chain mail, which may indicate use by the Ptolemaic Kingdom as well (Sekunda 2001, front cover, p. 69).

Chain mail was a Celtic invention of about 300, consisting of rows of interlocking iron rings, each ring passing through two above it and two below it to give a strong but flexible defence. Rows of punched rings usually alternated with rows of butted or riveted rings (Connolly 1998, p. 124), the latter being stronger. Each ring is usually 8–9mm in diameter. The shape of the later mail cuirasses adopted by both Romans and, presumably, Greeks was similar to the shoulder-piece corslet, with two shoulder flaps coming over the shoulders and being fastened down onto the chest. Chain mail corslets appear on the Pergamum frieze, where they probably represent armour captured from the Galatians. The date of *c.* 170 for this monument shows that this would have been the type of cuirass adopted by the Seleucids in the 160s. Wealthier Roman soldiers wore this form of cuirass, and it seems likely that all legionaries were issued with chain mail in *c.* 123, after Rome had inherited the wealth of the new province of Asia. It would have been very expensive for Antiochus IV to equip 5,000 soldiers in chain mail for the Daphne parade, which is one reason why Polybius remarks upon it.

Chain mail is an excellent defence, combining the flexibility of leather with the resilience of iron plate, and it lasted as a defence until the Middle Ages. It was even revived as a defensive material for tank crew in the First World War. It would have been quite heavy to wear a knee-length corslet of mail, but the defensive capabilities were excellent. Pointed weapons would be caught in a ring and held, while edged weapons also would not have much penetrative power, especially as the mail would have been worn over a leather jack. As far as the Greeks go, however, it was the last innovation before impotence led to a gradual absorption into the Roman Empire. Macedonia and Greece were annexed in 148, Seleucid Syria in 64 – although it had ceased to be any sort of power since the 120s – and Egypt in 30, although it too had existed since 168 only by the will of Rome.

# Conclusion

With the demise of the Hellenistic kingdoms, we come to the end of this survey of Greek arms and armour. We have covered nearly 1,500 years of continuous development, from the Mycenaeans to the rise of Rome. Over this period there were elements both of continuity and of change. On the side of continuity, the thrusting spear was the main weapon of choice apart from the Greek Dark Age of 1000 to 700, when the throwing spear took over, and the late period, after 350, when warfare was dominated by the *sarissa*. On the side of change there was body armour, which appeared as bronze plate, disappeared, came back as linen armour, then leather armour, bronze plate and scales, iron plate, composites and finally chain mail. In other areas we are not so certain. The bronze helmet seems to have been a constant, but there is no real evidence for its use in the Dark Age. The use of archers and slingers in the early periods is also shadowy.

The changes that there were came over a long period of time, and what we have seen does show Greek conservatism. Hoplite warfare was around for a long time because both sides in a battle agreed, perhaps subconsciously, to fight that way. Only when the Peloponnesian War came along and the fighting became more desperate did innovations start to appear again. Most innovations throughout the history of Greek warfare seem to have been home grown. The main exceptions were chariots and bronze helmets adopted (and adapted) from the Near East, and the Naue II Type sword adopted from the Urnfield culture of Central Europe. The boars' tusk helmet was Greek. The Greeks invented plate bronze body armour and greaves. Instead of adopting Eastern scale armour to any great extent, they used bronze plate and linen armour, although the latter probably was adopted from Egypt. This developed, however, into the Greek composite corslet which spread to Italy and beyond. In the Hellenistic period the Greeks developed plate iron armour, the *sarissa* and artillery. The expansion of Greeks and Greek power following the conquests of Alexander brought further contact with other cultures, and they did then adapt and adopt the use of Celtic shields, saddles and chain mail, Parthian horse armour and the cataphract, and Indian elephants.

Changes in equipment came about for various reasons. As larger armies were fielded by the Mycenaean palaces, the amount of body armour worn decreased, an economic factor which was repeated at the end of the fifth century. When this was taken to its logical conclusion in the fourth century, the state had to provide the arms and armour for its soldiers. Other changes were concerned more with technique. When bronze plate could be manufactured, it replaced the time-consuming construction of boars' tusk helmets, and was in its turn replaced by the still-stronger iron. Other changes concerned the opposition. In the big picture, when peltasts started to defeat hoplites, everyone had to change the way they thought about hoplite warfare. In the smaller picture, when Celts with slashing swords invaded Greece, everyone reinforced their helmets with extra brow defences!

What the Greeks finally could not adapt to, in the end, was the Romans. This was not just the fighting ability of the legions; it was the Roman mentality. Most Greek combat consisted of a pitched battle. Somebody won and somebody lost. Territory was exchanged and treaties made. That did not happen with Rome, as both Pyrrhus and Hannibal found out. If Rome lost, it just put together another army and kept on fighting until it won. In 197 the Romans defeated Philip V of Macedon and offered him terms, which he felt obliged to accept. In 171 at Callinicus, Perseus defeated the Romans and offered them terms, which they refused. They continued to fight until they crushed Perseus and deposed him in 168. The Romans had virtually unlimited manpower, as well as this willpower, and the Greek states were helpless against them (Sekunda 2001, p. 115).

# Glossary

| | |
|---|---|
| *antilabe* | the handgrip at the edge of a hoplite shield |
| *aryballos* | a small vase |
| *aspis* | a large round shield used by a hoplite |
| ballista | a bolt- or arrow-shooting machine |
| cataphract | a heavily armoured cavalryman riding an armoured horse |
| catapult | a machine for shooting arrows or stones |
| *ekdromoi* | lightly armed hoplites |
| greave | a guard for the lower leg |
| guilloche | embossed decorations like interlace |
| hoplite | heavily armed soldier with round shield fighting in a phalanx |
| *hoplon* | a large round shield used by a hoplite (or sometimes just a term for arms and/or armour, especially in the plural) |
| *hypaspist* | foot soldier of Alexander, probably armed in hoplite fashion |
| ideogram | sketch picture in Linear B writing |
| jack | a padded tunic (usually) worn under armour |
| *kausia* | a Macedonian beret |
| kegelhelm | early Greek cone-shaped helmet made in five pieces |
| *kopis* | a single-edged, recurved slashing sword (same as the machaira) |
| *kotthubos* | a leather arming jack with pteruges which could be worn as armour on its own (similar to the spolas) |
| *lekythos* | a tall thin vase |
| *machaira* | a single-edged, recurved slashing sword (same as the kopis) |
| omega line | a line on bronze armour imitating the line of the ribcage |
| panoply | suit of armour |
| parameridia | thigh guards for a cavalryman |
| pectoral | a piece of metallic armour (or decoration) covering the chest |
| *pelta* | a small round or crescent-shaped shield used by a peltast |
| peltast | lightly armed soldier, usually armed with javelins |
| phalanx | a body of heavy infantry fighting in close ranks |
| *porpax* | a bronze 'handle' in the middle of a hoplite shield, through which the left arm was placed |
| pteruges | strips of linen or leather worn at the waist as a protective skirt |
| repoussé | embossing onto metal, especially ridges for strength |
| rhyton | a drinking cup |
| *sarissa* | a long, two-handed, underarm spear like a pike |
| *sarissophoroi* | cavalry using a sarissa |

| | |
|---|---|
| *semeia* | a unit of men, probably the same as a syntagma or speira |
| *speira* | a unit of 264 men in a pike phalanx (same as a syntagma) |
| *spolas* | leather corslet/arming jack |
| stele/stelai | engraved or carved grave stones or slabs |
| *syntagma* | a unit of 264 men in a pike phalanx (same as a speira) |
| tang | the tongue of metal joining a sword to its hilt |
| telamon | a shoulder strap for carrying a shield or sword |
| *thureos* | a large oval shield of Celtic origin adopted by Greek light troops |
| *thureophoroi* | troops using a thureos |

All dates cited in this work are BC unless otherwise stated.

# Bibliography of Ancient Authors

(Loeb Editions used except where stated)

| | |
|---|---|
| Aelian | *On Animals* |
| Appian | *Mithridatic Wars* |
| | *Syrian Wars* |
| Archilochus | *Fragments* (In Loeb's *Greek Iambic Poetry*) |
| Arrian | *History of Alexander and Indica* |
| Asclepiodotus | *Tactics* |
| Biton | *Construction of War Engines and Artillery* (published in Marsden 1971) |
| Caesar | *The Gallic War* |
| Diodorus Siculus | *Histories* |
| Herodotus | *Histories* |
| Heron | *Belopoeica* (published in Marsden 1971) |
| Homer | *The Iliad* |
| | *The Odyssey* |
| Josephus | *Jewish Antiquities* |
| Livy | *From the Foundation of the City* |
| *Maccabees I & II* | (Jerusalem Bible) |
| Nepos | *Life of Hannibal* |
| | *Life of Iphicrates* |
| Pausanias | *Description of Greece* |
| Philon | *Belopoeica* (published in Marsden 1971) |
| Plutarch | *Life of Aemilius Paullus* |
| | *Life of Alcibiades* |
| | *Life of Alexander of Macedon* |
| | *Life of Cato the Elder* |
| | *Life of Cimon* |
| | *Life of Demetrius* |
| | *Life of Lucullus* |
| | *Life of Philopoemon* |
| | *Life of Pompey* |
| | *Life of Pyrrhus* |
| | *Life of Sulla* |
| | *Life of Theseus* |
| Polybius | *The Histories* |
| Silius Italicus | *Punica* |

| | |
|---|---|
| Strabo | *Geography* |
| Theophrastus | *Enquiry into Plants* |
| Thucydides | *The Peloponnesian War* |
| Tyrtaeus | *Fragments* (In Loeb's *Greek Elegiac Poetry*) |
| Varro | *De Lingua Latina* |
| Xenophon | *Anabasis* |
| | *Hellenica* |
| | *On Horsemanship* |
| | *Memorabilia* |

# References

Adcock, F.E. (1957). *The Greek and Macedonian Art of War* (University of California Press)

Ahlberg, G. (1971). *Fighting on Land and Sea in Greek Geometric Art* (Svenska Institutet i Athen)

Alexandre, O. (1973). 'Kranos Boiotiourges ex Athenon', *Archaeologike Ephemeris*

Alexiou, S. (1954). 'The Boars'-Tusk Helmet: A Recent Find', *Antiquity*, 28

Anderson, J.K. (1970). *Military Theory and Practice in the Age of Xenophon* (University of California Press)

—— (1975). 'Greek Chariot-borne and Mounted Infantry', *American Journal of Archaeology*, 79

Andronikos, M. (1977). 'Vergina: The Royal Graves in the Great Tumulus', *Athens Annals of Archaeology*, 10

Anglim, S., Jestice, P.G., Rice, R.S., Rusch, S.M. and Serrati, J. (2002). *Fighting Techniques of the Ancient World: 3000 BC–AD 500* (Greenhill Books)

Arias, P. (1962). *A History of Greek Vase Painting* (Thames and Hudson)

Astrom, P. (1977). 'The Cuirass Tomb and Other Finds at Dendra. Part I: The Chamber Tombs', *Studies in Mediterranean Archaeology*, 4

Baitinger, H. (2001). *Die Angriffswaffen aus Olympia: Olympische Forschungen XXIX* (Walter de Gruyter)

Bar-Kochva, B. (1970). *The Seleucid Army* (University of California Press)

—— (1973). 'On the Sources and Chronology of Antiochus I's Battle against the Galatians', *Cambridge Philological Society Proceedings*

Barnes, P. (1985). *Flax and Linen* (Shire Publishing)

Benton, S. (1939–40). 'Bronzes from Praisos', *Annual of the British School at Athens*, 40

—— (1940–5). 'The Dating of Helmets and Corselets in Early Greece', *Annual of the British School at Athens*, 41

*Bericht über die Ausgrabungen in Olympia* (1936–99). (11 vols)

Bernard, P. *et al.* (1980). 'Campagne de Fouille 1978, a Ai Khanum (Afghanistan)', *Bulletin de L'École Française D'Extrême Orient*, 68

Best, J.G.P. (1969). *Thracian Peltasts and their Influence on Greek Warfare* (Walters-Moordhoff)

Bevan, E.R. (1966). *The House of Seleucus* (2 vols) (Routledge and Kegan Paul)

Bikerman, E. (1938). *Insitutions des Seleucides* (Librarie Orientaliste Paul Geuthner)

Bishop, M.C. (1989). 'The Articulated Cuirass in Qin Dynasty China', *Antiquity*, 63

Boardman, J. (1978). *Greek Sculpture: The Archaic Period* (Thames and Hudson)

—— (1979). *Athenian Red Figure Vases: The Archaic Period* (Thames and Hudson)

—— (1980a). *Athenian Black Figure Vases* (Thames and Hudson)

—— (1980b). *The Greeks Overseas* (Thames and Hudson)

—— (1985). *Greek Art* (Thames and Hudson)

—— (1989). *Athenian Red Figure Vases: The Classical Period* (Thames and Hudson)

—— (1998). *Early Greek Vase Painting* (Thames and Hudson)

——, Brown, M.A. and Powell, T.G.E. (1971). *The European Community in Later Prehistory: Studies in Honour of C.F.C. Hawkes* (Routledge and Kegan Paul)

Bol, P.C. (1989). *Argivische Schilde: Olympische Forschungen XVII* (Walter de Gruyter)

Borchhardt, J. (1972). *Homerische Helme* (Philipp von Zabern)

Bosanquet, R.C. (1901–2). 'Excavations at Praesos I', *Annual of the British School at Athens*, 8

Bossert, H. Th. (1937). *The Art of Ancient Greece* (Zwemmer)

Bouzek, J. (1981). 'Die Anfange der Blechernen Schutzwaffen im Ostlichen Mitteleuropa', published in H. Lorenz, *Studien zur Bronzezeit: Festschrift für Wilhelm Albert Von Brunn* (Phillip von Zabern)

Buchholz, H-G. (1987). *Agaische Bronzezeit* (Wissenschaftliche Buchgesellschaft)

—— and Wiesner, J. (1977). *Archaeologia Homerica, Kriegwesen Teil 1* (Vandenhoeck and Ruprecht)

—— —— (1980). *Archaeologia Homerica, Kriegwesen Teil 2* (Vandenhoeck and Ruprecht)

Bugh, G.R. (1988). *The Horsemen of Athens* (Princeton University Press)

Bury, J.B. and Meiggs, R. (1980). *A History of Greece* (Macmillan Press)

Campbell, D.B. (2003). *Greek and Roman Artillery 399 BC–AD 363* (Osprey)

Carman, J. and Harding, A. (1999). *Ancient Warfare* (Sutton)

Carter, H. and Mace, A.C. (1923–33). *The Tomb of Tutankhamun* (Cassell)

Cartledge, P. (1977). 'Hoplites and Heroes: Sparta's Contribution to the Technique of Ancient Warfare', *Journal of Hellenic Studies*, 97

Cassola Guida, P. (1973). *Le armi difensive dei Micenei nelle figurazioni* (Edizioni dell'Ateneo)

Catling, H.W. (1955). 'A Bronze Greave from a 13th Century BC Tomb at Enkomi', *Opuscula Atheniensis*, 2

—— (1964). *Cypriot Bronzework in the Mycenaean World* (Clarendon Press)

Chadwick, J. (1976). *The Mycenaean World* (Cambridge University Press)

Choremis, A. (1980). 'Metallinos Oplismos apo tou tapho sto Prodromi tes Thesprotias', *Athens Annals of Archaeology*, 13

Coldstream, J.N. (1977). *Geometric Greece* (Ernest Benn)

Coles, J.M. and Harding, A.F. (1979). *The Bronze Age in Europe* (Methuen)

Colledge, M.A.R. (1967). *The Parthians* (Thames and Hudson)

Connolly, P. (1977). *The Greek Armies* (McDonald Educational)

—— (1978). *Hannibal and the Enemies of Rome* (McDonald Educational)

—— (1986). *The Legend of Odysseus* (Oxford University Press)

—— (1998). *Greece and Rome at War* (Greenhill Books)

—— (2000). 'Experiments with the Sarissa – the Macedonian Pike and Cavalry Lance: a Functional View', *Journal of Roman Military Equipment Studies*, 11

Courbin, P. (1957). 'Une tombe Géometrique d'Argos', *Bulletin de Correspondance Hellénique*, 81

Coussin, P. (1932). *Les Institutions militaires et navales* (Les Belles Lettres)

Debevoise, N.C. (1938). *A Political History of Parthia* (University of Chicago Press)

Dezso, T. (1998). *Oriental Influence in the Aegean and Eastern Mediterranean Helmet Traditions in the 9th–7th Centuries BC: The Patterns of Orientalization* (British Archaeological Reports, International Series 691)

Dintsis, P. (1986). *Hellenistische Helme* (Giorgio Bretschneider Editore)

Doumas, C. (1992). *The Wall-Paintings of Thera* (The Thera Foundation – Petros M. Nomikos)

Drews, R. (1993). *The End of the Bronze Age: Changes in Warfare and the Catastrophe ca. 1200 BC* (Princeton University Press)

Edrich, K.H. (1969). *Der Ionische Helm* (Published Dissertation – Göttingen University)

Elton, H. (2002). *Warfare in the Greek World, a Topical Bibliography* (http://www.fiu.edu/~eltonh/warfare/gwarfare.html)

Fellman, B. (1984). *Frühe Olympische Gurtelschmuckscheiben aus Bronze: Olympische Forschungen XVI* (Walter de Gruyter)

Feugere, M. (1994). *Casques antiques* (editions Errance)

Feyel, M. (1935). 'Un nouveau fragment du règlement militaire trouvé à Amphipolis', *Revue archaeologique*, 6, series 5, 31

Fortenberry, D. (1991). 'Single Greaves in the Late Helladic Period', *American Journal of Archaeology*, 95

Foster, P. (1978). *Greek Arms and Armour* (The Greek Museum, University of Newcastle-upon-Tyne)

French, E. (2002). *Mycenae: Agamemnon's Capital* (Tempus)

Furtwangler, A. (1966). *Olympia IV: Die Bronzen* (Adolf N. Hakkert)

Gjerstad, E. *et al.* (1935). *The Swedish–Cyprus Exhibition: Vols. I–IV* (Victor Pettersons)

Glover, R.F. (1948). 'The Tactical Handling of the Elephant', *Greece and Rome*, 17, 49

Gower, W. (1948). 'African Elephants and Ancient Authors', *African Affairs*, 47

Green, P. (1990). *Alexander to Actium* (Thames and Hudson)

Greenhalgh, P.A.L. (1973). *Early Greek Warfare* (Cambridge University Press)

—— (1980). 'The Dendra Charioteer', *Antiquity*, 54

Griffith, G.T. (1935). *The Mercenaries of the Hellenistic World* (Cambridge University Press)

—— (1956–7). 'MAKEDONIKA: Notes on the Macedonians of Philip and Alexander', *Proceedings of the Cambridge Philological Society*

—— (1981). 'Peltasts and the Origins of the Macedonian Phalanx', in *Ancient Macedonian Studies in Honour of C.F. Edson* (Institute for Balkan Studies)

Hackett, J. (1989) (ed.). *Warfare in the Ancient World* (Sidgwick and Jackson)

Hagemann, A. (1919). *Griechische Panzerung* (B.G. Tubner)

Hammond, N.G.L. (1966). 'The Battle of the Aoi Stena', *Journal of Roman Studies*, 56

Hanson, V.D. (1989). *The Western Way of War* (Hodder and Stoughton)

—— (1991) (ed.). *Hoplites: The Classical Greek Battle Experience* (Routledge)

—— (1999). *The Wars of the Ancient Greeks* (Cassell)

Hartmann, N. (n.d.). 'Bronze Armour and the Earliest Greek Kouroi' (Dissertation)

Harvey, P. (1937). *The Oxford Companion to Classical Literature* (Clarendon Press)

Hatzopoulos, N.B. and Loukopoulos, L.D. (1980). *Philip of Macedon* (Heinemann)

Head, D. (1981). 'The Myth of the Heavy Phalangite', *Sling Shot Magazine*, 94 (War Games Research Group)

—— (1982). *Armies of the Macedonian and Punic Wars* (War Games Research Group)

Healy, M. (1991). *The Ancient Assyrians* (Osprey)

—— (1992). *New Kingdom Egypt* (Osprey)

Hencken, H. (1971). *The Earliest European Helmets* (Harvard University)

Hoffman, H. and Raubitschek, A.E. (1972). *Early Cretan Armourers* (Philipp von Zabern)

Hood, M.S.F. (1953). 'A Mycenaean Cavalryman', *Annual of the British School at Athens*, 48

—— and De Jong, P. (1952). 'Late Minoan Warrior Graves from Ayios Ioannis and the New Hospital Site at Knossos', *Annual of the British School at Athens*, 47

Hornblower, J. (1981). *Hieronymus of Cardia* (Oxford University Press)

Humble, R. (1980). *Warfare in the Ancient World* (Cassell)

Jackson, A. (1999). 'Three Possible Early Dedications of Arms and Armour at Isthmia', *Isthmia VIII: The Late Bronze Age Settlement and Early Iron Age Sanctuary* (Princeton)

Jaeckel, P. (1965). 'Pergamenische Waffenreliefs', *Jahrbuch Waffen und Kostumkunde*

Jarva, E. (1995). *Archaiologia on Archaic Greek Body Armour* (Pohjois-Suomen Historiallinen Yhdistys)

Kahler, H. (1965). *Der Fries von Reiterdenkmal des Aemilius Paullus Monument in Delphi* (Gebr. Mann)

Karageorghis, V. (1975). *Alaas: A Protogeometric Necropolis in Cyprus* (Zavallis Press)

Karo, G. (1930). *Die Schachtgraber von Mykenai* (Bruckmann, Munich)

Kilian-Dirlmeier, I. (1993). *Die Schwerter in Griechenland (ausserhalb der Peloponnes), Bulgarien und Albanien* (Franz Steiner)

—— (1997). *Das Mittelbronzezeitliche Schachtgrab von Agina* (Philipp von Zabern)

King, C. (1970). 'The Homeric Corslet', *American Journal of Archaeology*, 74

Kroll, J.H. (1977). 'Some Athenian Armour Tokens', *Hesperia*, 46

Kromayer, J. (1903). *Antike Schlachtfeldes in Griechenland* (Weidmannsche Buchhandlung)

—— and Veith, G. (1928). *Heerwesen und Kriegfuhrung der Griechen und Römer* (C.H. Beck'sche)

Kunze, E. (1991). *Beinschienen: Olympische Forschungen XXI* (Walter de Gruyter)

Laffineur, R. (1999) (ed.). *Polemos: Le Contexte guerrier en Egée à l'âge du bronze*. Aegaeum 19 (two volumes) (University of Liège/University of Texas)

Lang, M.L. (1969). *The Palace of Nestor at Pylos in Western Messenia*, vol. ii. *The Frescoes* (Princeton University Press)

Lazenby, J.F. (1985). *The Spartan Army* (Aris and Phillips)

Liampi, K. (1998). *Der Makedonische Schilde* (Deutsches Archäologisches Institut Athens)

Liddell, H.J. and Scott, R. (1968). *A Greek–English Lexicon* (Clarendon Press)

Littauer, M.A. (1972). 'The Military Use of the Chariot in the Aegean in the Late Bronze Age', *American Journal of Archaeology*, 76

—— and Crouwel, J.H. (1983). 'Chariots in Late Bronze Age Greece', *Antiquity*, 58

Lorimer, H.L. (1950). *Homer and the Monuments* (Macmillan)

Lullies, P. (1957). *Greek Sculpture* (Thames and Hudson)

Lumpkin, H. (1975). 'The Weapons and Armour of the Macedonian Phalanx', *Journal of the Arms and Armour Society*, 58, 3

McDonald, W.A. and Wilkie, N.C. (1992) (eds). *Excavations at Nichoria in Southwest Greece, vol. ii: The Bronze Age Occupation* (University of Minnesota)

*Machines Time Forgot: Chariot* (2003). A Windfall Films/AAC Fact Prodution in association with Channel 4, France 5, History Channel and Discovery Channel

Madhloom, T.A. (1970). *The Chronology of Neo-Assyrian Art* (Athlone Press)

Mallwitz, A. and Herrman, H.-V. (1980). *Die Funde aus Olympia* (S. Kasas)

Marinatos, S. (1932). 'Ai Anaskaphai Goekoor en Kephallenia', *Archaiologike Ephemeris*

—— and Hirmer, M. (1960). *Crete and Mycenae* (Thames and Hudson)

Markle, M.M. (1977). 'The Macedonian Sarissa, Spear and Related Armour', *American Journal of Archaeology*, 81

—— (1978). 'Use of the Sarissa by Philip and Alexander of Macedon', *American Journal of Archaeology*, 82

Marsden. E.W. (1964). *The Campaign of Gaugamela* (Liverpool University Press)

—— (1969). *Greek and Roman Artillery: Historical Development* (Clarendon Press)

—— (1971). *Greek and Roman Artillery: Technical Treatises* (Clarendon Press)

—— (1977). 'Macedonian Military Machinery and its Designers under Philip and Alexander', in *Ancient Macedonia* vol. ii (Institute for Balkan Studies)

Merhart, G. von (1969). *Hallstatt und Italien* (Römisch–Germanischen Zentralmuseums)

Mills, E. (1989). 'Ancient Logistics', *Slingshot Magazine*, 43 (Wargames Research Group)

Montagu, J.D. (2000). *Battles of the Greek and Roman Worlds* (Greenhill Books)

Morgan, J.D. (1981). 'The Battlefield of Sellasia Revisited', *American Journal of Archaeology*, 85

Morkholm, O. (1966). *Antiochus IV of Syria* (Gyldendalske Boghandel–Nordisk Forlag)

Morkot, R. (1996). *The Penguin Historical Atlas of Ancient Greece* (Penguin)

Morris, C.E. (1990). 'In Pursuit of the White Tusked Boar: Aspects of Hunting in Mycenaean Society', in R. Hagg and G.C. Nordquist (eds), *Celebrations of Death and Divinity in the Bronze Age* (Argolid)

Mountjoy, P.A. (1984). 'The Bronze Greaves from Athens: A Case for a LHIIIC Date', *Opuscula Atheniensia*, 15: 11

Mylonas, G.E. (1964). 'Grave Circle B of Mycenae', *Studies in Mediterranean Archaeology*, 7

Nelson, R. (1978). *Armies of the Greek and Persian Wars* (War Games Research Group)

Ognenova, L. (1952). *Bulletin de l'Institut Bulgare*, 18

—— (1961). 'Les Cuirasses de bronze trouvées en Thrace', *Bulletin de Correspondance Hellénique*, 85

Osgood, R. and Monks, S. with Toms, J. (2000). *Bronze Age Warfare* (Sutton)

Papadopoulos, T.J. (1998). *The Late Bronze Age Daggers of the Aegean I: The Greek Mainland* (Franz Steiner)

Parke, H.W. (1933). *Greek Mercenary Soldiers: From the Earliest Times to the Battle of Issus* (Oxford University Press)

Parkinson, R. and Schofield, L. (1995). 'Images of Mycenaeans: A Recently Acquired Painted Papyrus from El-Amarna', in W.V. Davies and L. Schofield (eds), *Egypt, the Aegean and the Levant* (British Museum)

Persson, A.W. (1951). 'Garters–Quiver Ornaments?', *Annual of the British School at Athens*, 46

Pflug, H. (1989). *Antike Helme* (Rheinland Verlag)

Popham, M.R., Catling, E.A. and Catling, H.W. (1975). 'Sellopoulo Tombs 3 and 4, Two Late Minoan Graves near Knossos', *Annual of the British School at Athens*, 70

—— Sackett, L.H. and Themelis, P.G. (1980). *Lefkandi I: The Iron Age* (Thames and Hudson)

—— Touloupa, E. and Sackett, L.H. (1982). 'The Hero of Lefkandi', *Antiquity*, 56

Powell, T.G.E. (1959). *The Celts* (Thames and Hudson)

Pritchett, W.K. (1971). *Ancient Greek Military Practices Part I* (University of California) (Later republished as: *The Greek State at War Part I*)

—— (1974). *The Greek State at War Part II* (University of California)

—— (1979). *The Greek State at War Part III: Religion* (University of California)

—— (1985). *The Greek State at War Part IV* (University of California)

—— (1991). *The Greek State at War Part V* (University of California)

Reboredo Morillo, S. (1996). 'L'arc et les flèches en Grèce', *Dialogues d'histoire ancienne*, 22/2

Richter, G.M.A. (1915). *The Metropolitan Museum of Art: Greek, Roman and Etruscan Bronzes* (Metropolitan Museum of Art)

Robertson, M. (1979). *Greek Painting* (Skira Rizzoli)

Russell Robinson, H. (1975). *The Armour of Imperial Rome* (Arms and Armour Press)

—— (1976). *What the Soldiers Wore on Hadrian's Wall* (Frank Graham)

Sage, M.M. (1996). *Warfare in Ancient Greece: A Sourcebook* (Routledge)

Salmon, J. (1977). 'Political Hoplites?' *Journal of Hellenic Studies*, 97

Sandars, N.K. (1961). 'The First Aegean Swords and their Ancestry', *American Journal of Archaeology*, 65

—— (1963). 'Later Aegean Bronze Swords', *American Journal of Archaeology*, 67

—— (1964). 'The Last Mycenaeans and the European Late Bronze Age', *Antiquity*, 38

—— (1971). 'From Bronze Age to Iron Age: A Sequel to a Sequel', in J. Boardman, M.A. Brown and T.G.E. Powell (eds), *The European Community in Later Prehistory: Studies in Honour of C.F.C. Hawkes* (Routledge and Kegan Paul)

Savvopoulou, Th. (1990–5). 'Chalkino Kranos apo to Chorygi', *Archaeologike ex Athenon*, 23–8

Schaeffer, C. (1952). *Enkomi-Alasia* (French Archaeological Mission)

Schauer, P. (1982). 'Die Beinschienen der Späten Bronzen und Frühen Eisenzeit', *Römisch–Germanisches Zentralmuseums*, 29

Schefold, K. (1968). *Der Alexander-Sarcophag* (Propylaen)

Scullard, H.H. (1974). *The Elephant in the Greek and Roman World* (Thames and Hudson)

Sekellariou, A. (1974). 'Un cratère d'argent avec scène de bataille provenant de la IVe tombe de L'Acropole de Mycènes', *Antike Kunst*, 17

Sekunda, N. (1984). *The Army of Alexander the Great* (Osprey)

—— (1986). *The Ancient Greeks* (Osprey)

—— (1994a). *Seleucid and Ptolemaic Reformed Armies 168–145 BC, vol. 1. The Seleucid Army under Antiochus IV Epiphanes* (Montvert)

—— (1994b). 'Classical Warfare', *Cambridge Ancient History: Plates to Volumes V and VI* (Cambridge University Press)

—— (1995). *Seleucid and Ptolemaic Reformed Armies 168–145 BC, vol. ii. The Ptolemaic Army under Ptolemy VI Philometor* (Montvert)

—— (1999). *The Spartan Army* (Osprey)

—— (2000). *Greek Hoplite 480–323 BC* (Osprey)

—— (2001). *Hellenistic Infantry Reform in the 160s BC* (Ofycina Naukowa)

—— (2002). *Marathon 490 BC* (Osprey)

Sheratt, E.S. (1990). '"Reading the Text": Archaeology and the Homeric Question', *Antiquity*, 64

Snodgrass, A.M. (1965a). *Early Greek Armour and Weapons* (Edinburgh University Press)

—— (1965b). 'Hoplite Reform and History', *Journal of Hellenic Studies*, 85

—— (1965c). 'The Linear B Arms and Armour Tablets – Again', *Kadmos*, 4

—— (1967). *Arms and Armour of the Greeks* (Thames and Hudson); repr. as *Arms and Armor of the Greeks* (John Hopkins University Press, 1999)

—— (1971). 'The First European Body Armour', in J. Boardman, M.A. Brown and T.G.E. Powell (eds), *The European Community in Later Prehistory: Studies in Honour of C.F.C. Hawkes* (Routledge and Kegan Paul)

—— (1980). *Archaic Greece: The Age of Experiment* (J.M. Dent and Sons)

—— (2000). *The Dark Age of Greece* (2nd edn) (Edinburgh University Press)

Spence, I.G. (1993). *The Cavalry of Classical Greece* (Clarendon Press)

Sprague de Camp, L. (1963). *Ancient Engineers* (Tandem Publishing)

Stead, I.M. (1991). *Iron Age Cemeteries in East Yorkshire* (English Heritage)

Taracha, P. (1999). 'Reconstructing the Dendra Panoply', *Archeologia*, 50 (Warsaw)

Tarn, W.W. (1930). *Hellenistic Military and Naval Developments* (Cambridge University Press)

—— (1940) 'Two Notes on Seleucid History', *Journal of Hellenic Studies*, 60

—— (1979). *Alexander the Great* (Cambridge University Press)

—— and Griffith, G.T. (1952). *Hellenistic Civilisation* (Edward Arnold)

Ueda-Sarson, L. (2000). *Classical Greek Shield Patterns* (http://www.ritsumei.ac.jp/se/~luv20009/Greek_shield_patterns_1.html)

Venedikov, I. (1976). *Thracian Treasures from Bulgaria* (British Museum)

Verdelis, N.M. (1963). 'Graber in Tiryns', *Mitteilungen des Deutschen Archaeologischen Instituts, Athenische Abteilung*, 78

Vermeule, E. (1972). *Greece in the Bronze Age* (University of Chicago Press)

—— and Karageorghis, V. (1982). *Mycenaean Pictorial Vase Painting* (Harvard University Press)

Vernant, J.P. (1968). *Problèmes de la guerre en Grèce ancienne* (Mouton)

Vickers, M. (2002). *Scythian and Thracian Antiquities in Oxford* (Ashmolean Museum)

Vokotopoulou, J. (1995). *Guide to the Archaeological Museum of Thessalonike* (Kapon Editions)

Vutiropoulos, N. (1991). 'The Sling in the Aegean Bronze Age', *Antiquity*, 65

Wace, A.J.B. (1932). 'Chamber Tombs at Mycenae', *Archaeologia*, 32

Walbank, F.W. (1940). *Philip V of Macedon* (Cambridge University Press)

—— (1972). *Polybius* (University of California Press)

—— (1981). *The Hellenistic World* (Fontana)

Walberg, G. (1998). *Excavations on the Acropolis of Midea Vol I:1, The Excavations on the Lower Terraces 1985–1991* (William Gibsons)

Walters, H.B. (1899). *Catalogue of the Bronzes (Greek, Roman and Etruscan) in the British Museum* (British Museum)

—— (1915). *Select Bronzes, Greek, Roman, and Etruscan in the Department of Antiquities* (British Museum)

Wardle, K.A. and Wardle, D. (1997). *Cities of Legend: The Mycenaean World* (Bristol Classical Press)

Warren, P. (1989). *The Aegean Civilizations from Ancient Crete to Mycenae* (Phaidon)

Warry, J. (1980). *Warfare in the Classical World* (Salamander Books)

Webber, C. (2001). *The Thracians 700 BC–AD 46* (Osprey)

Whitley, A.J.M. (1988). 'Early States and Hero-Cults: a Reappraisal', *Journal of Hellenic Studies*, 108

Wilson, D. (1981). *The Anglo-Saxons* (Penguin)

Winter, F.E. (1971). *Greek Fortifications* (Routledge and Kegan Paul)

Wirgin, J. (1985). *The Emperor's Warriors* (City of Edinburgh Museums and Art Galleries)

Worley, L.J. (1994). *Hippeis: The Cavalry of Ancient Greece* (Westview Press)

Yadin, Y. (1963). *The Art of Warfare in Biblical Lands* (Weidenfeld and Nicolson)

Yalouris, N. (1960). 'Mykenische Bronzeschutzwaffen', *Mitteilungen des Deutschen Archaeologischen Instituts, Athenische Abteilung*, 75

Yaylali, A. (1976). *Der Fries des Artemisions von Magnesia am Mäander* (Ernst Wasmuth)

Zapheiropoulou, Ph.N. (2001). 'To Archaio Nekrotapheio Tes Parou Ste Geometrike kai Archaike Epoche', *Archaeologike Ephemeris*, 139

# Index